# Augmented Reality and Virtual Reality in Special Education

**Scrivener Publishing**
100 Cummings Center, Suite 541J
Beverly, MA 01915-6106

*Publishers at Scrivener*
Martin Scrivener (martin@scrivenerpublishing.com)
Phillip Carmical (pcarmical@scrivenerpublishing.com)

# Augmented Reality and Virtual Reality in Special Education

Edited by

**V. Ajantha Devi**

**Williamjeet Singh**

and

**Yogesh Kumar**

Scrivener Publishing

WILEY

This edition first published 2024 by John Wiley & Sons, Inc., 111 River Street, Hoboken, NJ 07030, USA and Scrivener Publishing LLC, 100 Cummings Center, Suite 541J, Beverly, MA 01915, USA

For more information about Scrivener publications please visit www.scrivenerpublishing.com.



**Wiley Global Headquarters**
111 River Street, Hoboken, NJ 07030, USA

For details of our global editorial offices, customer services, and more information about Wiley products visit us at www.wiley.com.



***Library of Congress Cataloging-in-Publication Data***

ISBN 978-139416-639-8

Cover Image VR Students: ID 316091653 | Dreamstime.com
Cover Background: Blue, Jasna Petrovic Zivkovic | Dreamstime.com
Cover design by Kris Hackerott

Set in size of 11pt and Minion Pro by Manila Typesetting Company, Makati, Philippines

Printed in the USA

10 9 8 7 6 5 4 3 2 1

# Contents

**Preface** **xiii**

**1 Digital Learning Environments—Constructing Augmented and Virtual Reality in Educational Applications** **1**
*Kapil Mehta and Chamkaur Singh*
1.1 Introduction 2
1.1.1 Organization of the Chapter 4
1.1.2 Multimedia Principles 5
1.1.2.1 Study One: Spatial Contiguity Principle 5
1.1.2.2 Study Two: Coherence Principle 6
1.2 Materials and Methods—Interaction between AR and VR 7
1.2.1 Immersion, Presence, and Embodiment 10
1.2.2 Interaction Methods 11
1.3 AR and VR Adaptability for Education 14
1.3.1 CoSpaces 16
1.3.2 Interior and Exterior Design 16
1.4 Constructing Framework of the ARLE System 18
1.4.1 Analysis 18
1.4.2 Design 19
1.4.3 Development 19
1.5 Digital Learning Environment Analysis in the Context of AR and VR 21
1.5.1 Physical Learning Environment 22
1.5.2 Psychological Learning Environment 22
1.5.3 Social Learning Environment 22
1.6 General Discussion and Future Aspects 23
References 28

**2 Role of AR and VR Technology in Transforming Education Ecology** 33
*Gagandeep Kaur, Harpreet Kaur, Sonia Goyal, Veerpal Kaur and Prabhleen Kaur*
2.1 Introduction 34
2.2 Related Works 36
2.2.1 Bibliometric Analysis 48
2.2.1.1 Search Key 48
2.2.1.2 Dataset Analysis 48
2.3 Source Analysis 49
2.3.1 Most Relevant Sources 49
2.3.2 Source Growth 49
2.4 Author Analysis 50
2.4.1 Corresponding Author's Country 50
2.4.2 Most Relevant Words 50
2.4.3 Wordcloud 52
2.4.4 Tree Map 53
2.4.5 Trend Topics 54
2.4.6 Thematic Map 54
2.4.7 Thematic Evolution 55
2.5 Strengths and Limitations of AR/VR in Education 56
2.5.1 Limitations of AR/VR Technology in the Education System 57
2.6 Conclusion 57
References 58

**3 Enhancing Social Skills Development Through Augmented Reality (AR) and Virtual Reality (VR) in Special Education** 65
*Ajantha Devi Vairamani*
3.1 Introduction 66
3.2 Theoretical Frameworks for Social Skills Development 67
3.3 Using AR for Social Skills Training 69
3.4 VR Simulations for Social Skills Development 70
3.5 Building Empathy and Perspective-Taking Through AR and VR 72
3.6 Virtual Social Interactions and Communication Training 73
3.7 Collaborative VR Environments for Social Skills Development 75
3.8 Assessing Social Skills Development in AR and VR Environments 76
3.9 Best Practices and Strategies for Implementing AR and VR in Social Skills Training 78

3.10 Real-World Examples of AR and VR Implementations in Social Skills Development: Case Studies 80
3.11 Potential Advancements and Future Research Directions for AR and VR in Social Skills Development 81
3.12 Conclusion 83
References 83

**4 Immersive Learning's Promise: The Educational Potential of Augmented and Virtual Reality 91**
***Priya Trivedi***
4.1 Introduction 91
4.2 The Impact of AR/VR on Education 92
4.3 Literature Survey 93
4.4 Some Uses of AR/VR in K–12 Education 94
4.5 Higher Education and AR/VR 94
4.6 AR/VR for Administrators and Educators 95
4.7 AR/VR Technologies: Current Applications in Education 95
4.7.1 K–12 Education: Increasing Opportunities and Improving Classroom Experiences 95
4.7.2 Curricula and Resource Collections for Immersive Learning 95
4.7.3 Special Education 96
4.7.4 Medical Education 96
4.7.5 Humanities, the Arts, and Other Academic Fields 97
4.7.6 Soft Skills and Career Development 97
4.7.7 Specialized Training and Technical Education 97
4.8 Teacher Preparation: Setting Up Teachers for Success 97
4.9 Invest in Health, Security, and Efficacy Research 97
4.10 Challenges Lie in Implementing VR in a Learning Environment 99
4.11 Policymakers and Recommendations 99
4.12 Conclusion 100
References 100

**5 Influence of Augmented Reality and Virtual Reality in Special Education in India 103**
***Ravichandran K.***
List of Symbols and Abbreviations 104
5.1 Introduction 104
5.1.1 Increased Usage of AR and VR in Education 104
5.1.2 The Significance of AR and VR in Special Education 104

5.1.3 Defining Special Education 105
5.1.4 Overview of Special Education as a Concept 105
5.1.5 Types of Disabilities Requiring Special Education Services 105
5.1.6 Significance of Personalized Learning Plans for Children with Disabilities 106
5.2 Review of Literature 106
5.2.1 Use Cases for AR in Special Education 106
5.2.2 Use Cases for VR in Special Education 106
5.2.3 VR Supports College Students with ASD during Social–Emotional Development 107
5.3 Methodology 107
5.4 Results 108
5.4.1 Demographics 108
5.4.2 ANOVA Test 109
5.4.3 One-Sample Kolmogorov–Smirnov Test 111
5.5 Discussion 113
5.6 Findings 114
5.6.1 ANOVA Findings 114
5.6.2 One-Sample Kolmogorov–Smirnov Test Findings 115
5.7 Conclusion 115
Acknowledgments 116
Conflict of Interest Statement 116
References 116

**6 Exploring the Untapped Potential of the Metaverse in Special Education: A Comprehensive Analysis of Applications and AI Integration 121**
***K. B. Priya Iyer and Ajantha Devi Vairamani***
6.1 Introduction 122
6.2 Pillars of the Metaverse 124
6.3 Importance of Special Education in the Metaverse 125
6.4 Inclusion of the Metaverse in Special Education 127
6.5 Benefits of Metaverse in Special Education 129
6.5.1 Helps Visually Impaired Kids with Sensory Enhancement 129
6.5.2 Reenacts Social Communication for Kids with Autism 129
6.5.3 Uses Visual Imagery to Teach Hearing- and Speech-Impaired Students 129
6.5.4 Makes Learning Accessible to Everyone 129
6.6 Metaverse vs. Conventional Learning 130

6.7 Accessibility Features in the Metaverse 131
6.8 Risks of Metaverse in Special Education 132
6.9 AI Integration in the Metaverse for Special Education 132
6.10 Challenges and Considerations 134
6.11 Future Directions and Potential Impact 135
6.12 Conclusion 136
References 137

**7 Fostering and Integrating Augmented Reality/Virtual Reality Experiences for Learners with Autism Spectrum Disorders (ASDs) 141**
***Usha Nandhini R. and P. Senthamizh Pavai***
List of Abbreviations 142
7.1 Introduction 142
7.2 Augmented Reality (AR) in Learning 143
7.2.1 Status of AR from the Beginning to the Present 144
7.2.2 Learning with AR in Special Education 144
7.2.3 How Does AR Support Special Education? 145
7.2.4 Benefits of AR 146
7.2.5 Issues with AR 147
7.3 VR in Learning 147
7.3.1 Status of VR from the Beginning to the Present 148
7.3.2 Learning with VR in Special Education 148
7.3.3 What is the Impact of Integrating VR Technology into Special Education? 149
7.3.3.1 Non-Immersive 149
7.3.3.2 Semi-Immersive 150
7.3.3.3 Fully Immersive 150
7.3.4 Benefits of VR in Special Education 150
7.3.5 Issues with VR 150
7.4 Variance between AR and VR 151
7.5 AR/VR Enhancement in Children with Autism 152
7.6 The Plan and Expansion of an AR/VR Application for Children with ASD 153
7.7 Setup Requirements for AR/VR 154
7.8 Suggestions to Address Technical Problems Encountered in AR/VR Applications 155
7.9 Experimental Implementation for Autistic Children Based on Research Articles 155
7.9.1 Experiment 1: Virtual Public Speaking 155
7.9.2 Experiment 2: Stimming—Repetitive Behaviors 156

7.10 Challenges and Solutions 156
7.11 Discussion 157
7.12 Conclusion 158
Acknowledgments 159
Conflict of Interest Statement 159
References 159

**8 Impact of AR/VR in the Learning Process of Children with Dyslexia 161**
***C.V. Suresh Babu and Vinutha S.***
8.1 Introduction 162
8.2 Background of the Study 165
8.2.1 Statement of the Problem 167
8.3 Medical Background 168
8.3.1 Significance of the Study 169
8.3.2 Suitable Alternative 171
8.3.2.1 Text-to-Speech Feature 172
8.3.2.2 Audiobooks 172
8.4 Research Aim, Objectives, and Hypothesis 172
8.4.1 Research on Dyslexia Bars 172
8.4.2 Research Questions 174
8.4.2.1 How Can Sound Therapy be Beneficial? 174
8.4.2.2 What Benefits does AR Offer? 174
8.4.2.3 What is the Situation of the Healthcare AR and VR Market Right Now? 176
8.4.2.4 Despite Its Many Drawbacks, Is VR Still Worthwhile? 176
8.4.3 Hypothesis on AR/VR 176
8.4.4 Objectives of the Solution 177
8.4.5 Delimitations of the Study 178
8.4.6 Limitations of Using AR/VR 179
8.5 Proposed Methodology 182
8.5.1 Implementation of AR/VR for Dyslexia Bars 183
8.5.2 Comparisons 185
8.6 Conclusion 186
References 187

**9 Immersive Experience in the Education of Special Kids Using the Metaverse Platform 189**
***Magesh Kasthuri***
9.1 Introduction 189

9.2 Technologies Used in Special Education 190
9.2.1 Artificial Intelligence 190
9.2.2 Virtual Reality 191
9.2.3 Augmented Reality 191
9.2.4 Robotics 192
9.2.5 Gamification Using Gadgets 193
9.2.6 Metaverse Platforms 193
9.3 Component View of the Metaverse in Special Education 194
9.4 System Architecture of Metaverse in Special Education 197
9.5 Recent Studies on Trends in Special Education 199
9.6 Why Use Metaverse in Special Education? 200
9.7 Challenges of the Metaverse in Special Education 202
9.8 Future Potential of the Metaverse in Special Education 204
9.9 Conclusion 205
Acknowledgments 206
Conflict of Interest Statement 206
References 206

**10 Privacy and Security Concerns with Augmented Reality/Virtual Reality: A Systematic Review 209**
***Sukhpreet Kaur, Saumya Rajvanshi and Gurleen Kaur***
List of Abbreviations 210
10.1 Introduction 210
10.2 Augmented Reality/Virtual Reality 211
10.2.1 Benefits of AR 212
10.2.1.1 Higher Attention 212
10.2.1.2 Student Engagement and Interest 212
10.2.1.3 Learning Environment 212
10.2.1.4 Indulging the Content 213
10.2.1.5 Collaboration 213
10.2.1.6 Memory 213
10.2.1.7 Sensory Development 213
10.2.1.8 Cost-Effectiveness 213
10.2.2 Classroom Examples of AR 214
10.2.2.1 Math 214
10.2.2.2 Chemistry and Biology 214
10.2.2.3 History 214
10.2.2.4 Coding 214
10.2.2.5 Educational AR Apps 215
10.2.2.6 Human Anatomy Atlas 215
10.2.2.7 Holo-Human 215

10.2.2.8 VR Frog Dissection 215
10.2.2.9 GeoGebra AR 215
10.2.2.10 Expeditions 215
10.2.2.11 Exoplanet 216
10.2.2.12 Star Walk 216
10.2.2.13 Touch Surgery 216
10.2.2.14 4-D Interactive Anatomy 216
10.2.2.15 Visible Body 216
10.2.2.16 Plantale 216
10.2.2.17 Boulevard AR 216
10.2.2.18 3DBear 217
10.3 Virtual Reality 217
10.3.1 Virtual Reality in Real World 217
10.3.2 Advantages 218
10.3.3 Disadvantages 219
10.4 Algorithms of AR Used in Education 219
10.4.1 Variance Inflation Factor (VIF) 219
10.4.2 The Hum-AR Library 219
10.4.3 SketchAR 220
10.4.4 Virtual Reality-Collaborating Classroom Grounded on Deep Learning Algorithm 220
10.4.5 Security Risks for AR 220
10.4.5.1 Cybersecurity Risks in AR 221
10.4.5.2 Attacks on AR Browsers 222
10.5 Reported Works 222
10.5.1 Comparative Analysis 224
10.6 Conclusion 228
Acknowledgement 228
Conflict of Interest Statement 228
References 228

**Index 233**

# Preface

In recent years, emerging technologies have been making significant strides in revolutionizing various aspects of education. Among these transformative innovations, augmented reality (AR) and virtual reality (VR) have emerged as game-changers in the realm of special education. The potential of these immersive technologies to enhance learning experiences for students with diverse learning needs and disabilities is both promising and inspiring.

The book *Augmented Reality and Virtual Reality in Special Education* is a comprehensive exploration of how AR and VR are reshaping the landscape of special education, creating new opportunities for personalized learning, inclusivity, and engagement. This book brings together experts, researchers, and educators from diverse fields to shed light on the latest developments, best practices, and cutting-edge applications of AR and VR in special education.

The book *Augmented Reality and Virtual Reality in Special Education* aims to empower educators, researchers, policymakers, and stakeholders in the field of special education to harness the full potential of AR and VR technologies. It aspires to inspire the reader with real-life success stories, research-driven insights, and evidence-based practices that demonstrate how these immersive technologies can lead to a more inclusive, engaging, and transformative educational experience for students with diverse learning needs and disabilities.

Chapter 1: "Digital Learning Environments: Constructing Augmented and Virtual Reality in Educational Applications" discusses the current shift in education towards utilizing digital media, particularly AR and VR, to create realistic and immersive learning environments. The chapter explores the theoretical foundations and benefits of augmented reality-based learning environment (ARLE) experiences in science and mathematics. It also highlights the role of VR in addressing educational applications and the potential of AR and VR to improve remote learning in higher education.

Chapter 2: “Role of AR and VR Technology in Transforming Education” examines the rapid advancement of artificial intelligence and its implications for various fields, including education. The chapter emphasizes the role of AR and VR in enhancing access to education, engaging students, and optimizing learning outcomes. It also discusses the potential of AR and VR to improve teaching methods and reform the educational system.

Chapter 3: “Enhancing Social Skills Development Through Augmented Reality (AR) and Virtual Reality (VR) in Special Education” focuses on the use of AR and VR technologies to address social skills development in individuals with special needs. The chapter presents theoretical frameworks and techniques for incorporating AR and VR in social skills training. Real-world examples and case studies demonstrate the effectiveness of AR and VR in fostering social engagement and self-confidence in individuals with autism spectrum disorder and communication challenges.

Chapter 4: “Immersive Learning’s Promise: The Educational Potential of Augmented and Virtual Reality” delves into the transformative potential of AR and VR in education. The chapter discusses the growing interest in AR and VR adoption worldwide and their impact on learners with disabilities or special needs. It explores how immersive technologies, such as virtual classrooms and simulations, can enhance learning experiences, student participation, creativity, and information retention.

Chapter 5: “Influence of Augmented Reality and Virtual Reality in Special Education in India” specifically examines the benefits of using VR and AR technologies for the treatment of autism in India. The chapter explores how VR can simulate everyday situations for early training scenarios tailored to the needs of children with autism. It also highlights the role of AR in enhancing message delivery and creating inclusive digital campuses in India.

Chapter 6: “Exploring the Untapped Potential of the Metaverse in Special Education: A Comprehensive Analysis of Applications, and AI Integration” introduces the concept of the metaverse and its potential applications in education. The chapter discusses the functions of AI in the metaverse and its possibilities for special education. It also explores various applications of the metaverse, from virtual classrooms to group problem-solving and experiential learning.

Chapter 7: “Fostering and Integrating Augmented Reality/Virtual Reality Experience for Learners with Autism Spectrum Disorders (ASD)” emphasizes the importance of integrating AR and VR technologies in the educational system for children with autism. The chapter discusses the challenges and responsibilities in creating high-quality AR/VR educational content tailored to the needs of these learners.

Chapter 8: "Impact of AR/VR in the Learning Process for Children Affected by Dyslexia" addresses the use of AR and VR technologies to support education for children with dyslexia and other learning difficulties. The chapter discusses the benefits and challenges of implementing AR and VR in teaching and learning, particularly in improving student engagement and learning outcomes.

Chapter 9: "Immersive Experience in the Education of Special Kids Using the Metaverse Platform" explores the use of the metaverse platform to create an immersive learning experience for children with special needs. The chapter highlights how machine learning can be used to customize the experience and accelerate the education of special kids through digital transformation.

Chapter 10: "Privacy and Security Concerns with Augmented Reality/Virtual Reality: A Systematic Review" focuses on the security risks and threats associated with AR and VR devices in educational contexts. The chapter discusses various techniques to mitigate these risks and provides a comparative analysis of reported works in this area.

In conclusion, this book presents a comprehensive examination of the applications, benefits, challenges, and potential of AR and VR in various educational contexts, with a particular focus on learners with special needs. It covers a wide range of topics, including theoretical frameworks, real-world examples, and considerations for privacy and security. The chapters collectively demonstrate the transformative role that AR and VR technologies can play in shaping the future of education.

1

# Digital Learning Environments—Constructing Augmented and Virtual Reality in Educational Applications

**Kapil Mehta[1]* and Chamkaur Singh[2]**

[1]*Department of Computer Science & Engineering, Chandigarh Group of Colleges, Landran, Mohali, Punjab, India*

[2]*Department of Computer Applications, Chandigarh Group of Colleges, Landran, Mohali, Punjab, India*

## *Abstract*

The current pattern shifts in education, which require students to study real-life scenarios and solve realistic problems utilizing digital media, have created a major challenge. Digital learning environments have transformed the way educational instructions are invented. Such learning atmospheres have evolved to meet various presentation styles, sensory modalities, and reality, with augmented reality (AR) being among the newest innovations where all parts of three dimensions can be brought together. As emerging technologies have grown in popularity, words like virtual reality (VR), AR, and mixed reality (MR) have become commonplace. Virtual reality is a hands-on, integrated learning tool that has a unique role to play in addressing educational applications. The major objective of this work is to design AR-based learning, which is thought to be in the field of science and mathematics in the learning environment, and to provide theoretical foundations for comprehending the benefits and restrictions of AR-based learning environments (ARLE) experiences. The proposed study demonstrates how information from multiple disciplines can be combined with VR to improve remote learning in higher education. In the framework of future technologies, we also discuss internal and external learning environments. The virtual scenario is part of the internal learning environment, whereas the circumstance in the room around the player is part of the external learning environment—the authentic learning experience before, during, and after gameplay. To offer a theoretical basis for future educational backgrounds for VR and AR, we investigate features and communications

**Corresponding author*: kapilmehta5353@gmail.com

V. Ajantha Devi, Williamjeet Singh and Yogesh Kumar (eds.) Augmented Reality and Virtual Reality in Special Education, (1–32) © 2024 Scrivener Publishing LLC

crucial to learning use in educational applications, as well as many learning theories. Several VR/AR learning instances are investigated, as well as analyzed, and various promising areas for additional study are suggested, including a stronger emphasis on convenience, the interaction between real-world and imaginary environments, and recommendations for efficient learning system foundations.

***Keywords:*** Augmented reality, virtual reality, mixed reality, education, augmented reality-based learning environment, higher education, remote learning

## 1.1 Introduction

In the era of technology and 4th industrial developments, educators think it is important to introduce new learning ideas and shift attitudes to spur creativity across the board. Promoting a curriculum that is driven by problem-solving, exploration, and experiential learning will change education from a normal teacher-centric classroom to a child-centered one. Numerous concepts have emerged in response to the rise of smartphones and other digital devices, together with the most recent advances. Virtual reality (VR), which enables users to incorporate themselves in an environment created by a computer, is one such idea. The definitions of VR, augmented reality (AR), and mixed reality (MR) have entered common discourse, thanks to the rising technology sector. In essence, VR submerges users in an entirely digitized environment, AR superimposes virtual objects in the fixed world, and MR combines virtual elements into the real world and frequently enables human interaction [1].

The COVID-19 pandemic has brought to light the necessity for distance learning to adapt so that it cannot only escape a crisis wave, but also maybe fit the new normal. Governments are becoming more aware of the possibility of cutting-edge technologies like VR and AR to discuss some of the drawbacks of correspondence courses over in-person instruction, including academic misconduct, a decline in socioeconomic aspects of learning, a lack of actual kinesthetic interactions, difficulties preserving students' attention, and the practice of technological boundaries. The deployment of these sophisticated and expensive technologies must be decided upon, not based on technical hype, but rather on results that have been supported by science.

Education research has consistently concentrated on the precise actions a tutor should take to help pupils learn through performance, increase their focus and motivation in class, and develop the necessary skills for this modern period. Students can learn via hearing and seeing, picturing, imagining, acting out, or memorization, according to Felder [1]. In the same way that learning styles differ, so do teaching methods; some instructors emphasize application, some on idea demonstration, and others on understanding. But in a laboratory, learning is dependent on both the training style of the teacher and the student's learning style. Education places a high value on learning experiences, which call for the mental imagery of ideas to better grasp parallels with less mental effort [2].

Rapid advancements in science and technology nowadays impact and alter people's lifestyles. The educational process and educational surroundings cannot remain unaffected by this transformation, aside from people. Comparing technologies utilized in education settings from the past to the present—the journey from the use of a chalkboard to the computer to the Internet—a trend may be noted toward connected phones with artificial intelligence. Education services could not be excluded from the sector since computer and Internet technologies, particularly in recent years, have such a wide range of applications in our daily lives.

Since today's students are classified as members of the Z generation or the digital generation, educators must keep up with technology advancements and employ the best available tools in learning environments. Education-related AR applications are one of these emerging technologies. There are several meanings of the term "AR" that scholars have established, according to an analysis of the literature. These definitions include the following:

The broadest definition of AR is that "it is a realistic setting where digital media items are employed instead of real-world things." It asserts that AR is a descendant of VR. This concept describes AR as an imaginary world that supplements present reality rather than creating it from scratch. In this setting, users may interact harmoniously with both virtual and actual items in AR surroundings. The interacting space between the virtual and physical worlds is created by AR. This is accomplished via AR. When definitions in the literature are compared, it can be said that AR is the process of enhancing the actual environment with digital things.

Applications for AR are being developed quickly every day, and utilization areas across many industries are beginning to expand. Major businesses have begun to prioritize adopting AR to provide their customers with a more embodied and genuine experience. This technology merges the virtual and physical worlds and may be found in a variety of industries, including food, automobiles, cosmetics, and construction. Today, it is crucial for businesses to identify target consumers, follow their behavior, and use technology for sustainable marketing and brand recognition. The most significant factor is that both public and private sector businesses invest in improved technology in more effective ways to sell or promote their services or goods, and they require competent individuals and businesses in this area. Businesses having access to technology may make use of these services, thanks to AR applications.

Although there are various uses for AR apps, the sector of education is the most significant. Over time, educators have become more interested in the novel educational prospects provided by AR technology [3]. The following fresh possibilities and benefits, when assessed, can be achieved [4–6]:

(a) To deliver additional flexible and exciting learning settings for students
(b) To experience a level of ecstasy they have never experienced
(c) To boost students' eagerness also enthusiasm to learn
(d) To encourage students to actively observe their learning processes and to generate hypotheses from these observations
(e) To improve students' academic achievement and assist them in developing social relationships inside the group, linking formal and informal education, and promoting group learning among pupils
(f) The application of AR promotes a sense of liberty, autonomy, and privacy
(g) To foster learning to open new educational options

Wearable technologies catch the eye when AR, which is widely used in the education sector, is evaluated. Smart sensors that can measure the movement of the body are abundant in wearables. Typically, these gadgets seamlessly sync with smartphones via Bluetooth, Wi-Fi, and mobile Internet connections. Sensors are used to link users to portable electronics. Regarding products the user always carries with them, wearable technology offers vital services in a variety of fields, particularly in entertainment, health, employment, information, education, sociability, and security.

### 1.1.1 Organization of the Chapter

This chapter is systematized in this manner: Section 1.1 introduces the concept of VR/AR applications in education. Section 1.2 characterizes the literature background involving materials and methods to interact between AR and VR. Section 1.3 elaborates the VR/AR adaptability in education. Section 1.4 emphasizes the framework of the ARLE System. The analysis of the digital learning environment in the context of AR and VR is presented in Section 1.5. General discussion and future aspects are concluded in Section 1.6.

### 1.1.2 Multimedia Principles

Two basic multimedia principles are implemented and investigated in the studies that we present. The spatial contiguity principle, which interacts with geographically connected physical and virtual aspects, and the coherence principle, which interacts with integrated visual and auditory depictions of contextually integrated virtual and physical elements.

#### *1.1.2.1 Study One: Spatial Contiguity Principle*

Examining the geographical integration of imaginary and real elements is the aim of the first investigation. The learning materials are entirely visual, and they emphasize how the spatial contiguity concept is applied in AR. The idea can be used to spatially integrate the viewing of both virtual and real-world objects in applications of AR. In the study, a genuine graphical environment is combined with virtual textual content. We wish to determine whether the spatial contiguity principle, specifically this implementation of the concept, has a favorable impact on cognitive parameters such as cognitive burden, task load, and knowledge.

By lowering visual search procedures and the duration of time that the various components must be maintained in working memory for mental fusion, we anticipate that adhering to the geographical contiguity principle through AR reduces superfluous processing, and hence extraneous cognitive burden (H1.1a). The accessible working memory capacity can be utilized for creative processing when information is integrated rather than isolated, increasing the relevant cognitive load (H1.1b).

We also propose that the task load is influenced by the geographical integration of the learning material. We anticipate that as the visualization is integrated, there will be less of a need to store discrete components in working memory for longer periods (H1.2a). Fewer eye movements are required due to the reduced need for visual search processes, which lowers the physical strain (H1.2b). In addition, since integrating the presentation requires fewer simultaneous search and processing steps (H1.2c), we anticipate that the temporal demand will be reduced. We suggest that the integrated presentation makes it simpler to comprehend the material, which results in better performance (H1.2d), as well as lesser work (H1.2e) and dissatisfaction (H1.2f). When information is spatially integrated, we could anticipate enhanced knowledge due to the reduced irrelevant cognitive load, workload-related variables, and the ensuing rise in relevant cognitive load (H1.3). A summary of all of Study One's hypotheses is given in Table 1.1.

**Table 1.1** Hypotheses in Study one: spatial contiguity principle.

| | |
|---|---|
| H1.1a | Lower unnecessary cognitive load results from learning with a unified display of real-world and virtual knowledge as opposed to learning with segregated demonstration. |
| H1.1b | Comparatively to learning with such a separate demonstration, learning with a unified presentation of real-world and virtual knowledge results in a higher relevant cognitive load. |
| H1.2a | Less mental effort is required to learn when actual and virtual facts are presented together rather than separately. |
| H1.2b | Less physical effort is required to learn when actual and virtual information are presented together than when they are presented separately. |
| H1.2c | Learning with the unified display of real-world and imaginary information was less time-consuming than learning from a separate presentation. |
| H1.2d | Learning with the unified display of real and imaginary information produces higher performance ratings than training with a separate presentation. |
| H1.2e | Learning with the unified display of real and imaginary knowledge demands less effort than learning from a separate presentation. |
| H1.2f | Less dissatisfaction is experienced during learning when actual and virtual facts are presented together rather than separately. |
| H1.3 | Learning with the combined display of real-world and imaginary content results in better information retention than studying with a separate presentation. |

#### *1.1.2.2 Study Two: Coherence Principle*

Examining the background coherence of imaginary information is the aim of another study. The application of the coherence principle in AR is the main topic of audio-visual instructional material. The idea may be used with both realistic and imaginary, visual and audio aspects in applications of AR. In the study, in addition to actual ambient noises, simulated sounds matched or did not match the subject matter of the added learning material to an application including simulated words, as well as images. In comparison to virtual auditory features, these noises are not directly related to the learning goal.

We propose that adhering to the coherence principle in AR and excluding noises results in decreased unnecessary dispensation and, consequently, in unnecessary cognitive load (H2.1a) due to the fewer items that must be processed. However, because of inspirational properties, matching sounds are anticipated for the rise in germane cognitive load in the limits through which non-matching sounds are unprovoked. For generative processing, functional memory capacities are made available that raise germane cognitive load having no addition in sounds (H2.1b).

Furthermore, we propose that adherence to the coherence principle affects work burden. We predict that when no noises are provided, both demands of psychological (H2.2a) and corporeal (H2.2b) are reduced because there is less sensory information that must be attended to and because fewer sensory organs are explicitly used. Because reduced physical information may be treated in a similar amount of period when new noises are absent (H2.2c), we also anticipate a reduction in temporal demand. We argue that the absence of extra noises increases perceptions of greater presentation (H2.2d) and reduced effort due to the reduced possibility for distraction through additional sensory information (H2.2e).

On the one hand, it is expected that frustration will be reduced when no disturbing sounds are added at all. On the other hand, expectations of frustration will be reduced when matching sounds are added, as opposed to non-resembling sounds whose reason for addition is unclear, which may result in even greater hindrance (H2.2f). When no sounds are added, we could also anticipate increased resulting knowledge due to reduced irrelevant cognitive load, as well as factors related to workload. Although, we could also anticipate that corresponding sounds produce advanced resulting knowledge other than non-matching sounds due to motivating effects and a reduction in frustration (H2.3). Table 1.2 provides a summary of Study Two's hypotheses.

## 1.2 Materials and Methods—Interaction between AR and VR

This study of the literature provides a thorough and worthy description of usages of VR and AR in the context of social education and serves as a starting point for a conversation and a more in-depth examination of VR/AR in learning. Although VR and AR use many of the same technology, such as tracking sensors and screens, they take two distinct methods to fuse the actual world with the virtual world. Virtual reality is a simulated imaginary

**Table 1.2** Study two: coherence principle.

| **Table hypotheses** | |
|---|---|
| H2.1a | Getting from materials that combine actual and simulated knowledge deprived of the inclusion of simulated noises results in a lower unnecessary cognitive burden. |
| H2.1b | Adding virtual sounds increases the germane cognitive load more than counting non-matching sounds, and knowledge material that combines real and simulated information depriving the addition of virtual sounds increases the germane cognitive load more than learning material without additional virtual noise. |
| H2.2a | Knowing from material that combines actual and simulated knowledge but no extra virtual noises results in decreased mental load. |
| H2.2b | Less physical effort is required when learning from material that combines actual and virtual knowledge without extra virtual noises. |
| H2.2c | Knowing from material containing both real and simulated information depriving the inclusion of simulated noises results in decreased temporal demand. |
| H2.2d | Learning from material that combines actual and virtual information without the inclusion of extra virtual noises results in greater perceived performance. |
| H2.2e | Less effort is required to learn knowledge that includes both real and virtual information with no extra virtual noises. |
| H2.2f | Learning content that combines real and virtual information without extra virtual sounds reduces irritation more than a learning material that just includes virtual sounds; adding matching sounds reduces frustration more than adding non-matching sounds. |
| H2.3 | Higher knowledge results from learning from material that combines real and virtual information without more virtual sounds, where the inclusion of matching sounds results in greater knowledge than the addition of non-matching sounds. |

environment that can be felt through sensor inputs (such as sights and noise) delivered by a system and in which actions partly influence those that occur in the surroundings [7]. On the other hand, AR enables the user to view the actual world while superimposing or compositing virtual things onto the real environment. As a result, rather than entirely replacing reality, AR enhances it [8].

Since at least the 1990s, researchers have been investigating the possibilities of immersive technologies as a teaching aid. Due to their immersive experiences, innovative information-sharing capabilities and potential to provide virtual experiences that expand access to educational opportunities that would otherwise be restricted by cost or physical distance, VR/AR technologies are a promising addition to the expanding field of education technology. However, it is only now that VR/AR hardware and software are sufficiently accessible and cost-effective for use in educational settings.

In comparison to its two-dimensional equivalents, VR/AR technologies offer a wide range of options to convey information in more interactive ways. Advanced VR systems can fully immerse users in a virtual environment where they can interact in real-time with both virtual things and other people. This type of encounter is conducive to experiential learning that either replicates real-world situations or provides complex material in novel ways. For instance, students can stand in the middle of a physics simulation or observe microscopic things in 3D. Users of VR can also enter 360-degree visual experiences that have already been recorded, either in the form of still photographs or videos, which they can observe but not alter or interact with.

Users can interact with virtual items that appear in their actual surroundings using AR, also known as MR. The scenarios where users must engage with virtual items, while also keeping situational awareness of their physical environment, benefit the most from this. Students may, for instance, follow digital overlays of instructions for difficult tasks like learning how to fix a complicated machine or performing a medical procedure. Like VR, AR enables users to view static virtual items or information within a real environment while still offering fewer interactive experiences. This is most advantageous when the actual thing itself has the greatest instructional value, such as when a virtual replica of a sculpture or historical artifact is displayed in a classroom or when extra text or photos are superimposed on a historical location.

In conventional AR, digital material is often superimposed onto a real-time opinion of the world, frequently as a view of a camera on moveable platforms or as a see-through display on AR systems like Microsoft HoloLens. In contrast, VR technology tries to immerse people in a wholly simulated environment with a variety of technologies to address one or more senses. As a result of its stereo display, spatial audio, and controllers (or hand-movement) for communications and response through haptic movements, head-mounted displays (HMDs) are frequently pointed to as immersive virtual reality (IVR). However, there are numerous other VR technologies with varying levels of immersion, such as projected walls and portable screens.

Although using technology in education is a common practice and the use of VR/AR in digital learning is non-novel, various aspects of its application might be enhanced. Particularly, there exists shaky consideration of the effectiveness of remembering advances made possible by VR or AR technology [9, 10]. The authors further expand on the usage of HMD VR in a learning management system's (LMS) environment to incorporate literature into our study, which was primarily finished in late 2018, and to fill in gaps identified since then [11].

Various techniques for enhancing learning materials' accessibility are explored for strongly connected (collaborative), multi-user, VR/AR theory, and communication. Multi-functional, responsive VR/AR material changes its usability, contribution to interactions, and yield for displays based on the accessing platform. The adaptability fits with the design for learning in virtual mode [12].

### 1.2.1 Immersion, Presence, and Embodiment

Presence is a crucial component in integrating someone into a virtual environment, which refers to how much a person acknowledges that a simulated world is real. Although the occurrence and immersion of the phrase are occasionally combined synonymously, few people recognize the below-mentioned meanings. As presence and embodiment are described as the "two profound affordances of VR" [13], we also define embodiment below:

(i) Immersion: What technology offers in terms of realism. The more technologies there are that span different modalities, the more immersive it becomes in comparison to real-world human senses. A 2D display, for instance, offers a less immersive experience than a stereoscopic display that follows the movement of the head [14].

(ii) Presence: Accept a fake world as a real one by being present. This consists of two basic deceptions that a person must accept: (1) the place deception (the idea that the location is truly real) and (2) the credibility deception (the idea that what is occurring is genuinely functioning) [15].

(iii) Embodiment: This refers to the psychological images of the body in space, which may be realistic or imaginary. Body ownership, self-contentedness, and activity all refer to the concept that the body in which one is being inhabited is one's own (the capacity to move and perceive one's own body) are the three fundamental elements of an embodiment. Embodiment is seen as a crucial component of learning [16].

### 1.2.2 Interaction Methods

Interactions in virtual environments (VEs) are defined by Bowman and Hodges as focusing on three core job categories: perspective navigation, assortment, and manipulation [17]. Furthermore, six interaction metaphors may be used to group these selection and manipulation strategies. These metaphors are described by LaViola *et al.* as bimanual (using two hands for interaction), hybrid, surface (using a 2-D multi-sensing surface), secondary (e.g., ray-cast select then conducting further multi-sense motions for editing instead of picking the item of choice), and gripping (e.g., utilizing a virtual hand) [18].

Furthermore, it is crucial to consider social media interactions in VR/AR because methodologies like "Together and Alone" and system-supported cooperative learning contend that learning is enhanced by closely knit collaborative interactions [19]. It is interesting to note that some of these cooperative dynamics may be explained by the social interdependence paradigm (positive = cooperative, negative = competitive), according to which "each individual's ability to achieve their goals is influenced by the activities of others."

This kind of "closely coupled cooperation" is demonstrated by "Rubik's Cube puzzles," the storyline developer works of the NICE project (Roussos *et al.* 1997), and numerous studies have shown that cooperative manipulation may occur inside VR/AR settings [20]. The virtual pavilion building project also broke tasks down into smaller tasks that needed to be completed by multiple users at once in both "same attribute" (for example, users choose an item that is heavier for a single user) and "distinct attribute" (for example, one user holds a ceiling joist and the other bolts a hole) tasks. Collaborative virtual environment (CVE) researchers further segment these types of different and similar features into synchronous (sub-jobs accomplished simultaneously) and asynchronous (sub-tasks completed sequentially) tasks.

When creating a virtual environment for cooperation, Pinho *et al.* add four factors to the CVE architecture as shown in Table 1.3 [21]. These factors are comparable to those that define reality-based interactions (RBIs), such as the need for bodily awareness, and skills for RBIs, and social immersive media, such as the need for socially scaled and familiar interactions [22].

The study results are listed in Table 1.4 alongside the interventions that were found, the stage at which they were found, their value and impact, the review article in which they were found, and a list of individual research that supported their findings.

The fact that engagement arose in every intervention, where it was measured, led us to believe that the novelty of the technology being employed directly improves engagement. If so, novelty itself is a possible intervention, and any recently popularized technology may have a comparable impact. If this is the case, it begs the question of whether novelty resistance develops over time and if it applies to all people or simply a subset of those with novelty. Does "accumulative novelty resistance"—the effect of adding new technologies to the learning process to boost students' interest and/or performance—have any impact because of satiation?

**Table 1.3** Considerations for "usable and beneficial" cooperative manipulation approaches.

| | |
|---|---|
| Awareness and consciousness | Showing a user the activities their buddy is carrying out |
| Evolution and expansion | Building supportive methods like logical progressions of one-user methods for benefiting from existing knowledge |
| Transition and transformation | Maintaining the sensation of immersion in the VE when switching between a one-user job and a supportive one without any explicit commands or breaks in the interactive process, in a fluid and organic manner |
| Reusability | Enabling the usage of the current code while supporting the creation of novel supportive interaction approaches |

**Table 1.4** Intervention research findings.

| Study no. | Stage | Intervention | Variable | Effect |
|---|---|---|---|---|
| 1 | Course design and planning of content | Use of AR technology without enough pedagogical preparation | Performance | Decrease |
| 2 | Cognitive load and time management | The use of intricate AR simulations for pupils who are unfamiliar with this intricate technology causes bewilderment and amazement | Performance | Decrease |
| 3 | Remote lectures and content delivery | Usage of AR in lectures and material delivery increases concentration and attention, making studying more engaging and gratifying | Engagement | Increase |
| 4 | Feedback and interactivity | Utilizing AR to visualize abstract concepts and learn calculus helps engineering students develop their mathematical and cognitive abilities | Performance | Increase |
| 5 | Social involvement, interaction | Better face-to-face and distant interactions and collaborations with the use of AR | Engagement | Increase |
| 6 | Remote practice, labs, kinesthetic learning | Medical students' learning rate and memorizing process were positively impacted by their use of AR | Performance | Increase |
| 7 | Remote evaluation | Medical students' learning rate and memorizing process were positively impacted by their use of AR | Performance | No change |

Virtual technologies are significant because they encourage active learning rather than passive learning and foster creativity in users. Construction education has undergone a tremendous transformation due to new technology and virtual tools. Following other practical disciplines, they made a considerable movement in teaching and specialized practices far from the conventional solo theory-based lecturing and toward group problem based learning (PBL). Learning from a particular project of construction as a case study is referred to as project learning. A few examples of group-based learning strategies include technical open-ended problem-solving answers, practical learning projects, and team-oriented interactions.

The idea of active learning and student engagement, which contends students know much and are better known for their professions by active consideration of sequence information, has had a considerable influence lately on the design of education in practical-based learning. Flipped classroom models were suggested by certain scholars for construction management. However, the architecture, engineering and construction (AEC), including the discipline of construction management, has not yet given this innovative, highly praised approach enough attention, especially for big classrooms. Additionally, this teaching approach is not supported by adequate digital resources. The issue is that the teacher is unable to bring a sizable class onto a construction site.

PBL is advised for several academic fields at universities. Many studies in a variety of disciplines, including AEC, are centered on the PBL assessment, and students are required to collaborate and improve their social and cooperative abilities. Based on the literature, Table 1.5 summarizes students' good and unfavorable PBL experiences.

## 1.3 AR and VR Adaptability for Education

More modern strategies are gradually replacing conventional teaching methods. To make learning more engaging and successful for kids, educators are always looking for fresh ideas. The educational experience is changing for both students and teachers due to new, creative training techniques, technological breakthroughs, and initiatives to make technology more accessible [20]. Since it generates a special, personalized experience that cannot be duplicated in the laboratory setting, VR in education specifically aids pupils in improved knowledge retention. The most popular VR platforms are tabulated in Table 1.6.

Using the Unity framework, 2D and 3D video games may be created. For better performance, students may design thoughts, imitations, games, and

**Table 1.5** Student involvement and barriers for grouping project assessments.

| Student involvement | Brief explanation | Reference |
|---|---|---|
| Benefit | More active encouragement and involvement. | Lee *et al.* [23] |
| Positive involvement | Make their task load and assigned additional tasks doable.<br>Give them time to discuss more information with the group.<br>Participating in group discussions would help them develop their critical thinking abilities. | Finlay and Faulkner [24] |
| Negative experience | The conversations took a lot of time and were shallow.<br>The lecture time dedicated to providing "facts" and direct responses was eliminated by the group learning approach.<br>Ineffective because it takes a while for the group to reach an agreement and, often, no results are produced. | Bahar-Özvaris *et al.* [25]<br>Herrmann [26] |
| Barriers | Free riders might not always be recognized.<br>Not all group members contribute equally to the assignment.<br>Creating engaging content | Hall and Buzwell [27] |

**Table 1.6** Popular VR platforms.

| | |
|---|---|
| Unity | Used for creating 2D and 3D gaming simulations for knowledge, skill, and performance. |
| PG&E | 3D maintenance simulation designed to educate through scalable and modular iPad and PCs. |
| Labster | The platform gives realistic knowledge that will help in performing experiments and ensures a risk-free learning environment. |

VR/AR tools. For instance, computer aided engineering (CAE) Vimedix AR assists learners to know sonography, which allows real-time visualization of the anatomy and ultrasound cut plane. The industrial, transportation, media distribution, architectural, engineering, and construction sectors are just a few of the real-world applications for the extensive selection of virtual solutions that Unity provides.

A 3D interactive program called PG&E Becker Pilot Service Training was created by Unity. The complexity of the parts and components might lead to a high mistake rate and a lengthy training period for the specialists. This causes both new and veteran frequency selective receiver (FSRs) to make a lot of support calls particularly about the rebuild process, which results in equipment damage and downtime. Users may create scenes and 3D landscape examples in the program editor and see the changes they make right away. Users may also publish games on a variety of networks using Unity, including TV, PC, and mobile devices. Unity also cooperates with AR, a technology used to build games for VR headsets that allows virtual things to appear in the real world.

Another website that provides students access to a genuine lab setting and allows them to conduct practical exams and hone their abilities in a safe and enjoyable environment to learn is Labster.

The majority of VR/AR solutions on the market lets students learn by doing while utilizing the capabilities offered by the technology. Each element may be customized to match a variety of learning objectives and class topics. Students can, for instance, use their knowledge in social sciences, STEM, coding, literature, languages, maker space, and the arts.

### 1.3.1 CoSpaces

For presentations in a variety of formats, such as charts or tables, graphs, and even timelines, infographics may be a good visual aid. CoSpaces is a useful VR/AR development tool that aids students in producing infographics by providing a grid canvas on which to position things. Charts, for instance, may be made in CoSpaces, utilizing the different library building elements. The tube that can be sliced as illustrated in Figure 1.1 or a chart that presents distributions like a histogram may be made using cuboid construction blocks in various heights.

### 1.3.2 Interior and Exterior Design

A house or apartment may be quickly and easily built in 3D using CoSpaces development tools. Students may learn about 3D modeling and creating by building and designing a virtual home or apartment. For instance, Figure 1.2

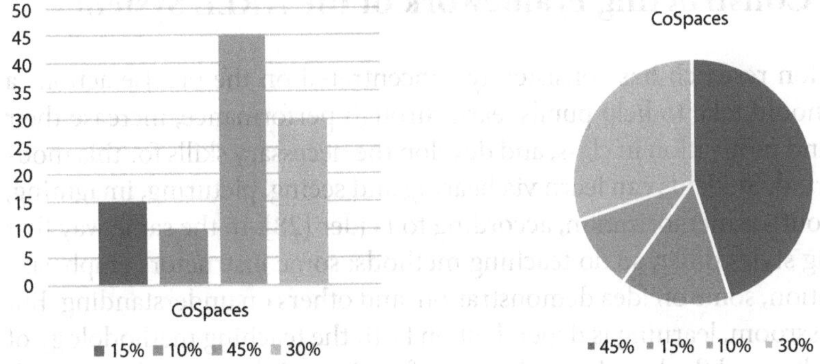


**Figure 1.1** Example of a chart made in CoSpaces using the cuboid tool.

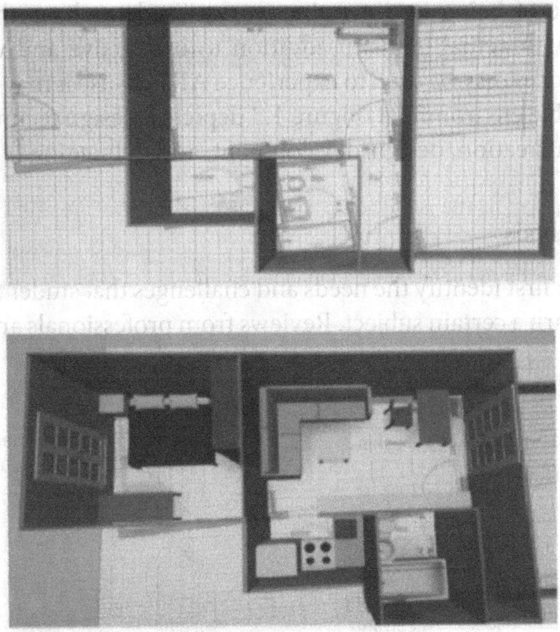

**Figure 1.2** Architecture and interior design using toolbox.

shows a floor plan picture from the upload area that can be imported and utilized as the foundation for a house or apartment.

Students and instructors can utilize a variety of items in the CoSpaces library in addition to the cuboid construction tool to re-enact and imitate lab investigations.

## 1.4 Constructing Framework of the ARLE System

Education research has consistently concentrated on the precise actions a tutor should take to help pupils learn through performance, increase their focus and motivation in class, and develop the necessary skills for this modern period. Students can learn via hearing and seeing, picturing, imagining, acting out, or memorization, according to Felder [28]. In the same way that learning styles differ, so do teaching methods; some instructors emphasize application, some on idea demonstration, and others on understanding. But in a classroom, learning is dependent on both the teaching methodology of the teacher and the learning technique of students. Education places a high value on learning experiences, which call for the mental imagery of ideas to better grasp parallels with less mental effort [29].

We selected AR over VR for educational purposes because it gives students a sense of being in a genuine world. Students have the option of interacting with actual items in addition to immersive and virtual ones. Different devices may be used to experience AR because it may be a mobile, system, or table environment. Figure 1.3 depicts a design technique, which includes idea creation, design/development, and debugging.

### 1.4.1 Analysis

It is crucial to first identify the needs and challenges that students encounter while they learn a certain subject. Reviews from professionals and educators

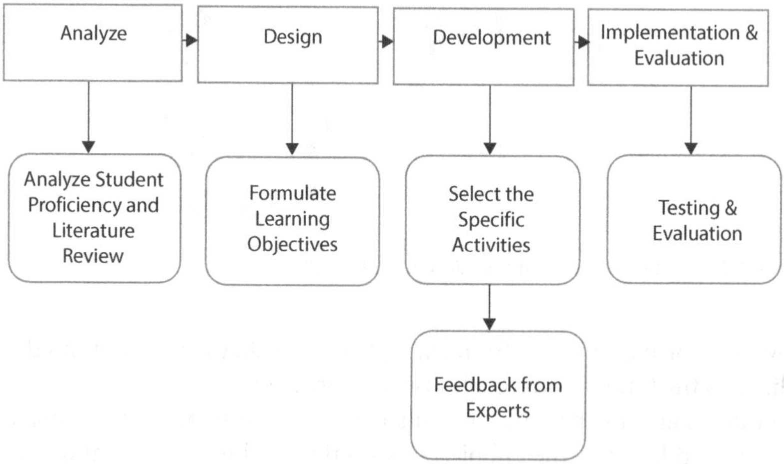


**Figure 1.3** Development steps of ARLE.

have been considered to establish the necessity of creating the application for that reason. For growth purposes, how the subject is taught in their regular classes has been considered. What product requirements and issues to be considered for designing an application have been examined?

### 1.4.2 Design

Making a teaching kit that is portable so that teachers may use it in regular classrooms is crucial for designing purposes. ARLE is created as a series of booklets, each having built-in graphs and marks on the last sheet so that helpful or accurate illustrations can be combined with notes for later use. Unity 3D has been utilized as a game apparatus and Vuforia as a scripting development kit for managing the content and scripting. The game engine Unity 3D is a user-friendly environment for designing and developing games. The program is user-friendly for novices and robust enough for specialists. Building 3D games and submissions for any portable unit is very simple with Unity. To expand the project in Unity, C# is used in the Mono-Develop Integrated Development Environment (IDE).

### 1.4.3 Development

During the development phase, the final product is produced, an estimation is made to aid in debugging, and adjustments are made as necessary. Additionally, the designer should create teaching equipment using phase of design characteristics, such as cost, materials, and safety considerations. To design portable, convenient, and visually appealing teaching equipment, consider these factors.

While doing exploratory research, the generated ARLE application can be estimated for use as a tool for education as an analysis conducted in [30–32] are examples. The "adapt and execute" method is employed in this practice to ensure continual improvement and adaptable reactions to changes. An assessment tool will be used to track learning and retaining time. The evaluation can be based on generic multiple choice question (MCQs) that would be approved by subject matter experts.

Afterward, a post-test will be administered instantly with the following instruction, 1 week later, and then 1 month later. A total of N students will be chosen, and they will be split into groups: a control group and a treatment group.

(a) Control Group: Group 1 constitutes the control group, which will study and be taught conventional methods.

(b) Treatment Group: Group 2 makes up the treatment group, which is further broken down into two subgroups: (1) CAD-based and (2) tabletop learning. To present information tailored to these learners' curricula, ARLE will be delivered to them.

The steps called Quasi-experimental research structure as shown in Figure 1.4 will cover the evaluation process as follows:

(i) A post-test will be practical and relevant to material that has been studied using various teaching strategies. Their topic lecturers and specialists will provide their approval for the questionnaire.
(ii) The quiz will assist in determining the knowledge that was learned. Students will take a test in the form of a questionnaire to gauge their ability to retain the facts they have learned after 1 week and 1 month of study.

The goal of the proposed effort is to provide students and teachers with an immersive learning and teaching experience that will benefit both parties. A mobile-based geometry application has been developed to help pupils grasp geometrical perspectives and help them visualize various angles.

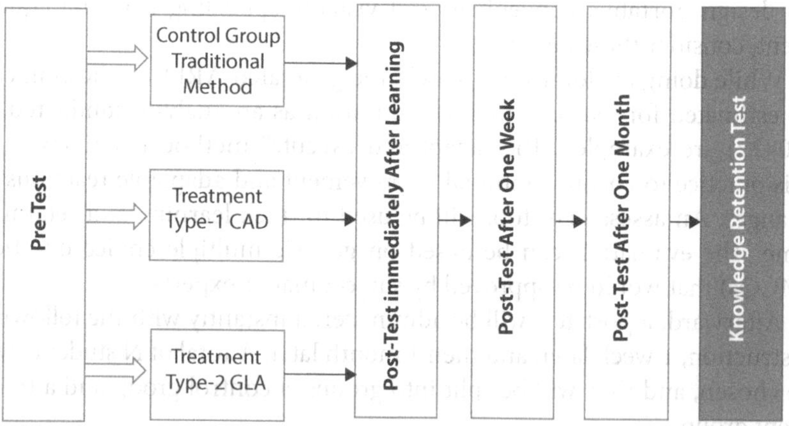


**Figure 1.4** Quasi-experimental research structure.

## 1.5 Digital Learning Environment Analysis in the Context of AR and VR

Physical, psychological, and social components are all present in the scenario that the player sees and experiences in digital learning environments. The virtual learning environment offers a wide range of pedagogical options. In the VR environment, learning is first and foremost learner-based. By using the information that they already know or are memorizing, the players of the game actively construct their learning while also accepting accountability for their actions. In the virtual learning environment, raising awareness regarding common misunderstandings in education is also prioritized. The VR setting offers a hands-on learning opportunity that will help the player or student understand. In some cases, if the player is instructing other players or engaging with other players, it is also possible to learn through cooperative learning. Structure and direction are essential for effective schooling. To advance in the educational system, students must meet learning objectives and outcomes that are explicitly specified.

The advantage of using AR and VR in the classroom is that these settings may be planned and programmed in advance. Students can thus engage in fun experimentation while still pursuing predetermined learning objectives. It has become somewhat passé to lecture school-age students. Modern teaching techniques are instead concentrated on creating a more enriching learning environment for kids, catching their attention and encouraging real participation. VR accomplishes this fundamentally by merely introducing diversity. Students are more likely to remain engaged when their study schedule is more varied. However, VR goes beyond this, immersing students in a powerful virtual setting that will keep their interest.

The more kids participate, try things out for themselves, see ideas in action, and enjoy active learning, the better. When reading textbooks and listening to lectures from teachers and instructors, it can be difficult to accomplish this. Therefore, more active structures will be required to support these more passive forms of learning, even though they will still be important. Instead of "learning by reading," VR and AR enable students to "learn by doing." This method of learning complements other knowledge delivery methods rather than replacing them, such as textbooks. In addition to being able to effectively retain knowledge, students must be able to consume it. According to studies, VR and AR actively enhance memory retention, making it simpler for the human brain to remember new information.

### 1.5.1 Physical Learning Environment

There are restrictions on the available space. The virtual learning environment might not provide students with enough opportunities to experience the room's architecture, for example, it would be hard to reproduce the smell and sound of a real obstacle in the game. The physical VR learning environment's [33] development is centered on describing how smoke will travel across the compartments. A stereotypical image of gestures or heroes wandering about the structure after breathing in smoke appears to exist. In reality, they would pass out within a few minutes, if not sooner.

### 1.5.2 Psychological Learning Environment

Knowing, remembering, avoiding, and making decisions are all cognitive and emotional activities that are tied to the psychological learning environment [34]. In the context of future technology, this may entail taking the game seriously, for instance, remembering how the building is laid out, looking for alternate paths, or determining what would be the polite thing to do. Virtual reality offers a managed and simulated environment for crises, particularly the attitudes toward them. Tasks are prioritized by thinking schemas, and a controlled setting provides options for action in a simulated stressful circumstance.

In addition, feelings of fear, surprise, or excitement experienced while playing the game are a component of the psychological learning environment. In the same example, the player must be able to recall the layout of the building, including where the rooms are located and how to unlock doors, to behave appropriately. The usage of VR/AR offers opportunities to pique players' interests and encourage problem-based learning.

As with the few scenarios, panic may preclude any reasonable activities or decisions that need to be taken in a matter of seconds; therefore, there are restrictions on the psychological dimension and the learning outcome.

### 1.5.3 Social Learning Environment

Interaction with the supervisor, other players, or non-player characters (NPCs) in the game is included in the social dimension [35] of the learning environment. Since these systems interact, it is impossible to completely separate the social and the psychological aspects of the learning environment. A person in the background of one of our VR solutions, which will be discussed later in this article, is working alone and unable to negotiate with anybody. The following table shows an external–internal digital environment of learning investigation in the context of VR and AR.

We give a comparison of two learning environments based on the data gathered from prior initiatives. Table 1.7 displays this information. Both software developers and educators already have access to VR technology. It might be difficult for individuals who want to invest heavily in VR technology to reduce investment risks because new spectacles are often released. In other words, investment in VR technology will not be current until the years after that. As a result, businesses must be able to split expenses while creating adequate learning materials for continuous usage. The creation of VR training facilities appears to be one of the trends for the future. Working jointly in multiplayer training situations from the pre-experience to the post-experience context is possible in this kind of setting for instructors and learners. Additionally, a training facility may feature AR training situations in a real-world setting. To teach new professionals from the start in realistic learning settings and provide updated education services for professionals, education institutions can use a mix of VR and AR training.

The most recent research look at the advantages and disadvantages of group project evaluation and note that it is difficult to gauge how much the students contributed to the primary effort. However, additional research offers some methods for detecting freeloaders and/or evaluating the contributions of other group members. They provide many techniques for peer assessment or evaluation to help lecturers determine the total value of each group member. These techniques primarily rely on a straightforward form that asks students 'to assign each group member a score from 1 to 100, with 100 being the highest, based on their participation in the efforts of the group. This form is an extra tool for evaluating the contributions of the students to their group projects. The following Table 1.8 shows the features of collaborative platform learning.

For administering big classrooms, LMSs provide practical online capabilities [43]. However, the present technologies do not completely enable a variety of pedagogical strategies, such as group projects focused on role-play [44].

## 1.6 General Discussion and Future Aspects

With the process of digitization, the design of learning environments in the field of education is addressed in this research along with a thorough investigation of the AR settings and apps that are often employed. According to the overall findings of the study, various tools and materials are now

**Table 1.7** An external–internal digital environment of learning analysis in the context of VR and AR.

| Learning environment | VR | AR |
|---|---|---|
| Physical external | Controllers for interactions, classrooms with limited space | Visual triggers for interactions, and field environment without any physical limitations |
| Physical internal | Physical actions | Does not exist, or is majorly connected with the external |
| Psychological external | Behavior can be fully monitored | Challenging to monitor players |
| Psychological internal | Controlled environment, possible to measure performance metrics | On-site training location, context, or situation-aware |
| Social external | Multiplayer functionality is required for difficult group dynamics and auditory education opportunities, such as training facilities. | Group work, instant teacher input, and more difficult |
| Social internal | Auditory instruction is feasible, especially in training facilities, and powerful AIs are used for natural language understanding (auditive teaching) | Instant feedback to learners, using headphones for auditory instruction, or using natural language understanding (auditive teaching) |
| Pedagogical external | Guidance is feasible, especially in training facilities, and iterations are conceivable | Iterations that are guided by pre-established instructional procedures are meaningless |

*(Continued)*

**Table 1.7** An external–internal digital environment of learning analysis in the context of VR and AR. (*Continued*)

| Learning environment | VR | AR |
|---|---|---|
| Pedagogical internal | Controlled design, problem-based instruction, and post-experiences: updated instruction and repetitions | Learner-centered, problem-based instruction; on-site experiences; just-in-time information (such as readily available silent information) |

**Table 1.8** Features of a collaborative learning platform.

| Factor | Benefit | References |
|---|---|---|
| Distribution | Learners may simply exchange ideas and provide each other with fast feedback. | Braojos *et al.* [36] |
| Collaboration and communication | Allow students to participate in group projects and real-time meetings with a multi-player option. | Cooper *et al.* [37] |
| Editing | Students can modify their pages rapidly. | Zheng *et al.* [38] |
| Simplicity | The Wiki page is a straightforward format-setting markup method (associating HTML). | Dominic *et al.* [39] |
| Accessibility | Simplicity for linking sources (e.g., YouTube). | Mannisto *et al.* [40] |
| Maintainability | It is simple to save databases, maintain previous versions, and keep track of changes. | Blau *et al.* [41] |
| Free-source | Anyone with access to Wiki can make changes to it. | Boje *et al.* [42] |

being employed in teaching techniques due to the entrance of technologies into educational settings. In context, it is obvious that integrating mobile devices and applications into settings of learning has lately gained popularity.

With the fast advancement of mobile technology, new media environments with higher levels of interaction provide users with an expanding range of services. Technologies that offer AR, can connect things in imaginary surroundings with actual physical existence objects. These innovations enable the overlay of virtual objects on actual photos. The components of an AR toolkit include a camera, a computer network, a marker, and physical objects.

Augmented reality technology in the education sector is the most significant field. Applications for AR assist students in learning and teaching abstract concepts, and they offer settings in which groups of students may exchange information. Additionally, research in the literature has proven that these settings considerably improve students' learning. Additionally, it was underlined that AR has a special role in the transfer of information and knowledge acquired in the imaginary environment to actual surroundings, as well as in improving students' experiences, interests, and incentives in the classroom. The most significant recommendations of this research are to employ AR apps and learning environments more frequently at different levels and course topics when its efficacy in education has been established to this extent.

The goal of the proposed effort is to provide students and teachers with an immersive learning and teaching experience that will benefit both parties. A mobile-based geometry application has been developed to help pupils grasp geometrical perspectives and help them visualize various angles. Additionally, students can receive problem-solving tips that will assist them in recalling all the necessary information to solve their problems. If learners fail to induce the correct line, angle, or representation as specified in the interrogation, ARLE can promptly and accurately correct them, identify the lines, as well as angles, and overlay the proper figure. The application can assess the effectiveness of AR in the education context for upper subordinate educators; however, AR is not restricted to a certain subject or idea. The created ARLE application can be further elaborated for different themes and subject areas if the usability findings are favorable.

Virtual reality offers players intense sentiments, thought-provoking encounters, and experiential learning opportunities that would last long after the actual play session. It is crucial to keep in mind that learning involves acquiring knowledge, abilities, and attitudes when creating educational games. We outlined the elements of the social, psychological, and physical learning environment to provide game designers with a framework for their work. The learning environment was further separated into two sections. It is impossible to separate the internal learning environment—the game's scenes and experiences—from the outward learning environment—the game's interior and surroundings. It is crucial to comprehend the fundamentals of game metrics, such as how long a game lasts, player characteristics, and other constraints of a digital learning environment, to be able to construct a meaningful game training facility.

Additionally, based on the main findings of the Virpagame, we can say that the VR environment offers players a rather realistic gaming experience when developing a game, for example, in fire prevention. A chance for a more precise learning experience is offered by AR solutions. It is crucial to do usability research for this VR/AR setup. The fire department has additional options, thanks to virtual learning environments. With the aid of pedagogical specialists, the game design should nonetheless proceed in the external learning environment. Researchers should also take learning outcome analyses into account. Without this, gaming would probably remain at the enjoyment level and the main objective of learning will not be accomplished. In that situation, we will consider if utilizing VR creates an encouraging environment of learning.

In this study, we investigate the use of VR and AR inside societal learning environments or education in general, while also identifying fresh R&D opportunities to investigate. We suggest that VR/AR educational platforms emphasize scalability across the critical areas: platform scaling, social expandability, and reality scalability, for enhanced universal design for learning (UDL) concerns and much available social engagement across learners utilizing the same social learning settings.

We also recommend giving more thought to investigating how virtual and physical worlds interact, as well as investigating learning theories that could more effectively direct VR/AR learning inside physical and virtual social learning environments. The research into the use of these skills for knowledge is inspiring in that it "provides evidence that VR-based instruction is an effective means of enhancing learning outcomes," which has led many researchers to be positive about the use of VR/AR in education. Students who attend educational institutions that aim to devote time and money in VR/AR are most likely to gain the most from such a learning environment. The biggest difficulty will be figuring out how to use technology to improve kids' learning in a way that does not only replicate or replace the actual learning environment, but also allows for events and access to resources that are not available in physical settings.

To create a more integrated environment, VR can be employed in education. The study discussed the current use of VR platforms in the fields of architecture, gas and oil, automation, and education. For instance, for young children to better grasp processes like transpiration, vapor, and condensation, the water cycle has been designed utilizing the CoSpaces VR platform. VR enables the user to feel more directly linked with their environment and aids in more effective learning than the usual movies or charts used to teach the water cycle.

A prototype for employing VR in teaching is the work being presented here. When utilized by students to study concepts and theories more easily, a VR interface can aid distant learners in the educational area. Inside a decorating university, students may utilize VR 3D creations to help them comprehend concepts on a deeper level. Before actual execution, it is also utilized for animations and virtual experiences of the concepts. Other than for educational purposes, marketers can make use of AR and VR. For a more engaging manner to present material, AR is often used in exhibits and event activations. Jobs can be developed and done in some ways and for various industries, including real estate, tourism, coaching and training, education, and the medical sector. Virtual reality may be utilized in the tourism industry for hotel tours and attractions, vacation destinations, and marketing of travel deals and packages. For medical procedures, VR helps lessen fear and anxiety associated with shots, injections, and blood draws in children, adolescents, and adults.

## References

1. J. Tokareva, "The difference between virtual reality, augmented reality and mixed reality," *Forbes*, 2018.
2. K. Mehta, V. M. Sood, C. Singh, and P. Chabra, "Machine Learning based Intelligent System for Safeguarding Specially Abled People," *2022 7th International Conference on Communication and Electronics Systems (ICCES)*, 2022, pp. 1199-1206, DOI: 10.1109/ICCES54183.2022.9835773.
3. Erbas, C. and Demirer, V. (2015). Eğitimde Sanal ve Arttirilmiş Gerçeklik Uygulamaları. In book: Eğitim Teknolojileri Okumaları 2015 Chapter: 7.
4. Chiang, T.H.C., Yang, S.J.H. and Hwang, G.J. (2014). An augmented reality-based Mobile learning system to improve student's learning achievements and motivations in Natural science inquiry activities, *Educ. Technol. Soc.*, 17(4), 352-365.
5. Information Technology and Communication Agency Report (2020). Retrieved from Information and Communication Technology in Special

Needs Education report | European Agency for Special Needs and Inclusive Education (european-agency.org).

6. Sezgin, S. (2016), "Eğitimde Giyilebilir Teknolojiler: Fırsatlar ve Eğilimler", *Educ. Fac. J. Mehmet Akif Ersoy*, 40, 405-418.
7. Mehta, Kapil, Yogesh Kumar, and Aayushi Aayushi. "Enhancing Time Synchronization for Home Automation Systems." *ECS Trans.*, 107.1 (2022): 6197.
8. Jerald J (2015) The VR book: a human-centered design for virtual reality Morgan & Claypool Publishers and ACM Books, San Rafael.
9. Mehta, Kapil, *et al.* "Enhancement of Smart Agriculture Using Internet of Things." *ECS Trans.*, 107.1 (2022): 7047.
10. Dede C, Richards J (2017) Conclusion—strategic planning for R&D on immersive learning. In: Lui D, Dede C, Huang R, Richards J (eds.) Virtual, augmented, and mixed realities in education. Springer, Berlin, pp 237–243. https ://doi.org/10.1007/978-981-10-5490-7_1.
11. Fowler C (2015) Virtual reality and learning: where is the pedagogy? *Br. J. Edu. Technol.*, 46(2):412–422.
12. Johnson-Glenberg MC (2018) Immersive VR and education: embodied design principles that include gesture and hand controls. *Front. Robot AI*, 5(July):1–19. https ://doi.org/10.3389/frobt .2018.00081.
13. Borrego A, Latorre J, Alcañiz M, Llorens R (2019) Embodiment and presence in virtual reality after stroke A comparative study with healthy subjects. *Front. Neurol.*, 10(October):1–8. https ://doi.org/10.3389/fneur .2019.01061.
14. Johnson-Glenberg MC, Megowan-Romanowicz C (2017) Embodied science and mixed reality: how gesture and motion capture affect physics education. *Cogn. Res. Princ. Implic.*, https ://doi.org/10.1186/s4123 5-017-0060-9.
15. Rai, Vinayak, *et al.* "Automated Biometric Personal Identification-Techniques and Applications." *2020 4th International Conference on Intelligent Computing and Control Systems (ICICCS)*. IEEE, 2020.
16. Hoang TN, Cox TN (2018) The sense of embodiment in virtual reality. *Presence Teleoper. Virtual Environ.*, 26(4):402–419.
17. Borrego A, Latorre J, Alcañiz M, Llorens R (2019) Embodiment and presence in virtual reality after stroke A comparative study with healthy subjects. *Front. Neurol.*, 10(October):1–8. https ://doi.org/10.3389/fneur 2019.01061.
18. Bansal, Abhishek, Kapil Mehta, and Sahil Arora. "Face recognition using PCA and LDA algorithm." *2012 Second International Conference on Advanced Computing & Communication Technologies*. IEEE, 2012.
19. LaViola JJ Jr, Kruijff E, McMahon RP, Bowman DA, Poupyrev IP (2017) 3D user interfaces: theory and practice (Usability) (2nd). Addison-Wesley, Boston.
20. Stahl G, Hakkarainen K (2020) Theories of CSCL. In: *International Handbook of Computer Supported Collaborative Learning*. Springer.
21. Rai, Vinayak, *et al.* "Cloud Computing in Healthcare Industries: Opportunities and Challenges." *Recent Innovations in Computing* (2022): 695-707.

22. Jacob RJK, Girouard A, Horn MS, Zigelbaum J (2008) Reality-based interaction: a framework for post-WIMP interfaces. In: *Proceedings of the SIGCHI Conference on Human Factors in Computing Systems.*
23. Lee, S.J.; Ngampornchai, A.; Trail-Constant, T.; Abril, A.; Srinivasan, S. Does a case-based online group project increase students' satisfaction with interaction in online courses? *Act. Learn. High. Educ.*, 2016, 17, 249–260. [CrossRef]
24. Finlay, S.-J.; Faulkner, G. Tête à tête Reading groups and peer learning. *Act. Learn. High. Educ.*, 2005, 6, 32–45. [CrossRef]
25. Bahar-Özvaris¸, S.e.; Çetin, F.Ç.; Turan, S.; Peters, A.S. Cooperative learning: A new application of problem-based learning in mental health training. *Med. Teach.*, 2006, 28, 553–557. [CrossRef] [PubMed]
26. Herrmann, K.J. The impact of cooperative learning on student engagement: Results from an intervention. *Act. Learn. High. Educ.*, 2013, 14, 175–187. [CrossRef]
27. Hall, D.; Buzwell, S. The problem of free-riding in group projects: Looking beyond social loafing as a reason for non-contribution. *Act. Learn. High. Educ.*, 2012, 14, 37–49. [CrossRef]
28. Snibbe SS, Raffle HS (2009) Social immersive media—pursuing best practices for multi-user interactive camera/projector exhibits. In: *Proceedings of the SIGCHI Conference on Human Factors in Computing Systems.*
29. S. Freitas and G. Veletsianos, "Crossing boundaries: Learning and teaching in virtual worlds," *Brit. J. Educ. Technol.*, vol. 41, no. 1, pp. 3-9, 2010.
30. R. M. Felder and L. K. Silverman, "Learning and teaching styles in engineering education", *Eng. Educ.*, pp. Vol. 78, no. 7, pp. 674–81, 2002.
31. T. Thornton, J. Ernst, and C. Clark, "Augmented reality as a visual and spatial learning tool in technology education," *Technol. Eng. Technol.*, pp. Vol. 71, no. 8, pp. 18–21, 2012.
32. B. Jeong and J. Yoon, "Competitive intelligence analysis of augmented reality technology using patent information", *Sustainability Summit* (Sustainability 2017, 9, 497), pp. Vol. 9,no. 4, pp. 1–22., 2017.
33. M. Ibanez, A. Di-Serio, D. Villaran-Molina, and C. Delgado-Kloos, "Augmented reality-based simulators as discovery learning tools: an empirical study", *IEEE Trans. Educ.*, pp. Vol. 58, no. 3, pp. 208–13, August 2015.
34. M. Restivo, F. Chouzal, J. Rodrigues, P. Menezes, B. Patrao and J. B. Lopes, "Augmented reality in electrical fundamentals", *Int. J. Online Eng. (IJOE)*, pp. pp. 68–72Vol. 10, no. 6,, EDUCON2014.
35. Mehta, Kapil, and Y. O. G. E. S. H. Kumar. "Implementation of efficient clock synchronization using elastic timer technique in IoT." *Adv. Math.; Sci. J.*, 9.6 (2020): 4025-4030.
36. Gutiérrez-Braojos, C.; Montejo-Gamez, J.; Marin-Jimenez, A.; Campaña, J. Hybrid learning environment: [1Collaborative or competitive learning? *Virtual Real.* 2019, 23, 411–423. [CrossRef]

37. Cooper, G.; Park, H.; Nasr, Z.; Thong, L.; Johnson, R. Using virtual reality in the classroom: Preservice teachers' perceptions of its use as a teaching and learning tool. *Educ. Media Int.*, 2019, 56, 1–13. [CrossRef]
38. Zheng, L.; Zhang, X.; Gyasi, J.F. A literature review of features and trends of technology-supported collaborative learning in informal learning settings from 2007 to 2018. *J. Comput. Educ.*, 2019, 6, 529–561. [CrossRef]
39. Dominic, M.; Francis, S.; Pilomenraj, A. E-learning in web 3.0. *Int. J. Mod. Educ. Comput. Sci.*, 2014, 6, 8. [CrossRef]
40. Männistö, M.; Mikkonen, K.; Kuivila, H.M.; Virtanen, M.; Kyngäs, H.; Kääriäinen, M. Digital collaborative learning in nursing education: A systematic review. *Scand. J. Caring Sci.*, 2019. [CrossRef] [PubMed]
41. Blau, I.; Shamir-Inbal, T.; Avdiel, O. How does the pedagogical design of a technology-enhanced collaborative academic course promote digital literacies, self-regulation, and perceived learning of students? *Internet High. Educ.*, 2020, 45, 100722. [CrossRef]
42. Boje, C.; Guerriero, A.; Kubicki, S.; Rezgui, Y. Towards a semantic Construction Digital Twin: Directions for future research. *Autom. Constr.*, 2020, 114, 103179.
43. Bedi, Tejpreet Singh, Santosh Kumar, and Rakesh Kumar. "Corrosion performance of hydroxyapatite and hydroxyapatite/titania bond coating for biomedical applications." *Mater. Res. Express*, 7.1 (2019): 015402.
44. Singh, Chamkaur, Neeraj Sharma, and Narender Kumar. "Analysis of software maintenance cost affecting factors and estimation models." *Int. J. Sci. Technol. Res.*, 8 (2019): 276-281.

# 2

# Role of AR and VR Technology in Transforming Education Ecology

**Gagandeep Kaur[1]*, Harpreet Kaur[2], Sonia Goyal[2], Veerpal Kaur[3] and Prabhleen Kaur[1]**

[1]*Chitkara University Institute of Engineering and Technology, Chitkara University, Punjab, India*
[2]*Punjabi University, Patiala, India*
[3]*School of Computer Science and Engineering, Lovely Professional University, Phagwara, Punjab, India*

***Abstract***

Artificial intelligence is advancing rapidly and has a wide range of implications for development. In recent years, technology has gained significant traction in all areas of life, including business logistics, telecommunications, the medical field, and education. A virtual or augmented reality (commonly abbreviated as AR or VR) enhances or substitutes a real-life environment with a virtual equivalent. In AR, digital elements are added to a live view, for instance, by using a smartphone's camera, while VR is a totally engrossing experience in which a real-world environment is replaced by a simulated environment.

Education is undergoing rapid transformation due to digital technologies. In the educational technology sector, immersive technologies like augmented reality and virtual reality (AR/VR) can allow users to interact with digitally rendered content in both physical and virtual environments. The rapidly expanding field of education technology, immersion experiences, new and engaging ways to share information, and the possibility of offering virtual experiences make AR/VR technologies promising for enhancing access to education that might otherwise be restricted to geographical distances or cost constraints. A key purpose of AR/VR in education is to engage students and foster greater understanding of learning content. By utilizing simulation, 3D imagery, and audio-visual effects, AR and VR technologies are being utilized to optimize learning outcomes. Universities and colleges will undoubtedly usher in unprecedented intelligent changes as an

**Corresponding author*: gaganmalhotra1791@gmail.com

V. Ajantha Devi, Williamjeet Singh and Yogesh Kumar (eds.) Augmented Reality and Virtual Reality in Special Education, (33–64) © 2024 Scrivener Publishing LLC

important base for cultivating talent and nurturing development forces in the new era. Applications of AR and VR can improve the skills and knowledge of students. When compared with traditional didactic methods, simulations/animations, AR/VR techniques demonstrate more engagement, competency, and skill improvement for learners. Researchers found AR/VR to have great potential in education and can have a huge impact on teaching reforms. The technique of AR augments and enhances our perception of reality with elements such as image, audio, and text; on the other hand, VR creates a simulated learning environment that engages and enables students to work on activities that are part of the curriculum.

***Keywords*:** Augmented reality, virtual reality, educational and training systems, priority, framework, access to education, basic education, innovation, distance education

## 2.1 Introduction

Augmented reality and virtual reality (AR and VR) technologies stand out as truly newsworthy ever since they were introduced [1]. They enhance the real value of the learning process. 3D virtual worlds have turned into a popular trend in the digital world because of their progression in computing technology and network infrastructure [57] as shown in Figure 2.1.

With the help of AR/VR, it has become possible for students, as well as teachers, to visualize concepts and adapt to new skills with ease [2]. These new advances are not restricted to a particular age group of learners. The role of AR in transforming education has grown to a place where at present

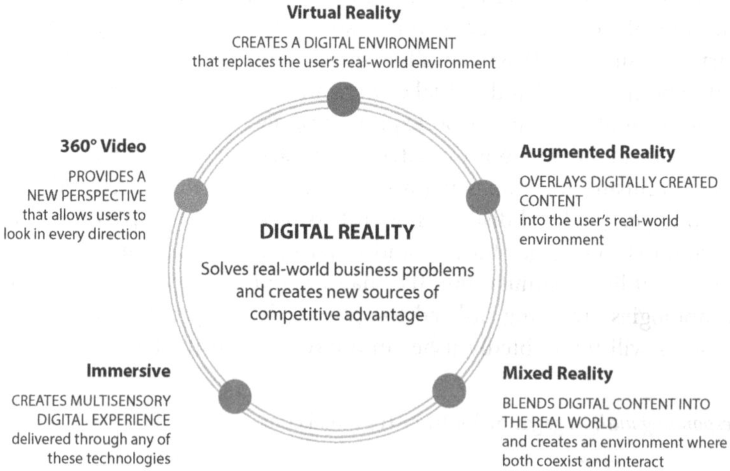


**Figure 2.1** Description of digital reality.

and across the globe, many areas or sectors use these two advancements in their everyday practice. As a result of the COVID lockdown [3], technology has been adopted rapidly in the education sector. As virtual classrooms and self-paced learning became the norm during lockdown, these technologies moved quickly from specific learning labs to simple mobile apps. Also, AR/VR may be used to recreate an analogous working environment that professionals would experience in the physical world. In addition, users with specialized abilities can utilize this virtual environment to practice, level up, and master their abilities whenever needed [4]. With cutting-edge work environment for millennials and gen Z workers, organizations will find it useful to incorporate AR/VR innovation for this tech-accommodating age. The purpose of AR is to guide students at distinct stages, while the purpose of VR is to provide students and educators with a radically different experience.

Augmented reality has been dominating the educational technology market with several successful implementations; VR is also a trending technology but has seen several commercial failures in the beginning. VR is a human–computer interface that provides the user with a sensory experience by simulating a realistic environment. The user can sense and interact with the simulated environment by touching, viewing, hearing, etc. Virtual reality has multiple application areas, and education is one of them. It is neither a new term in technology nor a new application tool in education. It was implemented for the first time in 1966 to showcase flight simulation to the US Air Force. A series of arcade games was developed by Virtuality Group in 1991, which became unpopular and had to be withdrawn. In 1993, a VR-based "Head Mounted Display" was designed by SEGA, which was never released. Several VR-based game systems were designed but were commercially a flop. Even though VR technology was not so popular in commercial implementation, it has found greater and more impactful results when deployed in education.

Some main roles and features of AR/VR are mentioned in this chapter. Both AR and VR assist with continuous feedback component, making learning more proficient and retainable. Their advancements help upgrade the efficiency and nature of instructor–student commitment or relationship. Virtual reality provides accessible and compelling online learning and evaluation experiences [5, 44, 45]. The novel democratization of learning on digital platforms is helping the differently-abled, and learners from rural regions, to get sufficiently close to information more effectively and plentifully. Notwithstanding content utilization, AR/VR in schooling is also valuable for supporting creativity of peers. Game-based learning builds commitment and inspiration, and VR can take this to a higher level [6].

VR innovation offers a realistic lab experience for users to practise their skills in a safe and controlled learning environment. It can assist learners with creating basic soft skills can will better prepare them for progress. Thus, these advancements give learners ways of extending their insight in different fields like reading, content creation, playing, genuine circumstances, and spatial ideas. These ideas will help in preparing them for various opportunities including field trips [7].

Hence, one might say that these innovations assist with making vivid universes where students can visualize concepts and master new abilities in a playful yet intuitive manner. The use of AR/VR in education empowers learners and can help address the most pressing concerns at present when training them [68]. These incorporate a shift away from fact-based teaching toward additional participatory ones, as well as a journey for better approaches to connect with students [8]. The primary market drivers for AR/VR in training are the high reception paces of virtual learning conditions, propels innovation of VR headsets, and benefits numerous new organizations in the corporate and education sectors. In contrast to 2D technologies, these technologies offer many capabilities for presenting data in more meaningful and engaging ways [9]. The use of AR and VR in schooling also assists a huge number of students in India, and overall, lightens some issues by making the learning process more playful, interesting, and delightful [10–12]. Thus, AR and VR are a stroke of luck for a country's educational sector and its potential seems never-ending. Machine learning can be used in AR/VR to recognize and understand the real-world environment [39, 40, 50–54]. It can also be used with other cryptographic techniques [41–43, 62, 63].

This chapter provides a detailed introduction to AR/VR and addresses their importance in the education sector in Section 2.1, followed by a comprehensive overview of current research and products in AR/VR that have potential pedagogical impact on educational systems and a bibliometric analysis of the field in Section 2.2. The study also highlights what AR/VR can offer learners and teachers, its strengths and limitations in Section 2.3, followed by conclusion and references.

## 2.2 Related Works

The following section describes works related to the field and details a bibliometric analysis. Jose *et al.* (2011) dissect the benefits presented by AR methods for distant labs to create and demonstrate the numerous potential outcomes of sensible online coaching within the areas of science and engineering. The undertakings of augmented reality for remote laboratories (ARRL) application are discussed. Admittance to the augmented remote laboratory (ARL) is also empowered by ARRL. This application is privately run on a client's computer and permission is granted to the distant lab through TCP/IP using AR methods that empower the interactive utilization of the lab gear [13].

Heen Chen *et al.* (2011) provided a concise overview of AR's potential and difficulties in engineering graphics education. Engineers can easily utilize a graphical language to impart engineering graphics guidance using an AR-based framework. The framework targets working on spatial awareness and interest in realizing, which will help maximize the benefits to students. The recreated and analyzed consequences of the model framework exhibit the viability of their methodologies [14].

Kangdon Lee *et al.* (2012) discussed AR, its ongoing circumstances, and how it functions in education and training. The work also highlighted proficiency, adequacy, and the possible effect of AR on the fate of schooling. A new wave of technologies and data transfers can provide improved AR experiences via computers or mobile devices, merging real-world experiences with augmented data to achieve logical coherence [15].

Dragos Iordache *et al.* (2012) target evaluating the degree to which explicit abilities of the augmented reality teaching platform (ARTP) support the comprehension of chemistry ideas, as well as their commitment to the evident value. In general, the collaboration worldview is demonstrated to impact the viability and proficiency of the educational experience [16].

Michael *et al.* (2013) undertook a study to assess how a 3D virtual environment could enhance student learning. This work was established in a virtual environment that relied on items that are available in the most commonly used 3D virtual world. According to assessments of the students' growth potential, 3D virtual environments could be used to accomplish constructivist learning results [17].

Hsin-Kai Wu *et al.* (2013) examined the ongoing status, scientific classifications, and advances of AR in schooling, along with its difficulties and solutions for these difficulties. Furthermore, they explained how various classifications of AR approaches may facilitate student learning, based on "roles," "tasks," and "locations." The author laid more stress that AR ought to be seen as a concept instead of a sort of innovation as it would be more valuable for teachers and researchers and likewise recognize specific elements and affordances of AR frameworks and applications [18].

Toshti H. *et al.* (2014) found that mobile learning frameworks based on AR have been proposed to guide request-based learning activities. Trials were conducted to determine whether the proposed approach regarding learning accomplishments and inspirations is viable. The exploratory outcomes demonstrated that the proposed approach can additionally foster students' learning achievements. Moreover, AR-based mobile learning was found to inspire students, showing essentially better outcomes in terms of consideration, certainty, and significance compared to traditional request-based versatile learning [19].

Le Q. T. *et al.* (2015) provided a framework for using mobile-based VR and AR to develop experiential safety training. The framework is structured around three modules: safety knowledge dissemination, safety knowledge reflection, and safety knowledge assessment. It comprises three key aspects of safety knowledge. The outcomes highlight that utilizing mobile-based AR/VR would further develop construction security and well-being, successfully enhancing risk-distinguishing proof abilities and familiarity with safe work methodology. In light of the above results, the researchers are convinced that the reconciliation of VR and AR with mobile registering can address the impediments of current development security training and significantly improve the future development faculty's well-being capability [20].

Caleb *et al.* (2016) summed up the possible significance and potential outcomes that games, AR/VR, and gaming can bring to nursing, patient consideration, and medical attendant schooling. Using game-based techniques in medical care mediation might improve outcomes, particularly in well-being prediction and patient consideration. Customizing gaming interventions to prioritise individual needs might enhance individuals' sense of control and serve as a motivating factor in achieving their wellness goals. Nurses might find it supportive to recognize current games and innovations and customize these as a feature of a patient-focused, objective-situated care arranging action [21].

Sarah Parsons *et al.* (2016) presented a reasonable survey that raises questions about the validity of VR for autism research by examining research papers that have used VR to enhance learning and to examine social responses. An analysis of the expected connection between virtual and real settings is given, along with an examination of specific planning elements and cooperation characteristics, which can help or hinder virtual environment learning and understanding. According to the findings, the field must investigate the factors that efficiently impact in answering in VR to understand when, and under what conditions, the reactions of people with mental imbalance can be considered appropriate [22].

Kavanagh *et al.* (2017) argued that most researchers use VR to inspire students and cite an extremely narrow range of factors such as constructivist teaching methods, cooperation, and gamification to guide their encounters. They also presented and looked at a large number of ongoing computer-generated simulation innovations, examining their capability to conquer a few of the issues recognized in the examinations, including cost and user experience [23].

Jorge Martin *et al.* (2017) discussed different virtual technology trends arising and spreading in schooling. Through examining the potential outcomes of incorporating advancements in education with VR and AR technologies, this work offers a far-reaching understanding of these technologies. The authors presented a brief description of how virtual innovations can be facilitated in fresher instructional situations and teaching practices. The benefits and drawbacks of incorporating virtual advances into instructional settings were also discussed [24].

A. Cascales Martínez *et al.* (2017) proposed to investigate the feasibility of utilizing multi-touch tabletops to teach applied math skills to students with disabilities. An examination of the effects of this innovation on students' performance is presented, as well as the relationship between the kind of need and the level of information provided by this innovation. The data indicates that the effectiveness of digital education is superior than that of conventional tactics. The use of the tabletop framework contributes significantly to expanding the information gained by the students, and the innovation can be effectively applied to unusual instructional requirements [25].

Wang Yu *et al.* (2018) dissected the application modes and specialized benefits of AR and VR in education. The discussion focused on the highlights of AR and VR, how the technology will impact teaching, how the learning environment will be further developed, the support and formation of aspects. The author emphasised the educational value and promptly demonstrated the potential foundation of AR/VR technology in educational applications. They also highlighted the use of AR/VR technology in the field of education [26].

I. Horváth *et al.* (2018) did an examination, which comprises conventional 2D interfaces and MaxWhere, a 3D VR instructive platform, to reveal insight into how these innovations impact the viability of different tasks and work processes comprising educators' undertakings. The consequences of the examination, assessed as far as a recently proposed system, highlight the end that, while utilizing MaxWhere rather than conventional 2D connection points, instructors, teachers, and trainers can achieve similar computerized work processes with significantly less client and machine operations. In light of these outcomes, the work sums up that MaxWhere, as an academic platform, offers clients various ways of achieving tasks that would somehow require very convoluted advanced work processes in additional conventional

2D conditions. In a nutshell, it can be expressed that other than MaxWhere's capacity to increment learning effectiveness, it likewise has a critical capacity to decrease the workload of educators and instructors [27].

Juan Gurzon *et al.* (2019) investigated significant issues like the exceptional requirements of clients or the effect of AR on schooling through the quantitative examination of facts and figures. The outcomes demonstrate that AR affects learning viability. There are AR frameworks in training that have been identified with significant benefits in terms of "learning gains" and "motivation." Consequently, stakeholders have an extraordinary opportunity to foster new and better frameworks to benefit all students by incorporating AR frameworks into instructive settings. The frequency of distributed studies examining the applications of augmented reality (AR) in education has increased since 2010. This is likely due to the integration of AR systems in mobile devices. Thus, it may be expected that AR advancements will also increase in use as cell phone usage spreads, particularly in developing countries [28].

George Papanastasiou *et al.* (2019) examined the impact of AR/VR innovations on students' 21st century skills and their general mastery by providing a brief and non-comprehensive overview of the momentum research studies. A primary motivation behind this work is to present workmanship approaches and examples of AR/VR frameworks, applications, and experiences that further enhance student learning and assessment of capabilities. AR/VR applications provide a powerful tool to boost learning and memory by providing immersive environments enriched with many notable characteristics, despite the presence of numerous limitations and challenges in their implementation [29].

N. Elmqaddem *et al.* (2019) analyzed whether VR is being used in education. Their goal was to check whether AR and VR have advanced to the point where they can be effectively coordinated in education programs and to understand why AR and VR can be, for the first time, genuinely incorporated into teaching and learning and to demonstrate their high commitment. It was concluded that AR and VR, along with their new upgrade, can facilitate a new way of learning that better addresses the needs of 21st century students who need diversion, intuition, cooperation, and control. In all cases, AR and VR will affect our way of communicating with this present reality and will be widely adopted in all areas within the next few years. Thus, VR will no longer be only a myth but a reality [30].

Mojtaba Noghabaei *et al.* (2020) surveyed architectural, engineering, and construction firms on how they are incorporating VR and AR. The principal goals of their review are to decide the trends in the reception of AR/VR advances in the business, to anticipate the future and vision of business specialists on the reception of these advancements, and to recognize the usage limits of these advancements. According to studies, industry experts anticipate solid development in the usage of AR/VR advances over the next 5 to 10 years. Moreover, the results show a significant expansion in AR/VR applications in the Architectural Engineering and Construction (AEC) industry over the past year [31].

Xiang Zhou *et al.* (2020) introduced an innovation that helped the biological microscope learning framework in view of AR/VR. Using AR/VR technology, this study aimed to provide students with another learning tool for microscope trials. The objective of this study was to reproduce microscope activity using vivid VR and image-based mobile AR. To simulate the process of using a microscope, a mobile AR innovation was utilized based on image data. Vivid VR innovation was utilized to develop an independent three-layered virtual learning environment and recreate genuine microscope tasks with an intuitive VR gadget for students to embrace the investigation without real trial instruments. The results proved that utilizing current technologies to help students' independent learning is successful in exploratory training [32].

Danny Schott *et al.* (2021), using clinical cases, presented a prototype of an AR and VR learning environment for liver anatomy education. Through a collaborative development process with surgeons and educators, they developed a virtual organ library. In this study, 19 liver informational indexes were used, including 3D surface models, 2D image data [48], pathology information, diagnosis, and treatment plans. In terms of volumetric and metadata, these indexes can be interactively arranged and analyzed individually. They also collected qualitative data through semi-structured interviews. Different teaching situations were shown that permit cooperative and helpful learning in different group constellations and gatherings. By integrating technologies such as VR and AR with surgical education content, the authors believe that their work offers a promising perspective [33].

A. Tokarev *et al.* (2021) conducted a practical study on improving VR educational instruments for school pre-proficient training. According to their examination, they developed a program to ensure skills in working with VR advances in accordance with Conceive – Design – Implement – Operate (CDIO) guidelines. The purpose of this program is to foster students' interest in concentrating on engineering, acquaint them with AR innovation, and show them the fundamentals of growing new specialized frameworks. The program incorporates six parts; one of each contains both a hypothetical and a practical part, which assists students with obtaining hypothetical and common-sense abilities for working with VR innovations. As a result of passing the fundamental course, students gain a comprehensive knowledge base and are more inclined to pursue virtual advancements in the future [34].

A. Raith *et al.* (2022) led a review that depicts confirmation of the idea for two AR-empowered instructive devices pointed toward a portion of the difficulties in medical services education using AR innovations: VIPER and ARTUR. Their examination gives a definite portrayal of the issues, the plan, the execution, as well as the approval of the AR models. The main objective of the study is to assess the perspectives of radiology professionals on the potential benefits of augmented reality (AR) and explore how virtual learning environments might assist radiographers in understanding radiographic methods. Through the development of the models, AR has demonstrated its effectiveness in visualizing rather complex strategies, such as the illumination system used in radiation treatment and the positioning of the patient during radiographic techniques. It shows that AR has extraordinary capability in education, as well as radiology training [35].

V. Sharma *et al.* (2022) claimed that, with the help of Game Learning Analytics (GLA), an AR-based serious game has been planned and assessed so that students can learn programming in a friendly and beneficial manner. They have conducted a careful survey with different college students. The consequence of this study is that students with less prior programming abilities can show a basic improvement after playing the game as it assists them with further developing their fundamental programming abilities. They have consolidated a game learning analytics framework in the game for different stakeholder benefits. Eventually, they gave the ideas and examined the ramifications for future work [36].

Q. Jin *et al.* (2022) conducted a comprehensive inquiry including key stakeholders and a series of collaborative design workshops with teachers and students. The principal objective of this study is to figure out how VR will enter university classrooms. The study identified key stakeholders for involving VR in advanced education, as well as key challenges and opportunities critical for current and future VR practices in college classrooms. This study contributes a point-by-point portrayal of current discernments and contemplations from a multi-partner viewpoint, giving new pieces of knowledge on planning novel VR advances in higher education. The authors believe that their work is a fundamental enhancement to the development of available and successful VR study halls under the college framework [37]. The crux of the above work has been described in Table 2.1.

**Table 2.1** Description of the related work.

| Contributors | Dataset | Framework | Outcome |
|---|---|---|---|
| Jose Manuel Andujar *et al.* [2010] | Students experiences | Virtual and remote laboratories: the ARL | The study emphasizes the use of VR in remote laboratories with a focus on practical training, and the results show that the Augmented Learning Laboratory ha an overall positive impact on student learning. |
| H. Chen *et al.* [2011] | Data related to engineering graphics | AR-based method | AR applications serve as effective teaching aids for engineering graphics courses and help students better understand complex spatial issues. |
| K. Lee *et al.* [2012] | - | The study describes the work related to AR/VR technology in the education sector | It shows the ongoing situation of AR in the education field and concludes that there are many positive effects of AR in education and learning. |
| D.D. Iordache *et al.* [2012] | Data related to the subject and students | ARTP | The consequences of this multiple-regression examination show that using ARTP in education empowers students to grasp each topic clearly with less exertion in learning. |
| M. Chau *et al.* [2013] | Data related to students | 3D virtual environments as an educational platform | The experiences of students in 3D virtual environments demonstrate that constructivist learning is effective when used in 3D virtual environments. |

*(Continued)*

**Table 2.1** Description of the related work. (*Continued*)

| Contributors | Dataset | Framework | Outcome |
|---|---|---|---|
| H.K. Wu *et al.* [2013] | - | - | It has analyzed the continuous status, logical order, and progression of AR in education. |
| T.H.C. Chiang *et al.* [2014] | Students experiences | An AR-based mobile learning system | In comparison to traditional learning approaches, AR-based mobile learning leads to significantly enormous guidance for consideration, certainty, and significance among students. |
| Q.T. Le *et al.* [2015] | - | Mobile-based VR and AR for experiential construction safety education | Based on the findings, mobile-based AR/VR would further develop construction safety and well-being in terms of identifying risk factors and becoming familiar with safe work practices. |
| C. Ferguson *et al.* [2016] | Dataset related to healthcare | AR, VR, and gaming applications | Expanding the utilization of game-based approaches in medical services mediations might prompt better results, especially in well-being anticipation methodologies and in persistent consideration settings. |
| S. Parsons *et al.* [2016] | - | A systematic study on VR | The conclusions suggest that the field should examine the different components that affect productive responses in VR. |

(*Continued*)

**Table 2.1** Description of the related work. (*Continued*)

| Contributors | Dataset | Framework | Outcome |
|---|---|---|---|
| S. Kavanagh *et al.* [2017] | - | A systematic review of VR in education | Several educational areas account for most of educational VR implementations, which indicate that VR is most commonly used to motivate students. |
| J. Martín-Gutiérrez *et al.* [2017] | - | Discussed VR trends in the education section | It discussed the benefits and impediments of involving virtual advances, as well as different virtual technology trends that are arising and spreading in education. |
| A. Cascales-Martínez *et al.* [2016] | Using an AR-enhanced tabletop system to promote learning of mathematics | Used an AR-enhanced tabletop system to promote learning of mathematics | It highlights that the tabletop educational adequacy is higher than that of utilizing traditional strategies. |
| W. Yu *et al.* [2018] | - | - | As AR/VR innovation advances in education and teaching, it not only aids in educational learning but also expands AR/VR application modes. |
| I. Horváth *et al.* [2018] | - | MaxWhere's 3D platform | The consequences of the examination highlight that the teacher can achieve similar computerized work processes with fewer clients and machine operations while utilizing MaxWhere rather than a conventional 2D connection. |

(*Continued*)

**Table 2.1** Description of the related work. (*Continued*)

| Contributors | Dataset | Framework | Outcome |
|---|---|---|---|
| Juan Garzón *et al.* [2019] | - | - | The outcomes demonstrate that AR can affect learning viability. |
| G. Papanastasiou *et al.* [2019] | - | Present state-of-the-art approaches and examples of AR/VR systems | AR/VR applications offer a convincing way to enhance learning and memory by providing drenched multimodal environments enhanced with a variety of significant features. |
| N. Elmqaddem *et al.* [2019] | - | - | VR will no longer be only a myth but a reality due to the new upgrade of AR/VR, which permits another way of discovering that better addresses the issues of the 21st century student. |
| Mojtaba Noghabaei *et al.* [2020] | Dataset related to industries | AR/VR technology | Based on the results of the studies, industry professionals predict that AR/VR advances will be utilized increasingly over the next 5 to 10 years. |
| X. Zhou *et al.* [2020] | - | Technology-aided biological microscope learning system based on AR/VR | This precisely showed that using current innovation to extend students' benefit in independent learning is furthermore an effective useful strategy for exploratory training. |

(*Continued*)

**Table 2.1** Description of the related work. (*Continued*)

| Contributors | Dataset | Framework | Outcome |
|---|---|---|---|
| Danny Schott *et al.* [2021] | With 19 liver datasets | Use of AR/VR for liver anatomy education | The purpose of this study is to describe a multi-user AR/VR learning environment designed to assist students in liver surgery education and to gain a better understanding of liver anatomy. |
| A. Tokarev *et al.* [2021] | - | - | With the completion of the central course, the student builds up a solid knowledge and competence base and can gain a premium level of expertise in virtual advances. |
| A. Raith *et al.* [2022] | Data related to healthcare | Microsoft HoloLens head-mounted display | It shows that AR has extraordinary capability in education, as well as radiology training. |
| V Sharma *et al.* [2022] | - | - | The consequence of this study is that students with less prior programming abilities show a basic improvement after playing the game as it assists them with further developing their basic programming abilities. |
| Q. Jin *et al.* [2022] | Qualitative analysis-based data from instructors and students | VR technology | This study contributes a point-by-point portrayal of current discernments and contemplations from a multi-partner viewpoint, giving new pieces of knowledge on planning novel VR and Human-Computer Interaction (HCI) advances in higher education. |

### 2.2.1 Bibliometric Analysis

In this section, a bibliometric analysis using the Biblioshiny package of RStudio has been conducted and various analyses have been drawn. The target dataset is collected from the Scopus database for analysis and below are the details of the extracted analysis.

#### *2.2.1.1 Search Key*

The search key is a combination of keywords. The dataset collected publications from the years 2000 to 2023 till date using keywords of the subject of this paper. The exact search key used is as follows:

*( TITLE-ABS-KEY ( "Augmented Reality" ) AND TITLE-ABS-KEY ( "Virtual Reality" ) AND TITLE-ABS-KEY ( "Education" ) ) AND PUBYEAR > 1999 AND ( LIMIT-TO ( LANGUAGE , "English" ) )*

A total of 1791 publications were collected in a CSV extracted file to be used in the Biblioshiny as a source of the analysis.

#### *2.2.1.2 Dataset Analysis*

The dataset analysis showed an *annual scientific production of 19.95%* for the used search key, which indicates that quite an impressive record of research work is being done in the field of education with AR/VR techniques. Figure 2.2 below shows a snapshot of the annual scientific production sourced from Biblioshiny.

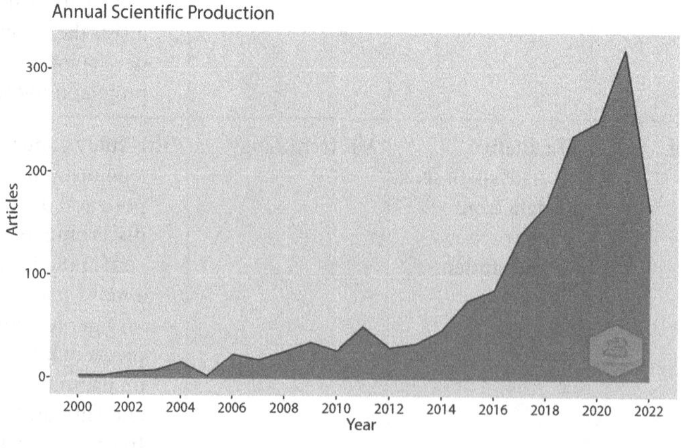


**Figure 2.2** Annual scientific production.

## 2.3 Source Analysis

The source analysis depicts information about the sources that are being used to publish the relevant papers.

### 2.3.1 Most Relevant Sources

The top 20 most relevant sources of publications under the search key topics are indicated in Figure 2.3. The Lecture Notes in Computer Science, ACM International Conference Proceedings series, and CEUR Workshop Proceedings are the top 3 among the relevant sources. Figure 2.3 shows more insightful information about the sources.

### 2.3.2 Source Growth

The source growth is presented in Figure 2.4, which indicates the impulsive growth of publications in Lecture Notes in Computer Science, whereas a gradual growth of publications has been seen in Studies in Health Technology and Informatics since 2002. Publications have begun to gain interest in Procedia Computer Science since 2014, whereas CEUR Workshop Proceedings and ACM International Conference Proceedings series have been gaining interest since 2016.

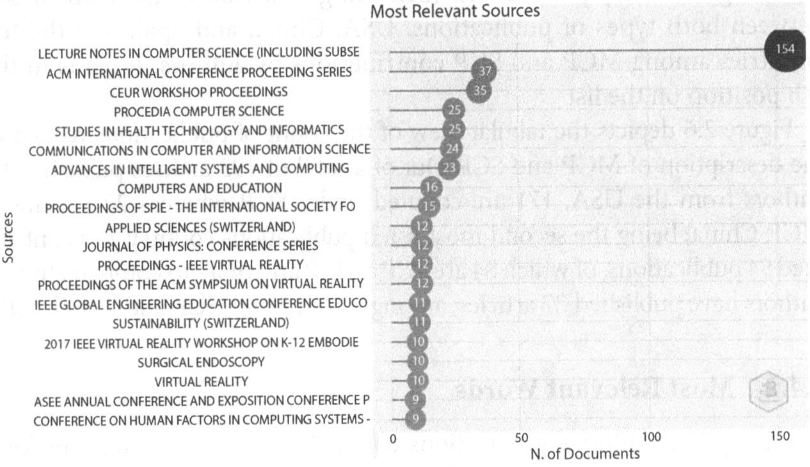


Figure 2.3 Source analysis.

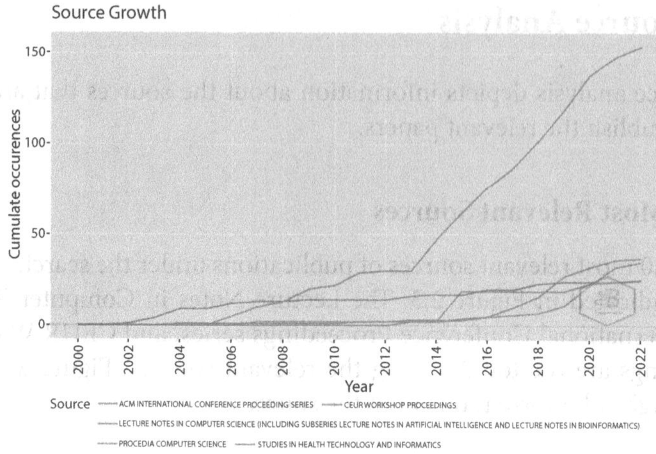


**Figure 2.4** Source growth.

## 2.4 Author Analysis

The author analysis gives an insight into the country of origin for most cited authors, locally cited, as well as inter-country specific publications and intra-country contributions.

### 2.4.1 Corresponding Author's Country

Figure 2.5 below depicts the multiple country publications (MCP) along with single country publications (SCP) to give a view of the comparison between both types of publications. USA, China, and Spain are the top countries among MCP and SCP contributions by authors. India is in the 9th position on the list.

Figure 2.6 depicts the tabular view of the count of publications related to the description of MCP and SCP. Out of a total of 193 articles published by authors from the USA, 171 are counted under SCP, whereas 22 are under MCP. China, being the second most listed publications country, has contributed 94 publications, of which 84 are SCP and 10 are MCP. To compare, Indian authors have published 27 articles, among which 23 are SCP and 4 are MCP.

### 2.4.2 Most Relevant Words

The analysis of authors' publications could also be seen through the keywords used in the publications. Figure 2.7 shows the most relevant words

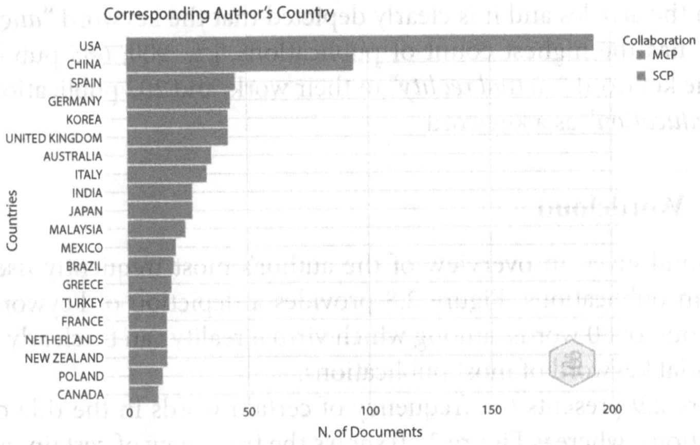


**Figure 2.5** Author analysis.

| Country | Articles | Freq | SCP | MCP | MCP_Ratio |
|---|---|---|---|---|---|
| USA | 193 | 0.20554 | 171 | 22 | 0.1140 |
| CHINA | 94 | 0.10011 | 84 | 10 | 0.1064 |
| SPAIN | 45 | 0.04792 | 36 | 9 | 0.2000 |
| GERMANY | 43 | 0.04579 | 32 | 11 | 0.2558 |
| KOREA | 42 | 0.04473 | 35 | 7 | 0.1667 |
| UNITED KINGDOM | 42 | 0.04473 | 28 | 14 | 0.3333 |
| AUSTRALIA | 35 | 0.03727 | 24 | 11 | 0.3143 |
| ITALY | 33 | 0.03514 | 25 | 8 | 0.2424 |
| INDIA | 27 | 0.02875 | 23 | 4 | 0.1481 |
| JAPAN | 27 | 0.02875 | 24 | 3 | 0.1111 |
| MALAYSIA | 24 | 0.02556 | 23 | 1 | 0.0417 |
| MEXICO | 20 | 0.02130 | 17 | 3 | 0.1500 |
| BRAZIL | 19 | 0.02023 | 19 | 0 | 0.0000 |

**Figure 2.6** Count of publications for MCP and SCP.

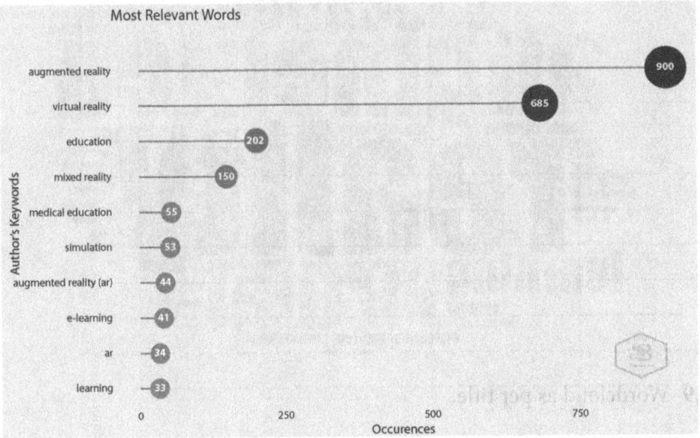


**Figure 2.7** Showing most relevant words.

used in the articles and it is clearly depicted that the keyword "*augmented reality*" has the highest count of publications, i.e., 900; 685 publications used the keyword "*virtual reality*" in their work; and 202 publications have used "*education*" as a keyword.

### 2.4.3 Wordcloud

Wordcloud gives an overview of the author's most frequently used keywords in publications. Figure 2.8 provides a depiction of keywords in a Wordcloud of 50 words, among which virtual reality can be clearly seen as a potential keyword of most publications.

Figure 2.9 presents the frequency of certain words in the title of most publications, whereas Figure 2.10 shows the frequency of certain words in the abstract of most publications.

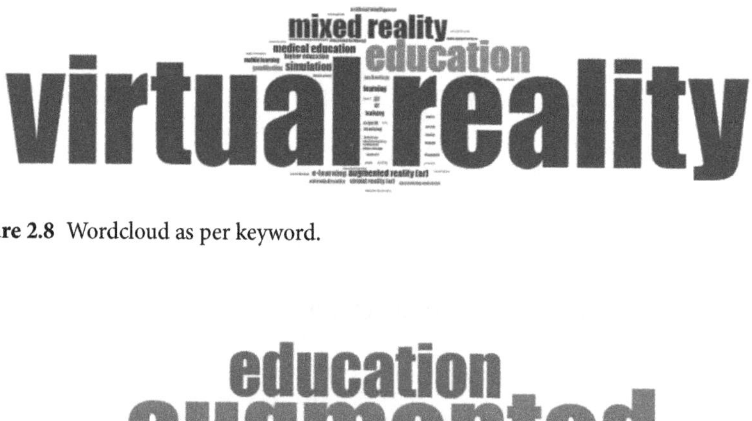


**Figure 2.8** Wordcloud as per keyword.

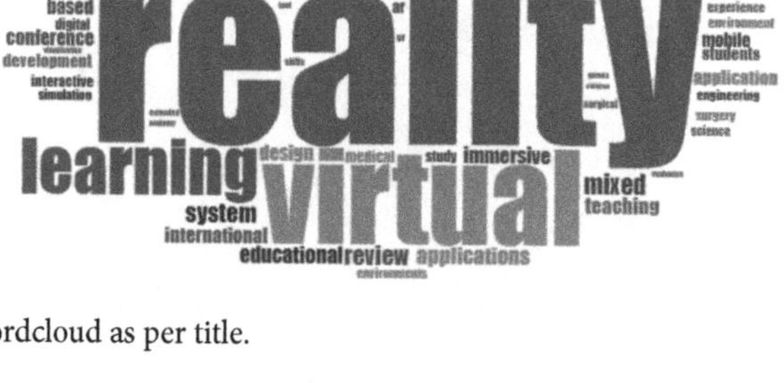


**Figure 2.9** Wordcloud as per title.

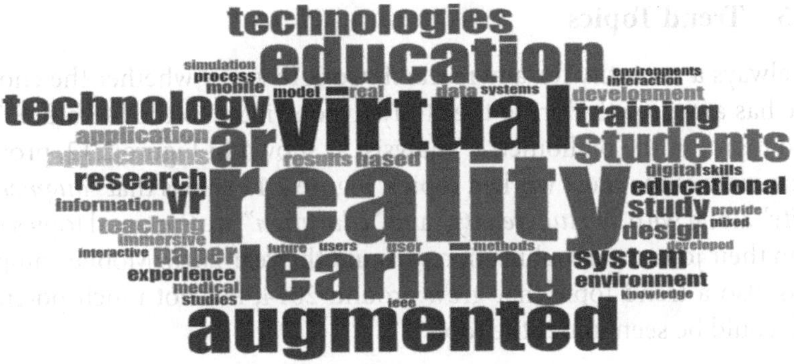


**Figure 2.10** Wordcloud as per abstract.

## 2.4.4 Tree Map

The Tree map shown in Figure 2.11 is one of the most used types of representation of keywords in publications as per their usage. The most used keyword is "*augmented reality*", which holds 31% of total publications followed by "*virtual reality*" and "*education*."

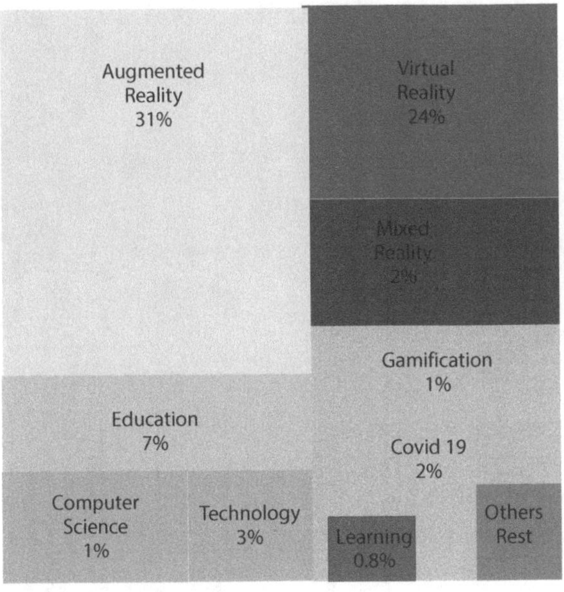


**Figure 2.11** Representation of the Tree map.

### 2.4.5 Trend Topics

It is always a necessity for any research work to know whether the chosen topic has any growth during the study to contribute to the literature. The trend topics in the bibliometric analysis, as shown in Figure 2.12, provide a clear view of the most worked topics. Figure 2.12 shows that "*augmented reality*" along with "*virtual reality*" and "*education*" are the trend topics that began their journey in publications around the year 2016. Mobile computing is also a trend topic that grew around 2014, but not much potential work could be seen under the topic.

### 2.4.6 Thematic Map

The thematic map shown in Figure 2.13 provides a precise view of trend topics as per the momentum gained by publications during the given period. The thematic map is bifurcated into four quadrants: the first quadrant tells the theme that is already developed and not much scope is there to study in the field, the second quadrant tells the peripherally developed themes that are least important and not so useful themes, the third quadrant tells the rarely explored themes, and the fourth quadrant tells the current trends and the high research scope themes that need the researcher's interest. The thematic map of the coined keywords for the trend analysis

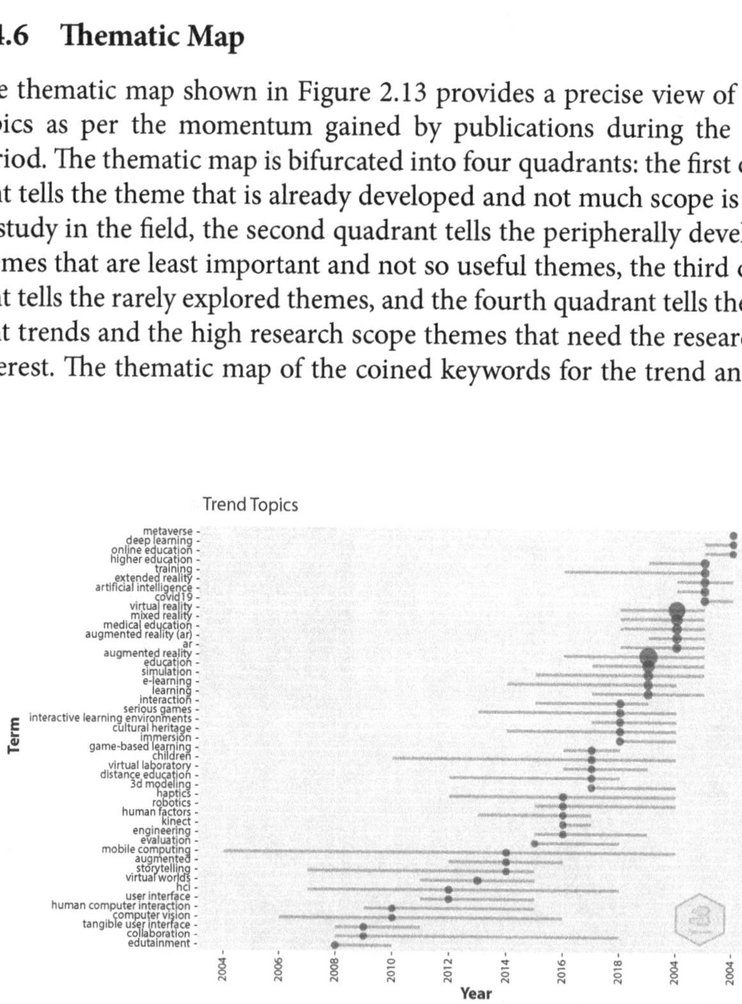


**Figure 2.12** Trend topics.

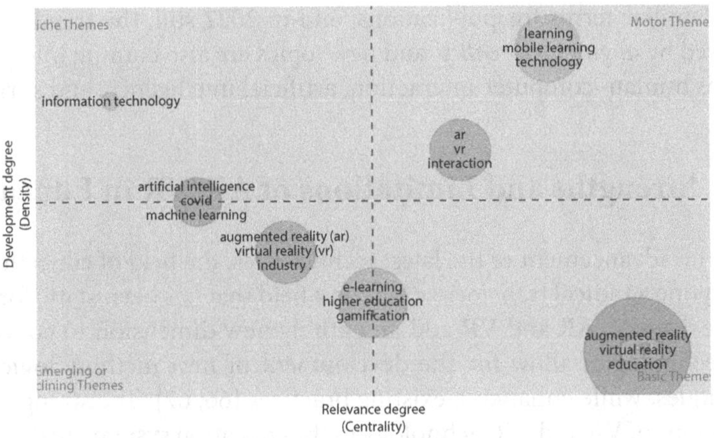


**Figure 2.13** Thematic maps.

is represented in the figure, where it can be visualized that AR, VR, and education are the undeveloped themes.

## 2.4.7 Thematic Evolution

The thematic evolution representation shows the trend of topics from 2000 to 2022. Figure 2.14 is sliced into four parts: from 2000 to 2016, *augmented reality* is a trend topic with a high number of articles published; from 2017 to 2019, *augmented reality, education,* and *embedded computing* are the most popular topics for publications; from 2020 to 2021, *augmented reality, experiential learning,* and *artificial intelligence* [55–58] are presented as the

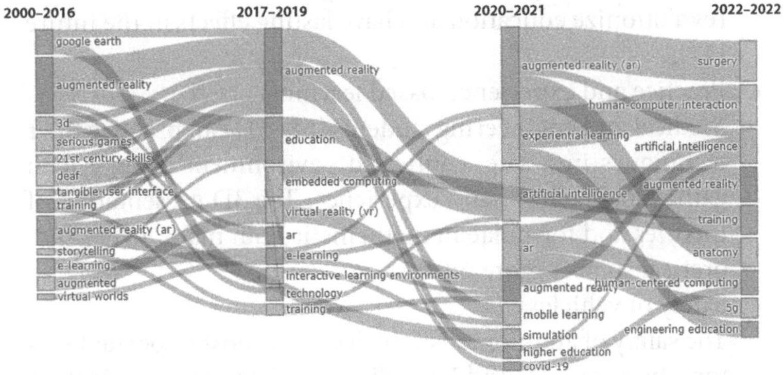


**Figure 2.14** Thematic evolution.

most familiar terms for publications; and in 2022 still, the trend is being followed by *augmented reality*, and new topics are also coming into picture such as human–computer interaction, artificial intelligence, and surgery.

## 2.5 Strengths and Limitations of AR/VR in Education

With the advancement of the latest technologies, the field of education has undergone a radical transformation. As a field that has been static for most of its existence, AR and VR add an entirely new dimension to education. The technologies allow for the development of new methodologies and techniques, while enhancing existing practices [66, 67]. The strengths and limitations of VR and AR technology in the education system are described here [38].

- Enhance student interest
  It has always been the teacher's responsibility to capture and maintain the students' attention in traditional classroom settings. VR and AR can drastically change this dynamic. It is very likely that the students' attention and interest will be greatly increased by adding a visual and interactive component to abstract information. They will be motivated to actively participate in the classroom, thereby improving the learning experience [46].
- Change the face of distance education
  Due to improved Internet access, professionalization, and standardization of the field, online learning has grown in popularity globally. With the right combination of online learning and experiential learning, an academic model can revolutionize education and have lasting effects in the future [47].
- Practice and experience-based learning
  Medical and engineering students [58–61] can practice their techniques in a safe, controlled environment using AR to gain valuable first-hand experience. The 3D presentation of theories and formulae in mathematics can make a very theoretical subject more interesting.
- Safety of vehicles
  The safety of autonomous vehicles is the most important factor. The use of AR and VR will be crucial in improving their safety [49, 64, 65].

### 2.5.1 Limitations of AR/VR Technology in the Education System

- Barriers to entry
  Although VR and AR technologies have advanced in leaps and bounds since their inception, they are still comparatively rare and prohibitively costly. The cost of accessing and utilizing them limits their availability to institutions and individuals with inadequate financial resources.
- The potential for isolation
  There is no doubt that interactive technologies can benefit learning outcomes in a significant way. By wearing VR goggles and learning in a virtual environment, you risk isolating yourself and undermining the element of human interaction that is so essential to the learning experience.
- Virtual environments are addictive
  VR addiction refers to a form of digital addiction associated with the use of virtual reality applications, which offer users a means of escaping the everyday stresses and concerns of life.

## 2.6 Conclusion

Over the past two decades, VR and AR technologies have developed in various ways. In recent years, these technologies have become an integral part of everyday life. There is strong evidence that AR and VR can be used to improve students' skills and knowledge. VR and AR apps provide students with a new and exciting way to explore content. Using technology, students can create interactive and interesting products that demonstrate their understanding and enhance their learning. The purpose of this work is to review VR and AR as educational technologies, to discuss their advantages and disadvantages, and to describe how VR and AR technologies can be utilized in the classroom to enhance the teaching process. AR/VR can also be utilized along with machine learning for analyzing and predicting the scope of improvement in the AR/VR systems for education. Cryptographic techniques can also be used to safeguard systems used to provide the simulated environment so that the information tracked and used by the system could not be utilized by any unauthorized member. Other applications of AR/VR have yet to be explored, which will be the future work of the presented study.

## References

1. Ardiny, H., & Khanmirza, E. (2018, October). The role of AR and VR technologies in education developments: opportunities and challenges. In: *2018 6th RSI International Conference on Robotics and Mechatronics (IcRoM)*, (pp. 482-487). IEEE.
2. Gaol, F. L., & Prasolova-Førland, E. (2022). Special section editorial: The frontiers of augmented and mixed reality in all levels of education. *Educ. Inf. Technol.*, 27(1), 611-623.
3. Maiti, M., Priyaadharshini, M., & VinayagaSundaram, B. (2021). Augmented Reality in Virtual Classroom for Higher Education During COVID-19 Pandemic. In: *Intelligent Computing*, (pp. 399-418). Springer, Cham.
4. Gaol, F. L., & Prasolova-Førland, E. (2022). Special section editorial: The frontiers of augmented and mixed reality in all levels of education. *Educ. Inf. Technol.*, 27(1), 611-623.
5. Pathania, M., Mantri, A., Kaur, D. P., Singh, C. P., & Sharma, B. (2021). A chronological literature review of different augmented reality approaches in education. *Technol. Knowl. Learn.*, 1-18.
6. Papadimitriou, F. (2022). An evaluation system for games related to geography and landscapes in education. In: *The Social Construction of Landscapes in Games*, (pp. 315-335). Springer VS, Wiesbaden.
7. Atta, M. T., Romli, A., & Majid, M. A. (2021, August). The Impact of AR/VR on Spatial Memory Performance of Learners: A review. In: *2021 International Conference on Software Engineering & Computer Systems and 4th International Conference on Computational Science and Information Management (ICSECS-ICOCSIM)*, (pp. 75-79). IEEE.
8. Reddy, K., Reddy, M. A., Kaur, V., & Kaur, G. (2022). Career Guidance System Using Ensemble Learning. Akhila and Kaur, Veerpal and Kaur, Gagandeep, Career Guidance System Using Ensemble Learning (July 14, 2022).
9. Roopa, D., Prabha, R., & Senthil, G. A. (2021). Revolutionizing education system with interactive augmented reality for quality education. *Mater. Today Proc.*, 46, 3860-3863.
10. Pathania, M., Mantri, A., Kaur, D. P., Singh, C. P., & Sharma, B. (2021). A chronological literature review of different augmented reality approaches in education. *Technol. Knowl. Learn.*, 1-18.
11. Paszkiewicz, A., Salach, M., Dymora, P., Bolanowski, M., Budzik, G., & Kubiak, P. (2021). Methodology of implementing virtual reality in education for industry 4.0. *Sustainability*, 13(9), 5049.
12. Maiti, M., Priyaadharshini, M., & VinayagaSundaram, B. (2021). Augmented Reality in Virtual Classroom for Higher Education During COVID-19 Pandemic. In: *Intelligent Computing*, (pp. 399-418). Springer, Cham.
13. Andujar, J. M., Mejías, A., & Márquez, M. A. (2010). Augmented reality for the improvement of remote laboratories: an augmented remote laboratory. *IEEE Trans. Educ.*, 54(3), 492-500.

14. Chen, H., Feng, K., Mo, C., Cheng, S., Guo, Z., & Huang, Y. (2011, December). Application of augmented reality in engineering graphics education. In: *2011 IEEE International Symposium on IT in Medicine and Education*, (Vol. 2, pp. 362-365). IEEE.
15. Lee, K. (2012). Augmented reality in education and training. *TechTrends*, 56(2), 13-21.
16. Iordache, D. D., Pribeanu, C., & Balog, A. (2012). Influence of specific AR capabilities on the learning effectiveness and efficiency. *Stud. Inform. Control*, 21(3), 233-240.
17. Chau, M., Wong, A., Wang, M., Lai, S., Chan, K. W., Li, T. M., ...& Sung, W. K. (2013). Using 3D virtual environments to facilitate students in constructivist learning. *Decis. Support Syst.*, 56, 115-121.
18. Wu, H. K., Lee, S. W. Y., Chang, H. Y., & Liang, J. C. (2013). Current status, opportunities and challenges of augmented reality in education. *Comput. Educ.*, 62, 41-49.
19. Chiang, T. H., Yang, S. J., & Hwang, G. J. (2014). An augmented reality-based mobile learning system to improve students' learning achievements and motivations in natural science inquiry activities. *J. Educ. Technol. Soc.*, 17(4), 352-365.
20. Le, Q. T., Pedro, A. K. E. E. M., Lim, C. R., Park, H. T., Park, C. S., & Kim, H. K. (2015). A framework for using mobile based virtual reality and augmented reality for experiential construction safety education. *Int. J. Eng. Educ.*, 31(3), 713-725.
21. Ferguson, C., Davidson, P. M., Scott, P. J., Jackson, D., & Hickman, L. D. (2015). Augmented reality, virtual reality and gaming: an integral part of nursing. *Contemporary Nurse*, 51(1), 1-4.
22. Parsons, S. (2016). Authenticity in Virtual Reality for assessment and inter-vention in autism: A conceptual review. *Educ. Res. Rev.*, 19, 138-157.
23. Kavanagh, S., Luxton-Reilly, A., Wuensche, B., & Plimmer, B. (2017). A systematic review of virtual reality in education. *Themes Sci. Technol. Educ.*, 10(2), 85-119.
24. Martín-Gutiérrez, J., Mora, C. E., Añorbe-Díaz, B., & González-Marrero, A. (2017). Virtual technologies trends in education. *Eurasia J. Math. Sci. Technol. Educ.*, 13(2), 469-486.
25. Cascales-Martínez, A., Martínez-Segura, M. J., Pérez-López, D., & Contero, M. (2016). Using an augmented reality enhanced tabletop system to promote learning of mathematics: A case study with students with special educational needs. *Eurasia J. Math. Sci. Technol. Educ.*, 13(2), 355-380.
26. Yu, W., Chi, S., & Shi, C. (2018, November). Research on Application Mode of AR/VR Technology in Education and Teaching. In: *Proceedings of the 2018 3rd International Social Sciences and Education Conference*, Diyarbakir, Turkey (pp. 14-17).

27. Horváth, I. (2018, August). Evolution of teaching roles and tasks in AR/VR-based education. In: *2018 9th IEEE International Conference on Cognitive Infocommunications (CogInfoCom)*, (pp. 000355-000360). IEEE.
28. Garzón, Juan & Pavón, Juan & Baldiris, Silvia. (2019). Systematic review and meta-analysis of augmented reality in educational settings. *Virtual Reality.*
29. Papanastasiou, G., Drigas, A., Skianis, C. *et al.* Virtual and augmented reality effects on K-12, higher and tertiary education students' twenty-first century skills. *Virtual Reality*, 23, 425–436 (2019).
30. Elmqaddem, N. (2019). Augmented reality and virtual reality in education. Myth or reality?. *Int. J. Emerg. Technol. Learn.*, 14(3).
31. Noghabaei, M., Heydarian, A., Balali, V., & Han, K. (2020). Trend analysis on adoption of virtual and augmented reality in the architecture, engineering, and construction industry. *Data*, 5(1), 26.
32. Zhou, X., Tang, L., Lin, D., & Han, W. (2020). Virtual & augmented reality for biological microscope in experiment education. *Virtual Reality & Intelligent Hardware*, 2(4), 316-329.
33. Schott, D., Saalfeld, P., Schmidt, G., Joeres, F., Boedecker, C., Huettl, F., & Hansen, C. (2021, March). A AR/VR environment for multi-user liver anatomy education. In: *2021 IEEE Virtual Reality and 3D User Interfaces (VR)*, (pp. 296-305). IEEE.
34. Tokarev, A., Skobelin, I., Tolstov, M., Tsyganov, A., & Pak, M. (2021). Development of VR educational instruments for school pre-professional education in a research university. *Procedia Comput. Sci.*, 190, 750-754.
35. Raith, A., Kamp, C., Stoiber, C., Jakl, A., & Wagner, M. (2022, April). Augmented Reality in Radiology for Education and Training—A Design Study. In: *Healthcare*, (Vol. 10, No. 4, p. 672). MDPI.
36. Sharma, V., Bhagat, K. K., Huang, H. H., & Chen, N. S. (2022). The design and evaluation of an AR-based serious game to teach programming. *Comput. Graphics*, 103, 1-18.
37. Jin, Q., Liu, Y., Yarosh, S., Han, B., & Qian, F. (2022, April). How Will VR Enter University Classrooms? Multi-stakeholders Investigation of VR in Higher Education. In: *CHI Conference on Human Factors in Computing Systems*, (pp. 1-17).
38. Choi, D. H., Dailey-Hebert, A., & Estes, J. S. (Eds.). (2016). Emerging tools and applications of virtual reality in education. Hershey, PA, USA: Information Science Reference.
39. Pokharel, B., Ganesh, K., Timilsina, B., Pokharel, Y., Makam, M., & Kaur, V. (2022). An Interactive AI-Powered Web Healthcare System. In: *2022 Second International Conference on Computer Science, Engineering and Applications (ICCSEA)*, (pp. 1-5). IEEE.
40. Verma, A., Shah, C. K., Kaur, V., Shah, S., & Kumar, P. (2022). Cancer Detection and Analysis Using Machine Learning. In *2022 Second International Conference on Computer Science, Engineering and Applications (ICCSEA)*, (pp. 1-5). IEEE.

41. Reddy, K., Reddy, M. A., Kaur, V., & Kaur, G. (2022). Career guidance system using ensemble learning. Akhila and Kaur, Veerpal and Kaur, Gagandeep, Career Guidance System Using Ensemble Learning.
42. Takkar, S., Kakran, A., Kaur, V., Rakhra, M., Sharma, M., Bangotra, P., & Verma, N. (2021). Recognition of Image-Based Plant Leaf Diseases Using Deep Learning Classification Models. *Nat. Environ. Pollut. Technol.*
43. Kaur, V., Gupta, K., Baggan, V., & Kaur, G. (2019). Role of cryptographic algorithms in mobile ad hoc network security: an elucidation. *International Journal of Recent Technology and Engineering (IJRTE)*. pp. 3750-3754.
44. Kaur, M., & Aron, R. (2020). Equal distribution based load balancing technique for fog-based cloud computing. In: *International Conference on Artificial Intelligence: Advances and Applications*, 2019 (pp. 189-198). Springer, Singapore.
45. Kaur, M., & Aron, R. (2022). An Energy-Efficient Load Balancing Approach for Scientific Workflows in Fog Computing. Wireless Personal Communications, 1-25.
46. Gill, S., Sharma, N., Gupta, C., & Samanta, A. (2021, November). Attendance Management System Using Facial Recognition and Image Augmentation Technique. In: *2021 International Conference on Intelligent Technology, System and Service for Internet of Everything (ITSS-IoE)*, (pp. 1-6). IEEE.
47. Saluja, K., Gupta, S., Vajpayee, A., Debnath, S. K., Bansal, A., & Sharma, N. (2022). Blockchain technology: Applied to big data in collaborative edges. *Meas.: Sens.*, *24*, 100521.
48. Tandon, R., & Gupta, P. K. (2021). A novel and secure hybrid iWD-MASK algorithm for enhanced image security. *Recent Advances in Computer Science and Communications*, (Formerly: Recent Patents on Computer Science), 14(2), 384-394.
49. Tandon, R., Verma, A., & Gupta, P. K. (2022). A Secure Framework Based on Nature-Inspired Optimization for Vehicle Routing. In: *International Conference on Advances in Computing and Data Sciences*, (pp. 74-85). Springer, Cham.
50. Harnal, S., Jain, A., Rathore, A. S., Baggan, V., Kaur, G., & Bala, R. (2023, March). Comparative Approach for Early Diabetes Detection with Machine Learning. In: *2023 International Conference on Emerging Smart Computing and Informatics (ESCI)*, (pp. 1-6). IEEE.
51. Kaur, G., Kaur, H., & Goyal, S. (2023). Correlation analysis between different parameters to predict cement logistics. *Innovations Syst. Software Eng.*, 19(1), 117-127.
52. Bindal, R., Sarangi, P. K., Kaur, G., & Dhiman, G. (2019). An approach for automatic recognition system for Indian vehicles numbers using k-nearest neighbours and decision tree classifier.
53. Kaur, G., Goyal, S., & Kaur, H. (2021, December). Brief review of various machine learning algorithms. In: *Proceedings of the International Conference on Innovative Computing & Communication (ICICC)*.

54. Kaur, G., & Kaur, H. (2017, July). Prediction of the cause of accident and accident prone location on roads using data mining techniques. In: *2017 8th International Conference on Computing, Communication and Networking Technologies (ICCCNT)*, (pp. 1-7). IEEE.
55. Harnal, S., Sharma, G., Malik, S., Kaur, G., Khurana, S., Kaur, P., ... & Bagga, D. (2022). Bibliometric mapping of trends, applications and challenges of artificial intelligence in smart cities. *EAI Endorsed Trans. Scalable Inf. Syst.*, 9(4), e8-e8.
56. Sarangi, P. K., Sahoo, A. K., Kaur, G., Nayak, S. R., & Bhoi, A. K. (2022). Gurmukhi numerals recognition using ann. In: *Cognitive Informatics and Soft Computing: Proceeding of CISC*, 2021 (pp. 377-386). Singapore: Springer Nature Singapore.
57. Kaur, V., & Singh, A. (2015). An Encryption Scheme Based on AES and SHA-512. *Int. J. Appl. Eng. Res.*, 10(10), 25207-25218.
58. Kaur, G., Choudhary, P., Sahore, L., Gupta, S., & Kaur, V. (2023). Healthcare: In the Era of Blockchain. In: *AI and Blockchain in Healthcare*, (pp. 45-55). Singapore: Springer Nature Singapore.
59. Kaur, V., & Kaur, R. (2022). An Elucidation for Machine Learning Algorithms Used in Healthcare. In: *Machine Learning for Edge Computing*, (pp. 25-36). CRC Press.
60. Harnal, S., Sharma, G., Malik, S., Kaur, G., Simaiya, S., Khurana, S., & Bagga, D. (2023). Current and Future Trends of Cloud-based Solutions for Healthcare. Image Based Computing for Food and Health Analytics: Requirements, Challenges, Solutions and Practices: IBCFHA, 115-136.
61. Tandon, R., & Gupta, P. K. (2021). Security and privacy challenges in healthcare using Internet of Things. In: *IoT-Based Data Analytics for the Healthcare Industry*, (pp. 149-165). Academic Press.
62. Kaur, G., Bindal, R., Kaur, V., Kaur, I., & Gupta, S. (2023, June). Bitcoin and cryptocurrency technologies: A review. In: *AIP Conference Proceedings*, (Vol. 2782, No. 1). AIP Publishing.
63. Kaur, V., & Singh, A. (2013). Review of various algorithms used in hybrid cryptography. *Int. J. Comput. Sci. Net.*, 2(6), 157-173.
64. Verma, A., Tandon, R., & Gupta, P. K. (2022). TrafC-AnTabu: AnTabu routing algorithm for congestion control and traffic lights management using fuzzy model. *Internet Technol. Lett.*, 5(2), e309.
65. Tandon, R., & Gupta, P. K. (2021). A novel encryption scheme based on fully homomorphic encryption and RR-AES along with privacy preservation for vehicular networks. In: *Advances in Computing and Data Sciences: 5th International Conference, ICACDS 2021*, Nashik, India, April 23–24, 2021, Revised Selected Papers, Part I 5 (pp. 351-360). Springer International Publishing.
66. Kukkar, A., Mohana, R., Sharma, A., & Nayyar, A. (2023). Prediction of student academic performance based on their emotional wellbeing and interaction on various e-learning platforms. *Educ. Inform. Technol.*, 1-30.

67. Liu, Y., Kukkar, A., & Shah, M. A. (2022). Study of industrial interactive design system based on virtual reality teaching technology in industrial robot. Paladyn, *Journal of Behavioral Robotics (JBR)*, 13(1), 45-55.
68. Kaur, G., Kaur, V., Sharma, Y., & Bansal, V. (2022, December). Analyzing various Machine Learning Algorithms with SMOTE and ADASYN for Image Classification having Imbalanced Data. In: *2022 IEEE International Conference on Current Development in Engineering and Technology (CCET)*, (pp. 1-7). IEEE.

# 3

# Enhancing Social Skills Development Through Augmented Reality (AR) and Virtual Reality (VR) in Special Education

**Ajantha Devi Vairamani**

*AP3 Solutions, Chennai, Tamil Nadu, India*

***Abstract***

Since persons with special needs occasionally find it difficult to participate in social situations and create long-lasting connections, social skills development is a crucial part of special education. Building immersive, interactive environments that enhance the development of social skills may be achieved using augmented reality (AR) and virtual reality (VR) technology to address these problems. This essay examines how AR and VR could improve social skills of children with special needs.

Theoretical frameworks provide a conceptual basis for understanding how AR and VR could promote social skills. Some techniques for incorporating AR and VR in social skills training include building empathy and perspective-taking skills, training in virtual social interactions and communication, collaborative VR settings, and assessment.

Real-world examples and case studies demonstrate the effective use of AR and VR in social skills development across various groups, including children with autism spectrum disorder (ASD) and persons with communication challenges. These examples show how AR and VR are effective in fostering social engagement, self-confidence, and the transfer of skills to real-world contexts.

Future opportunities in this field are also being investigated, and AR and VR are now more effectively used to foster social skills. The increase in immersion and realism, the creation of socially aware virtual agents, the customization of training sessions, the use of multimodal feedback and assessment, longitudinal studies, the design of interventions for particular populations, the encouragement of collaboration and social networking in VR, addressing ethical issues, the integration with

*Email*: ap3solutionsresearch@gmail.com

V. Ajantha Devi, Williamjeet Singh and Yogesh Kumar (eds.) Augmented Reality and Virtual Reality in Special Education, (65–90) © 2024 Scrivener Publishing LLC

other therapeutic modalities, and the guarantee that the technology is both accessible and affordable are all necessary to achieve this. In conclusion, AR and VR provide groundbreaking opportunities to enhance the development of social skills in special education. With the aid of these technologies, educators, therapists, and researchers may develop groundbreaking and successful programs that assist individuals with special needs in forming meaningful connections, navigating social situations, and thriving under a variety of social demands.

***Keywords:*** Collaborative VR environments, social skills development, communication issues, transfer of abilities, social networking in VR, accessibility

## 3.1 Introduction

Establishing relationships, taking part in fruitful social interactions, and prospering in society as a whole are examples of essential social skills (Smith, 2018). However, learning and using these abilities may be challenging for persons with particular educational challenges (Jones *et al.*, 2019). For these people, conventional social skills training techniques might not always be successful or inspiring (Johnson, 2020). Virtual reality (VR)and augmented reality (AR) technologies provide creative and exciting solutions in this area. Through the immersive and captivating experiences provided by AR and VR technologies, virtual worlds may be constructed, and real-world situations duplicated (Davis *et al.*, 2021). In the context of special education, these technologies have the power to radically transform how social skills are acquired (Brown & Miller, 2017). Augmented reality and VR may be used by educators and therapists to design relaxation-secure and regulated settings where people can improve their social skills. The numerous methods that AR and VR may improve, particularly the development of social skills in special education, are covered in this chapter. The theoretical foundations for the use of AR and VR to enhance social skills are examined (Johnson & Wilson, 2018). It also examines industry norms and useful applications of AR and VR software. The potential advantages and factors to be considered when using AR and VR technology to enhance the social development of people with special needs are emphasized in this chapter.

In the first section of the chapter, how AR and virtual reality VR fit into the theoretical frameworks that assist the development of social skills is investigated (Smith & Johnson, 2020). The analysis of particular AR and VR social skills training applications includes examples of AR-based activities and treatments, as well as VR simulations intended to improve social competence (Brown *et al.*, 2019). Additionally, it looks at how AR and VR could improve perspective-taking and empathy, two characteristics that are crucial for the development of social skills.

The chapter also considers the potential benefits of AR and VR for training in virtual social interactions and communication. It looks at the potential for creating realistic AR and VR experiences to improve social and communication skills (Thomas *et al.*, 2021). The chapter also considers how collaborative VR environments could help with group-based social skill training (Gonzalez *et al.*, 2018). An important topic covered in the chapter is evaluating social skills development in AR and VR situations, with an emphasis on assessment methodologies and factors to consider while monitoring outcomes (Johnson & Smith, 2019).

Adams *et al.* (2020) discussed measurement methods and instruments used to assess social competence in AR and VR applications. To support the effective use of AR and VR in the development of social skills, the chapter offers best practices and methodologies for incorporating these technologies into programs (Miller & Anderson, 2019). It gives suggestions for picking the proper AR and VR tools and programs in addition to guidelines for successful adoption (Gupta *et al.*, 2020). The chapter ends with the presentation of real-world case studies and success stories that demonstrate how AR and VR have improved the development of social skills in special education (Robinson & Smith, 2021).

Additionally, upcoming issues and patterns on AR and VR tools and identifying opportunities for advancements and additional studies are covered here (Clark *et al.*, 2022). The major goal of this chapter is to show how AR and VR technologies may significantly improve the development of social skills in special education. Teachers and therapists may offer outstanding and efficient learning opportunities that support the social skills development and success of people with special needs by utilizing the immersive and interactive qualities of these technologies.

## 3.2 Theoretical Frameworks for Social Skills Development

A few of the various skills that go into the development of social skills are cooperation, communication, empathy, perspective-taking, and problem-solving (Jones *et al.*, 2020). Theoretical frameworks shed light on the procedures and elements involved in developing and refining specific social abilities. When thinking of using AR and VR in special education to enhance social skills, it is essential to comprehend these theoretical underpinnings. Albert Bandura's Social Learning Theory, a crucial theoretical framework, emphasizes the significance of modeling and observational learning in the development of social skills (Bandura, 1977). This idea contends that people acquire new skills by observing the behaviors others, then imitating or changing those behaviors in themselves. To help students develop their social skills, AR and VR technologies can offer virtual settings where they can observe and mimic proper social behaviors (Brown *et al.*, 2019).

The Social Learning Theory served as the foundation for Albert Bandura's Social Cognitive Theory, which stresses the importance of cognitive processes in learning (Bandura, 1986). People actively review information, decide if certain actions are suitable, and participate in self-reflection based on their views and experiences. By presenting possibilities for problem-solving, decision-making, and self-reflection, AR and VR technologies can help children develop the cognitive processes necessary for social skills.

The capacity to comprehend that others can have beliefs, objectives, and points of view that are dissimilar from one's own is known as theory of mind. The development of empathy and social ties depends heavily on theory of mind. By allowing students to take on several roles and experience situations from various points of view, AR and VR technologies may be utilized to create scenarios that assist students in applying or using theory of mind and perspective-taking abilities (Lieberman, 2007). The social information processing hypothesis (Crick & Dodge 1994) holds that accurate reception, comprehension, and response to social information are essential. The focus of this theory is how people understand and react to social cues in social situations. With the use of AR and VR, teachers may give students supervised practice reading and responses to social cues, which will help them become more adept at deciphering social signs.

The Positive Behavior Support (PBS) technique, according to Horner *et al.* (2005), is centered on proactive interventions that encourage positive behaviors and lessen negative ones. It seeks to promote healthy behavior, share new knowledge, and create a safe atmosphere. The use of AR and VR in a PBS framework can provide children with the ability to perfect their skills, reinforce proper social behaviors, and progressively expose themselves to difficult circumstances in a safe and encouraging environment (Jones & Carr, 2004). It may be easier to plan and carry out AR and VR therapies for the improvement of social skills if you have a solid understanding of these theoretical frameworks. Teachers and therapists can develop more effective and focused treatments that address the unique social skills requirements of children with exceptional needs by combining ideas from these frameworks. These frameworks may also be used to direct testing and evaluation of social skills development in AR and VR scenarios, ensuring that interventions are supported by data and congruent with acknowledged theories of social skills development.

## 3.3 Using AR for Social Skills Training

Augmented reality offers unique opportunities for social skills training by offering interactive and immersive experiences inside real situations (Chen *et al.*, 2017). Thanks to AR, which superimposes digital content over the physical environment, users may interact with virtual things while still feeling linked to the real world.

AR may be applied in many ways to teach social skills, such as:

Students can practice and develop their social skills by simulating social encounters. These simulations can be created through AR. Using AR software, for instance, virtual characters or avatars may be projected onto real-world settings, allowing students to engage with them and act out role-playing and problem-solving scenarios. These simulations give students a safe, controlled environment where they may experiment with different social behaviors and receive quick feedback (Chen *et al.*, 2017).

Nonverbal Communication Skills: AR has the potential to improve nonverbal communication skills, which are essential for successful social interactions. Applications through AR may emphasize and explain a variety of nonverbal signs, including facial expressions, body language, and tone of voice. Thus, they become more adept at comprehending the motives and feelings of others (Bacca *et al.*, 2014). Augmented reality may be used to teach students how to recognize and understand these indicators or nonverbal cues.

Social Storytelling and Narratives: Augmented reality may be used to deliver interactive, visually pleasing social storytelling and narratives that teach social skills. Applications through AR can display animated people, environments, and text overlays to aid students in navigating social situations and to offer direction, prompts, and reinforcement for learning. This method, in accordance with Bacca *et al.* (2014), enables students to acquire and practice social skills in a pleasant and suitable way.

Exercises to Develop Perspective: Augmented reality can assist students in developing perspectives by immersing themselves in different viewpoints or changed representations of the environment. Students can develop empathy in interpersonal interactions and a greater knowledge of other people's viewpoints through this immersive learning environment (Chen *et al.*, 2017).

Real-Time Coaching and Feedback: As social skills are practiced, AR could provide immediate coaching and feedback. Augmented reality applications can encourage children to engage in more positive social behaviors by observing their interactions in real-time and making ideas, reminders, or suggestions. As a result of this continual feedback loop, individuals are encouraged to reflect and adapt, which promote social skills' enhancement (Chen *et al.*, 2017).

Rewards and gamification: To make social skills training more motivating and engaging, gamification components may be used into AR. Augmented reality applications may provide a dynamic and engaging learning environment by mixing challenges, stages, prizes, and scoring systems. According to Bacca *et al.* (2014), this gamified method encourages active involvement, persistence, and social skills training and development.

The fact that AR has a lot of promise for teaching social skills must be emphasized, but it should also be part of a thorough and attentive intervention strategy. The finest AR applications should be chosen with the help of teachers, therapists, and other specialists. They should also set goals, provide scaffolding, and encourage students to apply their newly acquired skills to real-world situations (Chen *et al.*, 2017).

## 3.4 VR Simulations for Social Skills Development

Virtual reality simulators offer a fun and interesting way to improve social skills. Students can practice and improve their social skills in a realistic and controlled setting by utilizing VR to create virtual surroundings and scenarios (Parsons & Mitchell, 2002). The following are some ways that VR simulations might improve social skills:

Social situations and role-playing: Students can take on a range of roles and engage with virtual characters in VR simulations of diverse social contexts, such as job interviews or social gatherings (Gutiérrez-Maldonado *et al.*, 2013). In a secure and encouraging setting, this allows children the chance to practice their communication skills, problem-solving techniques, and proper social behaviors.

Virtual reality simulations can help students understand and manage their emotions while also fostering empathy (Krijn *et al.*, 2004). As a consequence, they will be better able to manage their emotions. Students learn how to identify, manage, and successfully express their emotions by being immersed in virtual worlds that trigger a variety of emotional reactions. By putting pupils in the shoes of people from different origins or circumstances, VR may help to simulate experiences that promote empathy.

According to Rizzo *et al.* (2000), VR may be used to teach students how to identify and interpret social indicators including body language, voice tone, and facial expressions. Students can practice recognizing and reacting to these cues in authentic situations by using VR simulations. Students are able to transfer or apply their talents because of the realistic experience that VR's immersive nature provides.

It is crucial to remember that under the supervision of educators and therapists, VR simulations should be used in conjunction with a thorough program for social skills development. To be effective, they must be combined with other intervention tactics and customized to meet the special needs of children (Smith & Goodman, 2019). For students with special needs, instructors may develop fun social skills training programs by utilizing VR's immersive and interactive features.

Problem-Solving and Conflict Resolution: By exposing students to social issues and conflicts, VR simulations allow them to hone their problem-solving and conflict resolution abilities (Neguţ *et al.*, 2016). Students can practice resolving conflicts, offering compromises, and reaching agreements in a virtual setting. Virtual reality enables students to learn and grow successfully by providing quick feedback and advice.

Cooperation and Peer Interaction: Even when students are geographically separated, VR simulations can enhance peer contact and cooperation (Freina & Ott, 2015). Students can participate in cooperative activities including team-building exercises, group discussions, and cooperative problem-solving by joining shared virtual spaces. This online community environment encourages teamwork, the growth of social skills, and peer engagement.

According to Blascovich *et al.* (2002), VR simulations act as a link between virtual experiences and practical use. Students may progressively apply their social skills to situations in the real world after receiving VR instruction. Students may develop competence and confidence in their social skills by often participating in VR simulations and getting feedback, increasing the possibility that they will apply such skills successfully in real life.

According to Sanchez *et al.* (2017), it is essential to create VR simulations for social skills development that are based on methods that have been scientifically proven to be effective and are specifically cater to the needs of individual students. To make sure that VR simulation experiences are in line with the unique learning aims and objectives of the students, teachers, therapists, and other professionals play a significant role in directing and supporting their use. In-depth and efficient social skills training in VR can help students with special needs navigate social situations.

## 3.5 Building Empathy and Perspective-Taking Through AR and VR

Building empathy and perspective-taking abilities is crucial for social development, and AR and VR technologies offer unique opportunities to do so (Banakou *et al.*, 2018).

To promote empathy and enhance perspective-taking, AR and VR can be used to implement the strategies listed below:

Immersive Encounters: According to Slater *et al.* (2014), AR and VR provide consumers with immersive experiences that let them view and participate in events from several angles. These technologies enable people to observe and absorb a variety of experiences, difficulties, and emotions by translating them into virtual settings, which promote empathy and perspective-taking.

Virtual Simulations: According to Schaub *et al.* (2020), AR and VR simulations can mimic real-life situations to aid users in understanding various points of view. Virtual reality simulations, for instance, might transport viewers into a world of people with disabilities or expose them to issues that impoverished groups deal with. These simulations offer a first-person viewpoint, which fosters greater understanding and empathy.

Cultural Immersion: According to Pan and Hamilton (2018), virtual interactions with different cultures and locations might completely immerse consumers in AR and VR experiences. Increased sensitivity to cultural variety can increase empathy and lessen prejudice in society. This awareness can be achieved through engaging with digital avatars of people from different backgrounds, taking part in cultural activities, or virtually traveling to various countries.

Narrative experiences and storytelling: According to Chirico *et al.* (2017), AR and VR may be used to produce immersive narrative that encourages empathy and perspective-taking. People can learn to understand the opinions, feelings, and experiences of others through listening to narratives from a variety of points of view. Augmented reality and VR storytelling encourage empathy and understanding by eradicating prejudices and creating emotional connections.

Virtual Roleplaying: Users of AR and VR systems can take on a variety of views and personalities when participating in virtual roleplaying activities (Lange *et al.*, 2018). People can practice perspective-taking and develop an awareness of the experiences of others by assuming diverse origins and points of views. Virtual roleplaying, being in a secure environment, makes it feasible to explore various social dynamics and cultural backgrounds.

Virtual Reality Therapy: According to Freeman *et al.* (2017), AR and VR technologies provide people with a safe space in which to tackle their own problems, prejudices, or phobias. Simulating circumstances that trigger certain feelings or experiences may aid in the development of empathy and a greater appreciation of one's own and other people's viewpoints.

In instructional and awareness-raising efforts, VR and AR technologies are employed (Lin *et al.*, 2020). Individuals may learn about the struggles encountered by poor groups through interesting activities and informative materials, which foster empathy and motivate people to take action for social change.

It is crucial to use AR and VR ethically and responsibly due to its emotional effect, accuracy, and cultural sensitivity (Bohil *et al.*, 2011). Teachers, therapists, and other professionals are crucial in sparking insightful debates and ideas on empathy-enhancing AR and VR experiences. By utilizing the immersive and interactive qualities of AR and VR, these technologies can inspire empathy among individuals, foster perspective-taking, and lessen discrimination, ultimately resulting in the growth of a more understanding and compassionate society.

## 3.6 Virtual Social Interactions and Communication Training

Virtual social interactions and communication training through VR offer valuable opportunities for individuals to enhance their social skills (Krijn *et al.*, 2004).

Here are some key aspects of virtual social interactions and communication training:

Simulating Real-World Social Situations: With the use of VR, users may interact with characters or avatars in surroundings that closely simulate real-world social contexts (Pan *et al.*, 2021). In a safe and encouraging setting, people may hone their social skills by simulating face-to-face conversations.

Safe and Calm Environment: According to Baus *et al.* (2016), VR offers a calm and safe environment for people to practice social interactions. As a result, people may test out various communication techniques, gain confidence, and cultivate useful social skills without worrying about the possible implications of their actions in real-life settings.

Real-Time Feedback and Coaching: VR simulations can provide real-time coaching and feedback during social interactions, according to Huang *et al.* (2020). The virtual environment can assess verbal and nonverbal indicators, giving rapid advice on communication efficiency, acceptable body language, voice tonality, and reaction timing. This feedback loop makes it easier to reflect and make changes, which boost social skills.

Targeted Skills Development: According to Pertaub *et al.* (2002), VR may concentrate on certain social skills that people may find difficult to practice and cultivate. Individuals can obtain specialized instruction and practice skills like active listening, turn-taking, starting conversations, and keeping eye contact by using virtual settings and guided exercises. Repetitive practice in a virtual setting fosters skills growth and development.

Exposure to a Variety of Social Scenarios: Virtual reality may expose people to a variety of social scenarios, including difficult or unusual circumstances, to aid in the development of flexibility, adaptation, and resilience in social interactions (Freina & Ott, 2015). Through VR, people may develop their social skills by learning how to negotiate various social circumstances, resolve disputes, and interact with other personalities.

Roleplaying and Perspective-Taking: According to Gutierrez-Maldonado *et al.* (2019), VR allows users to adopt a variety of roles and views during virtual social interactions. This fosters empathy for other people's perspectives and improves perspective-taking abilities. People may learn about the experiences and feelings of others by assuming the roles of various characters in the virtual world, which improves their empathy and social understanding.

Collaborative Virtual Environments: By enabling people to participate in virtual cooperation and group activities, VR enhances collaborative experiences (Slater *et al.*, 2000). As people experience social dynamics in a group context, this encourages the development of social skills linked to collaboration, bargaining, and shared decision-making.

Generalization to Real-Life Environments: Social skills learned through virtual social interactions and communication training in VR may be used in real-life environments (Chow *et al.*, 2019). By bridging the gap between virtual and real-life interactions for successful social integration, people may develop confidence and use their abilities in real-world social settings with repeated practice and progressive exposure.

Virtual social interactions and communication training should be incorporated into a comprehensive curriculum that blends virtual experiences with practice and feedback. When creating and executing efficient VR-based social skills treatments, the advice of educators, therapists, or other specialized specialists is essential (Freina & Ott, 2015). Utilizing VR's immersive and interactive features, people may improve their social skills, communication talents, and ability to flourish in social situations.

## 3.7 Collaborative VR Environments for Social Skills Development

Collaborative VR environments present unique possibilities for the development of social skills as they allow individuals to engage in virtual group activities, teamwork, and cooperative experiences (Kokkinara & Slater, 2019).

Here are some key aspects of utilizing collaborative VR environments for social skills development:

Shared Virtual Spaces: Collaborative VR environments allow for the simultaneous occupancy of numerous users in the same virtual area, allowing for avatar-based interaction and communication (Pan & Hamilton, 2018). The participants feel more connected and engaged because of the shared virtual spaces' presence and social presence.

Collaboration and Cooperation: Tasks and challenges in collaborative VR environments call for collaboration and cooperation (Bohil, Alicea, & Biocca, 2011). Participants cooperate to resolve issues, accomplish common objectives, and finish tasks. Communication, cooperation, coordination, and shared decision-making are key social skills that may be developed through collaborative VR activities.

Nonverbal Communication and Body Language: People can use nonverbal communication and body language signals to connect with one another in collaborative VR settings (Tarr & Warren, 2020). Participants may communicate nonverbally much like they would in face-to-face conversations, thanks to avatars' ability to imitate head motions, gestures, and facial expressions. This intimate social interaction encourages comprehension of nonverbal signs and heightens social dynamics awareness.

Empathy and Perspective-Taking: Collaborative VR environments give players the chance to adopt other viewpoints and engage in roleplaying activities (Kilteni *et al.*, 2013). People can practice perspective-taking and foster empathy by taking on the identities of various avatars or characters and experiencing various situations from a variety of perspectives. This encourages comprehension, empathy, and respect for various viewpoints.

By providing situations including disputes or disagreements, collaborative VR settings provide opportunities for people to strengthen their negotiating and conflict resolution abilities (Dascal *et al.*, 2017). Participants can practice conflict resolution, negotiation, and effective communication tactics in the virtual environment (Freitas *et al.*, 2018). The development of positive strategies for resolving conflicts is encouraged by this experiential learning.

Collaborative VR environments that incorporate social norms and etiquette can direct participant behavior and promote suitable social interactions (Depping *et al.*, 2020). Individuals have the chance to acquire and practice appropriate social behaviors in a controlled environment by setting up virtual social rules and expectations (Pan & Hamilton, 2018). This improves social skills and prepares people for social situations in the real world.

Real-time feedback and reflection possibilities are provided by collaborative VR settings (Freitas *et al.*, 2018). To provide feedback and pointers for development, the virtual environment can evaluate participant interactions, communication styles, and social behaviors (Bombari *et al.*, 2020). People may evaluate their performance and make changes to improve their social skills, thanks to the feedback mechanism.

Individuals can gain confidence in their social skills by gradually exposing themselves to collaborative VR settings (Depping *et al.*, 2020). Participants can begin with easier activities and work their way up to more difficult social situations, which help them develop over time (Freitas *et al.*, 2018). This gradual exposure eases anxiety and promotes skills improvement.

It is crucial to create cooperative VR settings with specific social skills in mind and to ensure that educators, therapists, or other experts are providing the necessary direction and facilitation (Bombari *et al.*, 2020). To optimize its efficacy, collaborative VR should be incorporated into a comprehensive therapeutic program including real-world practice and feedback (Dascal *et al.*, 2017). Individuals may improve their social skills, collaboration skills, and social relationships in a helpful and engaging way by taking advantage of the interactive and immersive nature of collaborative VR settings.

## 3.8 Assessing Social Skills Development in AR and VR Environments

Accurately and meaningfully assessing social skills development in AR and VR environments requires careful consideration and specific approaches (Hartanto *et al.*, 2021). Here are some strategies and considerations for assessing social skills development in AR and VR environments:

Observation and behavior analysis are two methods that may be used to evaluate participant behavior in AR and VR social interactions. These methods include verbal and nonverbal communication, social engagement, collaboration, problem-solving, and adherence to social norms (Bombari *et al.*, 2020). This qualitative method offers insightful information about the social abilities and behaviors of the participants.

Self-Report Measures: Using standardized questionnaires or scales, participants can self-evaluate the growth of their social skills (Diemer *et al.*, 2015). Self-report questionnaires allow individuals to express how they personally feel about their own interpersonal abilities, including empathy, perspective-taking, social comfort, and dispute resolution.

Assessments conducted before and after AR and VR therapies can assist in determining whether the intervention was successful in enhancing participants' social skills (Hartanto *et al.*, 2021). Standardized tests or assessments with an emphasis on social skills can be used to monitor improvements in participant social interaction skills, behaviors, and attitudes.

Performance-Based Tasks: Creating tasks or activities that focus on social skills within AR and VR environments enables direct evaluation of participants' social competence (Kandalaft *et al.*, 2013). Roleplaying, problem-solving, perspective-taking, or communication activities may be a part of these assignments. Assessors might use predetermined criteria or rubrics to evaluate participants' performance.

Virtual Behavioral Analytics: According to Chirico *et al.* (2020), AR and VR technologies can record information on users' interactions and activities inside a virtual environment. By examining participants' speech patterns, body language, social engagement, and adherence to social standards, virtual behavioral analytics can provide unbiased insights into the development of their social skills.

Based on the unique objectives of the social skills intervention, it is crucial to choose the best evaluation techniques and to consider the advantages and disadvantages of each strategy (Hartanto *et al.*, 2021). Combining several evaluation techniques can provide researchers with a thorough grasp of how participants' social skills develop in AR and VR settings.

Peer and teacher evaluations are important in measuring the development of social skills in AR and VR environments (Chirico *et al.*, 2021). Participants' communication, collaboration, empathy, and social engagement can be evaluated by peers or teachers who watch them interact in AR and VR settings. These assessments provide various viewpoints and can support other assessment techniques.

It is essential to evaluate how social skills acquired in AR and VR settings translate to actual social situations (Hartanto *et al.*, 2021). Comments, observations, or self-reports from others in participants' regular contexts (such school or the community) might shed light on how social skills learned in AR and VR settings are applied in real-world situations.

For a thorough knowledge of social skill development in AR and VR settings, longitudinal research is crucial (Bombari *et al.*, 2020). Researchers and practitioners may monitor participants' progress, spot developmental patterns, and assess the long-term efficacy of AR and VR treatments on social skill development by completing evaluations at various intervals.

Establishing the validity and reliability of assessment methods used in AR and VR settings is crucial for ensuring correct evaluation (Chirico *et al.*, 2021). Assessments should consider ecological validity, individual variability, and cultural sensitivity. A complete and well-rounded evaluation of participants' social skills development in AR and VR settings may be achieved by integrating several assessment methodologies.

## 3.9 Best Practices and Strategies for Implementing AR and VR in Social Skills Training

When implementing AR and VR in social skills training, careful planning and consideration are essential to maximize effectiveness (Feng *et al.*, 2021).

Here are some best practices and strategies to consider when integrating AR and VR into social skills training:

Clearly defining learning objectives is crucial (Dascal *et al.*, 2017). Specifically identify the social skills or competencies that AR and VR experiences aim to develop. Establishing clear learning objectives that align with participants' needs and desired outcomes will guide the design and implementation of the AR and VR interventions. Customize AR and VR content to individual needs (Parsons *et al.*, 2017). Tailor the experiences to participants' specific developmental levels, social challenges, and individual goals. Customization ensures that the training is relevant, engaging, and impactful for each participant.

Provide adequate training and support to participants and facilitators (Feng *et al.*, 2021). Ensure that they receive proper training in using AR and VR technologies, becoming familiar with the equipment, software, and virtual environment navigation. Offering guidance on maximizing the benefits of AR and VR for social skills development is crucial. Foster a safe and supportive environment for participants (Dascal *et al.*, 2017). Emphasize that virtual space is judgment-free, where individuals can practice and learn without fear of embarrassment or failure. Encourage open communication and establish a positive learning atmosphere.

Incorporate real-time feedback during AR and VR social skills training (Parsons *et al.*, 2017). Utilize interactive features, such as virtual coaches, performance assessments, or instant feedback mechanisms, to provide immediate guidance and support participants' learning and improvement. Gradually increase the complexity of social scenarios in AR and VR (Feng *et al.*, 2021). Start with simpler situations and progressively introduce more challenging interactions as participants gain proficiency. Gradual exposure and progression allow individuals to build confidence, master foundational skills, and apply them to more complex social contexts.

To maximize the effectiveness of AR and VR experiences in social skills training, it is important to consider the following best practices and strategies (Bacca *et al.*, 2014):

Integrate real-world practice alongside AR and VR experiences to promote the transfer and generalization of social skills. Encourage participants to apply the skills they learn in AR and VR settings to real-life interactions and provide opportunities for reflection, feedback, and reinforcement in authentic situations.

Help participants generalize the social skills acquired in AR and VR to various settings and contexts. Establish connections between virtual experiences and real-life scenarios and provide guidance on transferring learned skills to different social situations encountered in school, home, or community environments.

Incorporate collaborative learning opportunities within AR and VR experiences. Foster teamwork, cooperation, and communication skills by encouraging participants to engage in joint problem-solving, roleplaying, or cooperative tasks that enhance social engagement and interaction. Regularly evaluate and assess the effectiveness of AR and VR interventions in social skills training. Collect feedback from participants, educators, and therapists to monitor progress, identify areas for improvement, and make necessary adjustments to optimize the training program.

Consider ethical guidelines when using AR and VR in social skills training. Ensure privacy, obtain appropriate consent, and prioritize the emotional safety and well-being of participants. Respect cultural diversity, avoid stereotypes, and promote inclusivity within virtual experiences. Collaborate with professionals, such as educators, therapists, and experts in social skills training or special education. Their expertise and guidance can help ensure that the AR and VR interventions align with evidence-based practices and meet the specific needs of participants.

By implementing these best practices and strategies, AR and VR can be effectively integrated into social skills training, offering individuals immersive, engaging, and impactful learning experiences to enhance their social competence.

## 3.10 Real-World Examples of AR and VR Implementations in Social Skills Development: Case Studies

Different AR and VR applications have been created to help the development of social skills in various demographics. Here are some instances:

Virtual Speech is a VR application that aims to enhance communication and public-speaking abilities (Depping *et al.*, 2017). Users may practice speaking in an immersive environment with a variety of speech circumstances and a realistic virtual audience. Users may improve their communication skills by receiving real-time feedback on their speaking ability, body language, and engagement.

Children with autism spectrum disorder (ASD) may use the AR-based game Social Detective, according to Kaspar *et al.* (2014). To practice social cue identification, emotional comprehension, and acceptable social responses, it uses AR to present interactive social scenarios. Children's social skills development is supported by compelling visual and aural cues.

Platforms like VAST Autism use VR technology to provide speech and language treatment for those with communication challenges, according to Levy *et al.* (2016). Users may practice communication, social interaction, and language skills in virtual settings while receiving real-time feedback from therapists, which improve the efficacy of therapy.

Project Perfect World: According to Schultheis *et al.* (2020), Project Perfect World employs VR to improve the social skills and mental health of children with physical limitations. Children participate in activities that foster social interaction, self-confidence, and inclusivity via simulated experiences like riding a bike or playing sports.

SimSensei: According to Rizzo *et al.* (2011), SimSensei is an interactive virtual person that evaluates and helps users develop social skills. SimSensei is a virtual therapist who converses with people using VR. It evaluates body language, voice intonation, and facial expressions to offer immediate feedback and recommendations for enhancing communication abilities.

Second Life: According to Reich *et al.* (2013), Second Life is a virtual environment where users may create avatars and communicate with others. It has been used to teach social skills to people with autism by providing a secure and regulated environment for roleplaying, communication, and social interactions.

These case studies show numerous ways that AR and VR may be used to build social skills and cater to different groups. They demonstrate how these technologies may be used to design engaging and productive learning environments that develop social competency and improve people's capacity for interpersonal communication and interaction.

## 3.11 Potential Advancements and Future Research Directions for AR and VR in Social Skills Development

The advancement of AR and VR technologies has the potential to significantly improve social skills development. Here are some prospective study directions and potential breakthroughs in this area:

Future developments could concentrate on enhancing the immersion and realism of AR and VR experiences. To produce more realistic and interesting virtual worlds and avatars, this may entail improvements in visuals, haptic feedback, and sensory stimulation (Pan *et al.*, 2016).

Virtual agents that interact with people in AR and VR settings are being researched as socially intelligent virtual agents. The authenticity and efficacy of social skills training are increased by these agents' capacity to display more sophisticated behaviors, comprehend, and react to emotions, and offer individualized feedback and direction (Bickmore *et al.*, 2016).

Training that is Personalized and Adaptable: When teaching social skills, customization and adaptation are essential. Future studies can concentrate on creating AI algorithms that customize AR and VR experiences according to user demands, preferences, and advancement. This would make it possible to create training plans that are specifically tailored to societal concerns at hand while also enhancing learning outcomes (Sallinen *et al.*, 2020).

Expanding the selection of feedback and evaluation modes can improve the efficacy of AR and VR in the development of social skills. To give more thorough and reliable assessments of social skills, research can investigate the integration of multimodal feedback, including facial expression analysis, speech recognition, and physiological responses (Riek *et al.*, 2019).

Longitudinal Studies and Transferability: To investigate the long-term impacts of AR and VR treatments on the growth of social skills, long-term research must be conducted. Future studies can examine how well social skills developed in AR and VR settings translate to actual social interactions and gauge how well acquired abilities hold up over time (Smith *et al.*, 2019).

With AR and VR, these developments and next research paths show significant potential for further strengthening the development of social skills.

Training in Social Skills for Specific Populations: Developing specialized AR and VR therapies for certain populations with social skills issues, such as those with ASD, social anxiety, or communication impairments, might be the focus of a future study. Designing interventions with their particular needs, sensitivities, and ambitions in mind would be the main objective (Mazzone *et al.*, 2020).

Exploring the possibilities of collaborative VR environments and social networking platforms for the development of social skills is a promising subject. To improve their social interactions and forge new relationships, people can participate in cooperative activities, group discussions, or social networking in VR settings (Dunst *et al.*, 2019).

Ethical Guidelines and Considerations: It is essential to set moral standards and best practices for the use of AR and VR technologies in social skills development as they grow further. Understanding the ethical ramifications, privacy issues, and potential hazards linked with AR and VR treatments might be the subject of research. Creating norms and guidelines would guarantee responsible and secure execution (Felnhofer *et al.*, 2021).

Future studies can look into how AR and VR technologies can be used in conjunction with other therapeutic modalities like cognitive–behavioral therapy or social skills groups. A complete and synergistic approach to the development of social skills can be achieved by integrating AR and VR with conventional therapies (Botella *et al.*, 2019).

Cost-effectiveness and Accessibility: New hardware and software for AR and VR can make these technologies more usable and affordable. To reach a wider spectrum of people who can benefit from social skills training, future research can concentrate on building inexpensive and user-friendly AR and VR technologies that can be readily adopted in educational and therapeutic contexts (Hsieh *et al.*, 2021).

By pursuing these developments and investigating these research avenues, AR and VR can continue to revolutionize the development of social skills by providing cutting-edge interventions that enable people to enhance their social interactions, communication abilities, and all-around social competence.

## 3.12 Conclusion

In conclusion, there is significant promise for AR and VR to improve the development of social skills in special education. In a safe and encouraging atmosphere, these technologies offer immersive and interactive settings that let people practice and improve their social skills, communication abilities, and perspective-taking abilities. The use of theoretical frameworks offers a foundation for comprehending and creating AR and VR treatments for the improvement of social skills. Practical methods for implementation include using AR for social skills training, VR simulations for skills development, encouraging empathy and perspective-taking, teaching virtual social interactions and communication, creating collaborative VR environments, and monitoring the development of social skills in AR and VR environments.

The successful application of AR and VR in social skills development across varied populations, including children with ASD and people with communication issues, is shown via real-world examples and case studies. These instances demonstrate how these tools are efficient in fostering social interaction, self-assurance, and the application of knowledge in practical situations. Future research should concentrate on developments like enhancing immersion and realism, creating socially intelligent virtual agents, implementing adaptive and personalized training, integrating multimodal feedback and assessment, conducting longitudinal studies, creating interventions specifically for particular populations, investigating collaboration and social networking in VR, addressing ethical issues, and establishing guidelines as AR and VR technologies continue to advance.

AR and VR have the potential to completely transform the way social skills are developed in special education by embracing these developments and exploring these new lines of inquiry. These groundbreaking and useful techniques enable people to successfully negotiate social situations, build deep connections, and flourish in a variety of social environments. The social well-being and general quality of life for people with special needs might be considerably improved with continued study into and application of AR and VR.

## References

1. Adams, J. M., DePaul, M. R., Kern, L., & Rodriguez, B. J. (2020). Using a virtual classroom simulation to train educators to implement a token economy. *J. Behav. Educ.*, 29(1), 68-89.

2. Bacca, J., Baldiris, S., Fabregat, R., & Graf, S. (2014). Augmented reality trends in education: A systematic review of research and applications. *Educ. Technol. Soc.*, 17(4), 133-149.
3. Bacca, J., Baldiris, S., Fabregat, R., Graf, S., & Kinshuk. (2014). Augmented reality trends in education: A systematic review of research and applications. *Educ. Technol. Soc.*, 17(4), 133-149.
4. Banakou, D., Hanumanthu, P. D., & Slater, M. (2018). Virtual embodiment of white people in a black virtual body leads to a sustained reduction in their implicit racial bias. *Front. Hum. Neurosci.*, 12, 1-10.
5. Bandura, A. (1977). *Social learning theory*. Englewood Cliffs, NJ: Prentice-Hall.
6. Bandura, A. (1986). *Social foundations of thought and action: A social cognitive theory*. Prentice-Hall.
7. Baus, O., Bouchard, S., & Rizzo, A. A. (2016). Why immersive? In O. Baus, A. A. Rizzo, & S. Bouchard (Eds.), *Clinical Virtual Reality: A Systematic Review* (pp. 1-6). Springer International Publishing.
8. Bickmore, T. W., Pfeifer, L. M., & Jack, B. W. (2016). Taking the Time to Care: Empowering Low Health Literacy Hospital Patients with Virtual Nurse Agents. In *International Conference on Intelligent Virtual Agents* (pp. 63-74). Springer.
9. Blascovich, J., Loomis, J., Beall, A. C., Swinth, K. R., Hoyt, C. L., & Bailenson, J. N. (2002). Immersive virtual environment technology as a methodological tool for social psychology. *Psychol. Inq.*, 13(2), 103-124.
10. Bohil, C. J., Alicea, B., & Biocca, F. A. (2011). Virtual reality in neuroscience research and therapy. *Nat. Rev. Neurosci.*, 12(12), 752-762.
11. Bombari, D., Schmid Mast, M., & Canadas, E. (2020). From social sensing to social acting: An integrative approach to social intelligence in augmented reality and virtual reality. *Front. Psychol.*, 11, 1-11.
12. Botella, C., Bretón-López, J., Quero, S., Baños, R. M., García-Palacios, A., & Zaragozá, I. (2019). Treating social anxiety disorder with the evidence-based cognitive-behavioral therapy protocol ETASS: Study protocol for a randomized controlled trial using Internet-delivered virtual reality. *Trials*, 20(1), 143.
13. Brown, A., & Miller, J. (2017). The potential of virtual reality for individuals with autism spectrum disorder. In C. T. Miller (Ed.), *Interventions for Autism Spectrum Disorders* (pp. 345-367). Springer.
14. Brown, D. J., McCoy, A. R., & O'Sullivan, L. (2019). Virtual reality for pediatric pain. *Children*, 6(11), 117.
15. Chen, C. M., Huang, S. H., & Chang, C. K. (2017). A tablet-based augmented reality system for supporting children's social skills development. *Educ. Technol. Soc.*, 20(1), 133-145.
16. Chirico, A., Cipresso, P., Yaden, D. B., Biassoni, F., Riva, G., & Gaggioli, A. (2017). The potential of virtual reality for the investigation of awe. *Front. Psychol.*, 8, 1-6.

17. Chirico, A., Ferrise, F., Cordella, L., Gaggioli, A., & Baños, R. M. (2021). The potentials of virtual reality in social neuroscience: Insights from multimodal approaches. *J. Clin. Med.*, 10(2), 299.
18. Chow, H. M., Healey, M. K., Conway, A. R., & Kovacs, K. (2019). Augmented reality helps with prospective memory in young and older adults. *Front. Psychol.*, 10, 2056.
19. Clark, F., Schumann, M., & Mosterman, P. J. (2022). Virtual reality for special needs. In *Handbook of Virtual Environments for Occupational Safety and Health* (pp. 389-405). CRC Press.
20. Crick, N. R., & Dodge, K. A. (1994). A review and reformulation of social information-processing mechanisms in children's social adjustment. *Psychol. Bull.*, 115(1), 74-101.
21. Dascal, J., Reid, M., IsHak, W. W., Spiegel, B., Recacho, J., Rosen, B., & Danovitch, I. (2017). Virtual reality and medical inpatients: A systematic review of randomized, controlled trials. *Innov. Clin. Neurosci.*, 14(1-2), 14-21.
22. Davis, H., Fitzgerald, E., Lee, H., & Park, T. (2021). Augmented reality in education: A review of theories, applications, and challenges. *J. Educ. Technol. Soc.*, 24(4), 274-288.
23. Depping, A. E., Cash, E. R., Danforth, A., & Yoo, J. (2017). Virtual Speech: A Virtual Reality Application for Public Speaking Anxiety. *Int. J. Innov. Sci. Math. Educ.*, 25(5), 57-67.
24. Depping, M. K., Egger, M., Kühnel, S., Niermann, H. C., & Haudenhuyse, R. P. (2020). Virtual reality training to enhance the social skills of adolescents with autism spectrum disorders: A systematic review. *J. Autism Dev. Disord.*, 50(12), 4382-4398.
25. Diemer, J., Alpers, G. W., Peperkorn, H. M., Shiban, Y., & Mühlberger, A. (2015). The impact of perception and presence on emotional reactions: A review of research in virtual reality. *Front. Psychol.*, 6, 26.
26. Dunst, C. J., Hamby, D., Howse, R. B., Wilkie, H., Annas, K., Lin, X., & Zelenka, K. (2019). Early Childhood Intervention Professional Development and Practice Guides and Natural Learning Environment Practices. In *Educ. Train. Autism Dev. Disabil.* (Vol. 54, No. 2, pp. 187-200).
27. Felnhofer, A., Kothgassner, O. D., Beutl, L., Hlavacs, H., Kryspin-Exner, I., Hlavacs, H., & Kothgassner, O. D. (2021). Ethical challenges and considerations of the use of virtual and augmented reality in psychological research and clinical practice. *Int. J. Environ. Res. Public Health*, 18(4), 1669.
28. Feng, X., Song, J., Su, R., Xie, W., Zhang, S., & Li, Z. (2021). The effect of virtual reality technology on learning outcomes in K-12 education: A meta-analysis. *Educ. Technol. Res. Dev.*, 69(3), 1619-1654.
29. Freeman, D., Reeve, S., Robinson, A., Ehlers, A., Clark, D., Spanlang, B., & Slater, M. (2017). Virtual reality in the assessment, understanding, and treatment of mental health disorders. *Psychol. Med.*, 47(14), 2393-2400.

30. Freina, L., & Ott, M. (2015). A literature review on immersive virtual reality in education: State of the art and perspectives. In *The International Scientific Conference eLearning and Software for Education (eLSE)* (Vol. 1, pp. 133-141).
31. Freitas, S. M., de Vasconcelos, L. G., Hounsell, M. S., Ferreira, A. S., & dos Santos, J. A. (2018). A review on virtual reality for learning in the field of psychology. *Comput. Educ.*, 123, 69-87.
32. Gonzalez, M. C., Reznitskaya, A., McLaren, B. M., & Arthur, M. (2018). Exploring the potential of collaborative virtual reality for co-constructing ideas in science. *J. Educ. Psychol.*, 110(7), 1045-1065.
33. Gupta, A., Chouksey, M., Singh, D., & Srivastava, A. (2020). Emerging technologies for special needs: A review. In *2020 11th International Conference on Computing, Communication and Networking Technologies (ICCCNT)* (pp. 1-5). IEEE.
34. Gutiérrez-Maldonado, J., Ferrer-García, M., & Caqueo-Urízar, A. (2013). Design and validation of a virtual reality-based program for the induction of empathy. *J. Med. Internet Res.*, 15(6), e135.
35. Gutierrez-Maldonado, J., Gutierrez-Martinez, O., Loreto-Quijada, D., Nieto, R., & Ferrer-Garcia, M. (2019). A preliminary test of the effectiveness of role-play virtual reality in social skills training. *Front. Psychol.*, 10, 331.
36. Hartanto, D., Kampmann, I. L., Morina, N., & Emmelkamp, P. M. (2021). Social interactions in virtual reality: A systematic review and meta-analysis. *Neurosci. Biobehav. Rev.*, 128, 254-268.
37. Horner, R. H., Carr, E. G., Strain, P. S., Todd, A. W., & Reed, H. K. (2005). Problem behavior interventions for young children with autism: A research synthesis. *J. Autism Dev. Disord.*, 35(4), 423-446.
38. Hsieh, P. C., Aceves, D., & Pan, Z. (2021). Exploring Virtual Reality Technology in Education: Definitions, Key Features, and Emerging Issues. In *Handbook of Research on Virtual and Augmented Reality in Education* (pp. 1-25). IGI Global.
39. Huang, X., Nagao, K., & Pradhan, B. (2020). VR-based soft-skill training: A review. *Int. J. Hum.-Comput. Stud.*, 137, 102378.
40. Johnson, R. (2020). Social skills interventions for students with autism: A review of the literature. *Focus Autism Other Dev. Dis.*, 35(3), 157-165.
41. Johnson, R., & Smith, J. (2019). Evaluating social skills interventions for students with autism spectrum disorders: A systematic review and meta-analysis. *J. Autism Dev. Disord.*, 49(3), 852-873.
42. Johnson, S., & Wilson, C. (2018). An exploration of theoretical frameworks for using virtual reality in education. *J. Interact. Learn. Res.*, 29(3), 405-429.
43. Jones, P., Chadwick, D., & Williams, G. (2019). Social skills training for young people with intellectual disabilities: A systematic review. *J. Intellect. Disabil.*, 23(1), 92-112.
44. Jones, P., Williams, G., & Flewitt, R. (2020). Social and emotional learning for students with special educational needs: A systematic review. *Eur. J. Spec. Needs Educ.*, 35(2), 266-283.

45. Kandalaft, M. R., Didehbani, N., Krawczyk, D. C., Allen, T. T., & Chapman, S. B. (2013). Virtual reality social cognition training for young adults with high-functioning autism. *J. Autism Dev. Disord.*, 43(1), 34-44.
56. Kaspar, K., König, P., Schwandt, J., König, S., König, P., & Janke, V. (2014). Social Detective: An augmented reality game for teaching children with autism spectrum disorders to read facial expressions. In *7th International Conference on Pervasive Computing Technologies for Healthcare (PervasiveHealth)* (pp. 247254). IEEE.
47. Kilteni, K., Groten, R., & Slater, M. (2013). The sense of embodiment in virtual reality. *Presence: Teleoperators Virtual Environ.*, 22(4), 373-387.
48. Kokkinara, E., & Slater, M. (2019). Measuring presence in virtual reality: A meta-analysis. *Front. Rob. AI*, 6, 1-17.
49. Krijn, M., Emmelkamp, P. M., Biemond, R., de Wilde de Ligny, C., Schuemie, M. J., & van der Mast, C. A. (2004). Treatment of acrophobia in virtual reality: The role of immersion and presence. *Behav. Res. Ther.*, 42(2), 229-239.
50. Krijn, M., Emmelkamp, P. M., Olafsson, R. P., & Biemond, R. (2004). Virtual reality exposure therapy of anxiety disorders: A review. *Clin. Psychol. Rev.*, 24(3), 259-281.
51. Lange, B., Flynn, S. M., & Rizzo, A. A. (2018). Augmentation of social skills through virtual reality and serious games. In *The Oxford Handbook of Social Media and Music Psychology* (pp. 1-30). Oxford University Press.
52. Levy, E. S., McMahon, S. E., Salas, R. A., & Moore, E. J. (2016). Virtual Reality and Social Skills Training for Adolescents with Autism Spectrum Disorder. *J. Autism Dev. Disord.*, 46(12), 3701-3710.
53. Lieberman, M. D. (2007). Social cognitive neuroscience: A review of core processes. *Annu. Rev. Psychol.*, 58, 259-289.
54. Lin, C. T., Ke, J. W., & Chiang, Y. H. (2020). A survey of augmented reality and virtual reality applications in the creative arts field. *Sustainability*, 12(21), 1-19.
55. Mazzone, L., Benvenuto, A., Vassena, L., Fava, L., & Minervini, L. (2020). Autism spectrum disorders. *Child Adolesc. Ment. Health*, 25(3), 156-160.
56. Miller, L. M., & Anderson, F. (2019). Augmented reality applications in education. In *Handbook of Research on Learning Outcomes and Opportunities in the Digital Age* (pp. 292-322). IGI Global.
57. Neguţ, A., Matu, S., Sava, F. A., David, D., & Mogoase, C. (2016). Virtual reality measures in neuropsychological assessment: A meta-analytic review. *Clin. Neuropsychol.*, 30(2), 165-184.
58. Pan, X., & Hamilton, A. F. (2018). Why and how to use virtual reality to study human social interaction: The challenges of exploring a new research landscape. *Br. J. Psychol.*, 109(3), 395-417.
59. Pan, X., Gillies, M., Barker, C., Clark, D. M., & Slater, M. (2021). Social anxiety disorder: Remembering past virtual experiences and facilitating future interactions to improve social interactions in real-life. *J. Anxiety Disord.*, 77, 102359.

60. Pan, X., Hamilton, A. F., Kleinsmith, A., & de Sa, V. R. (2016). The Impact of Different Visual–Haptic Feedback Methods on Users' Perception and Motor Behavior in Virtual Reality. *IEEE Trans. Visual Comput. Graphics*, 22(11), 2426-2435.
61. Pan, Z., & Hamilton, H. J. (2018). Virtual reality's effect on empathy: A systematic review and meta-analysis. *Cyberpsychol. Behav. Social Networking*, 21(12), 737-743.
62. Parsons, T. D., & Mitchell, J. (2002). The potential of virtual reality in social skills training for people with autistic spectrum disorders. *J. Intellect. Disabil. Res.*, 46(5), 430-443.
63. Parsons, T. D., & Rizzo, A. A. (2017). Affective outcomes of virtual reality exposure therapy for anxiety and specific phobias: A meta-analysis. *J. Behav. Ther. Exp. Psychiatry*, 56, 152-161.
64. Pertaub, D. P., Slater, M., & Barker, C. (2002). An experiment on public speaking anxiety in response to three different types of virtual audience. *Presence: Teleoperators Virtual Environ.*, 11(1), 68-78.
65. Premack, D., & Woodruff, G. (1978). Does the chimpanzee have a theory of mind? *Behav. Brain Sci.*, 1(4), 515-526.
66. Reich, S. M., Subrahmanyam, K., & Espinoza, G. (2013). Friending, IMing, and Hanging Out Face-to-Face: Overlap in Adolescents' Online and Offline Social Networks. *Dev. Psychol.*, 49(1), 180-191.
67. Riek, L. D., Rabinowitch, T. C., Chakrabarti, B., & Robinson, P. (2019). The Social Signal Value of Inconsistent Nonverbal Cues. *Cognit. Sci.*, 43(1), e12712.
68. Rizzo, A. S., Buckwalter, J. G., Neumann, U., Kesselman, C., & Thiebaux, M. (2000). Virtual environments for targeting cognitive processes: An overview of projects at the University of Southern California. In Riva, G., & Galimberti, C. (Eds.), *Towards cyberpsychology: Mind, cognition, and society in the internet age* (pp. 3-10). IOS Press.
69. Rizzo, A., Scherer, S., DeVault, D., Gratch, J., & Hartholt, A. (2011). Detecting depression and PTSD with virtual humans. In *International Conference on Virtual Rehabilitation (ICVR)* (pp. 1-7). IEEE.
70. Robinson, L. E., & Smith, M. (2021). Augmented reality, virtual reality, and gaming in children's physical activity and exercise. In J. M. Erwin (Ed.), *Advances in Pediatrics* (Vol. 68, pp. 275-294). Elsevier.
71. Sallinen, M., Lehtonen, E., Ronimus, M., Salmi, P., & Korkiakangas, T. (2020). Adaptive Games for Social and Emotional Learning: A Systematic Review. *J. Educ. Comput. Res.*, 58(6), 1502-1526.
72. Sánchez, J., Subirats, L., & Tost, D. (2017). Teaching empathy through virtual reality: A systematic literature review. *Educ. Inf. Technol.*, 22(1), 351-368.
73. Schaub, M. P., Wenger, A., Berg, O., Beck, T., Stark, L., & Quednow, B. B. (2020). A simulated mind-reading intervention can effectively reduce cannabis use: Results of a randomized controlled trial. *Front. Psychiatry*, 11, 1-12.

74. Schultheis, M. T., Pazzaglia, A. M., Manos, T. L., & Rizzo, A. A. (2020). Project Perfect World: A Virtual Reality Application to Enhance Social Skills and Promote Self-Determination in Children with Physical Disabilities. *J. Spec. Educ. Technol.*, 35(1), 5-17.
75. Slater, M., Spanlang, B., Sanchez-Vives, M. V., & Blanke, O. (2010). First person experience of body transfer in virtual reality. *PLoS One*, 5(5), e10564.
76. Slater, M., Usoh, M., & Steed, A. (2000). Depth of presence in virtual environments. *Presence: Teleoperators Virtual Environ.*, 9(2), 130-144.
77. Smith, J. (2018). The importance of social skills training for students with disabilities. *Interv. Sch. Clin.*, 53(4), 235-240.
78. Smith, J., & Johnson, R. (2020). The impact of social skills interventions on students with autism spectrum disorder: A meta-analysis. *Focus Autism Other Dev. Dis.*, 35(1), 3-12.
79. Smith, M. J., & Goodman, E. L. (2019). Virtual reality in social skills training for individuals with autism spectrum disorders. In A. A. Alberti, & N. G. Schnell (Eds.), *Virtual Reality for Psychological and Neurocognitive Interventions* (pp. 101-123). Springer.
80. Smith, M. J., Ginger, E. J., Wright, K., Wright, M. A., Taylor, J. L., Humm, L. B., ... & Fleming, M. F. (2019). Virtual Reality Job Interview Training in Autism Spectrum Disorder: A Randomized Controlled Trial. *J. Autism Dev. Disord.*, 49(6), 2228-2238.
81. Tarr, M. J., & Warren, W. H. (2020). Virtual reality in behavioral neuroscience and beyond. *Trends Cognit. Sci.*, 24(11), 926-939.
82. Thomas, K., Hudson, M., He, Z., & Ferguson, N. (2021). Best practices for implementing virtual reality interventions in educational settings. *Comput. Educ.*, 172, 104370.

# 4

# Immersive Learning's Promise: The Educational Potential of Augmented and Virtual Reality

**Priya Trivedi**

*Department of Botany, Indore International College, Indore (M.P.), India*

***Abstract***

Technological advancements have become pervasive in people's lives despite the disadvantages that also come with their use. Technology assists human society in its quest to advance, from assisting in accurately navigating the streets to landing on Mars. Dan Brown even concluded in his book "Origin" that the next step in evolution is a combination of technology and humans. Conversations concerning virtual reality (VR) and augmented reality (AR) technology are rife right now in the realm of educational technology (edtech). According to a 2019 study by the International Data Corporation (IDC) on the adoption of AR and VR, their development will pick up speed across the globe. The effect VR and AR are having on learners with disabilities or special needs cannot be understated given the broad use of these educational technology tools. Taking this into account, the book chapter discusses the importance of VR and AR in the education sector, as well as their uses.

***Keywords:*** Edtech, augmented reality (AR) and virtual reality (VR), disabilities or special needs

## 4.1 Introduction

Digital innovations are continually transforming the educational sector. A 2019 Gallup poll found that just over 13% of educators at public schools in the country use digital tools occasionally and that 65% use them daily, with 85% expecting "great benefit" from doing so in the future [1].

*Email:* priyatrivedi2679@gmail.com

V. Ajantha Devi, Williamjeet Singh and Yogesh Kumar (eds.) Augmented Reality and Virtual Reality in Special Education, (91–102) © 2024 Scrivener Publishing LLC

Teachers and organizations are searching for creative methods of integrating technological solutions into classroom interactions as the use of educational technology (edtech) increases. Immersive technologies like augmented reality (AR) and virtual reality (VR), which let users interact with digitally created content in both real-world and virtual environments, present a tremendous opportunity for the advancement of digital learning. By reducing physical barriers, enhancing teamwork and interactive instruction, and enabling personalized educational methods that may assist students at all levels to thrive, these innovations increase the potential of educational settings ranging from K–12 classrooms to middle schools. The idea of using AR and VR as teaching tools is not new. Immersive learning, however, has just lately developed from a modest experimentation to a multimillion-dollar industry with rapidly rising utilization.

In classrooms around the nation, interactive virtual field trips, research projects, lifelike modeling, and other initiatives are used. Mobile devices offer a wide range of fundamental experiences, and better headsets get better while being cheaper. Additionally, the equipment needed to produce and experience immersive entertainment is becoming more affordable and user-friendly. To establish the framework for fully immersive educational environments in the future, this paper evaluates the present situation and possible advantages of AR/VR in education and presents a number of ways they are being used throughout disciplines and academic levels.

## 4.2 The Impact of AR/VR on Education

Since the 1990s, researchers have been examining the possibilities of virtual worlds as a teaching aid. AR/VR techniques have excellent potential because of their contribution to the expanding field of educational technology's multidimensional nature, creativity abilities, and potential to provide complete immersion that broadens learning possibilities that might otherwise be constrained by price or distance. However, AR/VR technologies and software have only recently been widely available and reasonably priced for use in educational settings. AR/VR technologies provide a wide variety of choices to deliver knowledge in more engaging learning environments compared to their two-dimensional counterparts. Modern AR systems enable users to actively participate in a computerized setting where they can communicate in an environment that combines both virtual and live objects and other users. This form of engagement promotes experiential learning that either replicates real-world situations or provides difficult material in novel ways.

For example, students can observe tiny things in three dimensions or stand in the middle of a physics simulation. Additionally, VR users have access to 360-degree viewing opportunities, which have been previously recorded as still photographs or films, so they can view them, but not interact with or alter them. This less immersive (but often less expensive) method may be advantageous when an experience's primary determinant is its perceived appearance or sense of presence, like when visiting a historical place.

Augmented reality, also known as a form of mixed reality (MR), allows users to engage with virtual things that show up in their actual surroundings. This works best in situations when users must interact with virtual objects while maintaining awareness of their surroundings in space. For example, students can adhere to digital instructions overlays when undertaking difficult assignments such as discovering ways to fix a challenging piece of equipment or conducting a medical operation. While delivering fewer interactive experiences than VR, AR allows users to observe fixed virtual objects or information within a real environment. This is most beneficial when the real thing has the most educational value, such as when a virtual reproduction of a work of art or historical object is exhibited in an educational environment or when additional text or images are added on a historical site. Immersive technology is becoming more and more popular with pupils, educators, parents, managers, and institutions as a teaching aid [2–4].

## 4.3 Literature Survey

In a 2016 study by the electronics giant Samsung and GfK comprising 1,000 US teachers, 93% said that their students would be enthusiastic about adopting VR, and 83% believed that these tools may improve learning outcomes [5]. According to a 2017 research [6] conducted by firms that provide digital and VR materials and the DigiLitEY academic network, 64% of parents and 70% of children in the US between the ages of 8 and 15 said that they were interested in VR. According to a 2018 Common Sense Media research, 84% of the parents who had used VR themselves and 62% of parents overall thought it might give educational experiences to their kids [7]. According to the results of another 2018 poll [8], less than 50% of higher education institutions have either completely implemented or are considering doing so. In a 2020 poll performed by Perkins Coie and the XR Association, education was listed as the second industry most likely to see disruption from immersive technology in the near future [9].

## 4.4 Some Uses of AR/VR in K–12 Education

Immersive solutions are becoming more common among K–12 educators and administrators as a result of these technologies' distinctive characteristics. AR/VR systems have the potential to enhance, partially replace, or completely replace learning in conventional classrooms. The most frequently used application in K–12 settings right now is improving the learning environment. For instance, teachers can accompany students on lifelike virtual tours or allow them to interact with 3D models using AR. However, for blended and online learning, schools are also utilizing AR/VR technologies. The change to digital and blended education brought about by the COVID-19 epidemic highlighted the advantages of location-independent instructional resources. Students who use immersive technologies can interact in real-time with peers and instructors while taking part in remote learning activities in a passive manner. Smartphone AR, for example, enables students to view a piece of art on the ceiling or something in their living room. While AR- or VR--based laboratories would enable students to undertake practical learning research regardless of whether they were present or not in a classroom or lab that is fully furnished. Reduced interruptions during remote learning are another benefit of fully immersive VR systems, which help students focus during sessions.

Additionally, AR/VR technologies present intriguing methods for involving kids with attention-deficit/hyperactivity disorder (ADHD), autism spectrum disorder (ASD), dyslexia, or other cognitive or learning difficulties, both in the classroom and remotely. For instance, VR experiences can assist young people with ASD in overcoming their fears. Augmented reality can also help kids with learning impairments by modifying or improving tangible learning resources like textbooks or flashcards [10–13].

## 4.5 Higher Education and AR/VR

Virtual reality and AR technologies have similar value in more sophisticated learning settings. Immersive technologies are being used in the classroom by academics at colleges and universities across all subject areas. In a 2018 internet poll of colleges and institutions, more than two-thirds had either partially or completely adopted AR/VR solutions, and an additional third were experimenting with them. In certain colleges and institutions, employees and students have even been given access to unique spaces where they may use AR and VR technologies to produce their own content. These specialized labs give students and teachers new opportunities to experiment with immersive learning, along with whatever hardware they own or borrow [14, 15].

## 4.6 AR/VR for Administrators and Educators

Both learning spaces and broader educational systems could benefit from immersive technology. In addition to improving student learning, immersive learning techniques can also benefit teachers by giving them access to helpful materials. Educators can practice their trade with fake, virtual pupils through virtual training before doing so in an actual classroom where their choices may have a significant impact on students' lives. Executives and officials may benefit from utilizing immersive solutions for community involvement, communication, and cooperation as technology continues to advance and flourish [16].

## 4.7 AR/VR Technologies: Current Applications in Education

Technologies like AR and VR have a lot of potential to improve education at every level and throughout disciplines. New use cases in learning settings are always developing as immersive technologies develop. The current breakthroughs laying the groundwork for immersive educational technology's future are highlighted in this section.

### 4.7.1 K–12 Education: Increasing Opportunities and Improving Classroom Experiences

Children's learning environments could become more interesting, efficient, and fair, thanks to immersive technologies. Some of the most recent advances in this field include libraries of fully immersive materials suitable for educational purposes, customized content for specific disciplines, as well as educational levels, and technologies made specially to support students with learning issues.

### 4.7.2 Curricula and Resource Collections for Immersive Learning

Many AR/VR technologies currently available for K–12 education provide pre-set curricula and libraries of immersive experiences that teachers can customize to meet certain learning objectives. Publicly accessible materials from governmental organizations, educational-focused collections from immersive content libraries, and specialist services from businesses, especially those specializing in integrating AR/VR in immersive experiences, are all examples of existing offers.

### 4.7.3 Special Education

All pupils, including those with cognitive and educational challenges, can gain from AR/VR capacity to offer personalized learning solutions. Additionally, there are immersive special education programs available, especially for ASD students.

Program Virtual Reality Opportunities to Implement Social Skills (VOISS), an institute of education-funded effort, is housed at the University of Kansas Centre for Research on Learning and the Department of Special Education. Through VR experiences, the project helps middle school students with learning difficulties hone and strengthen their social skills [17]. With a headset or web-enabled device, the software offers teachers and students a low-risk, controlled setting to rehearse a variety of typical scenarios. For young people with ASD, Floreo provides VR-based learnings in life and social skills. Users can practice social cues and conversation skills in a gamified setting using interactive story scenarios. A tablet or other mobile device application allows teachers or other authority figures to monitor progress and direct the experience. The activities emphasize making friends, practicing real-world interactions, and learning emotional-regulation skills.

Higher education solutions combine the benefits of immersive learning with the ability of AR and VR to lower barriers in physical space. As a result, students are given more chances to explore and learn on their own with the help of instructors because compared to their K–12 peers, they are often more decentralized. Higher educational institutions, especially, have come to rely more on AR/VR technologies to enhance guidance in less readily apparent subjects, such as arts and sciences and artwork, in addition to more specialized fields like business and law. While science, technology, engineering, and universal medical education have historically been at the forefront of immersive learning, this trend is changing.

### 4.7.4 Medical Education

Medical education requires a large degree of practical, in-person instruction to educate students sufficiently for anything ranging from speaking with patients to carrying out difficult procedures. More and more medical and healthcare educators are utilizing AR/VR systems to provide inexpensive, moderately risky, frequently attractive alternatives to the industry's current practices [18].

### 4.7.5 Humanities, the Arts, and Other Academic Fields

The use of AR/VR in higher education enhances cross-disciplinary learning beyond the physical sciences. The immersive, fascinating, and knowledge-rich interactions these technologies offer are being widely used by academics and researchers from various sectors [19].

### 4.7.6 Soft Skills and Career Development

Aside from the benefits they provide in particular fields of study and topic areas, AR/VR techniques can aid students in acquiring important soft skills that will start preparing them for a successful future. Students entering professions like law, business, and medicine, where interaction, negotiation, and reasoning skills are just as crucial as technical expertise, will find this to be especially helpful [20].

### 4.7.7 Specialized Training and Technical Education

Similar to how soft skills training can boost talents and specialization in technical education by establishing a condensed, inexpensive learning environment, learners can be exposed to relevant and even potentially dangerous activities during immersive experiences to better equip them for conducting research in real-life situations. By eliminating the need for expensive travel or onsite training, the use of AR/VR technologies increases the availability of technical education [21].

## 4.8 Teacher Preparation: Setting Up Teachers for Success

Immersive experiences that focus on education have audiences beyond children and college students. These technologies' strengths, which make them useful in K–12 and higher learning, also put them in a position to support educators' professional development.

## 4.9 Invest in Health, Security, and Efficacy Research

Immersive learning tools have clear educational potential, but there are still some open questions that will have to be answered. First, there are a lot of unanswered questions regarding the effects of AR and VR technologies on children's health and safety. This does not necessarily imply that the technologies are dangerous due to a lack of investigation. However, more research on the psychological effects (such as children's capacity to differentiate between fictional situations or virtual environments and the real world), as well as the physiological effects (such as dizziness, vision problems, or catastrophic injuries from head-worn devices), will indeed help parents and educators make better decisions. Because 30% of families are "extremely worried" regarding possible negative health impacts on their children, according to the nonprofit Common Sense Media, the use of VR technology in the classroom may run into opposition. Second, because the method of teaching is still comparatively new and rapidly developing, there is only a small body of research demonstrating the benefits of VR and AR on learning outcomes. More study is required to determine the optimum times and ways to use these technologies for learning, as well as the most effective ways to convert current pedagogical methods to immersive tools [22].

The encouragement of a scientific study for the secure and efficient utilization of these gadgets for children would make it simpler for parents, school leaders, and educators to make wiser choices about how to implement immersive creativity, particularly those that employ head-worn screens, in the classroom. The Department of Education's Institute for the Research and Development of Educational Sciences (ES) should fund studies that explicitly look at how immersive technology affects children's health and safety.

This investigation should also examine the amount and occurrence of possible side effects or impacts of immersive technology—such as psychological problems or dizziness it may cause—to ensure that students may profit from the academic benefits of fully immersive activities without suffering unwanted repercussions. The findings of this study should be used by education departments and health and human services to develop guidelines for creating and implementing immersive education opportunities for various age groups. Age restrictions, guidelines for age-appropriate content, kinds of devices, and length of individual encounters should all be taken into account.

The Institute of Educational Sciences should fund research into effective ways to employ AR/VR technologies to improve learning outcomes in addition to safety and health. This study should look at uses in K–12 classrooms, higher education, and online learning. Instructors, administrators, and students may profit from having a thorough grasp of the effects that these technologies have on learning outcomes when choosing how and when to incorporate AR/VR applications and tools into present educational resources.

Furthermore, as previously stated, this research may affect broader federal government recommendations and suggestions.

## 4.10 Challenges Lie in Implementing VR in a Learning Environment

To exploit the use of VR to its maximum learning potential, academics agree that there needs to be an effective pedagogy associated with it. This is true even though VR can be forced into present education paradigms with some success. According to Hu-Au and Lee (2018), teachers should not just try to replicate "face-to-face pedagogic educational learners" as this will only result in ineffective implementation [23]. Understanding how to develop and administer educational courses that are properly matched to this technology will be crucial, Elmqaddem (2019) notes [24]. According to Scavarelli *et al.* (2020), the biggest challenge in using VR is "figuring out how to best utilize this type of technology to more effectively improve the learning experience for learners in an approach that is not simply developing, or supplanting, the physical environment," [25]. Virtual reality is by no means a panacea for the intricate demands and needs of the education industry. In fact, using VR has its own set of difficulties. Even though VR is becoming more popular, it remains a niche technology that both educators and students might not be familiar with. Teachers should progressively bring the use of VR within their classrooms, Southgate *et al.* (2018) advised, keeping in mind the novelty element and the need to address it before beginning the actual class activities [26].

## 4.11 Policymakers and Recommendations

Technologies like AR and VR have the power to completely alter the way learners develop at all levels. Immersive learning's bright future, however, is not certain. The achievement of AR/VR technologies in academic environments will depend on a variety of factors that go beyond the technology itself, thus policymakers should take steps to foster an atmosphere of innovation in this field. To fully realize the benefits of AR/VR as a teaching tool, it is crucial to speak about important issues relating to technical expertise, quality of educational materials, health, security, and accessibility.

## 4.12 Conclusion

Technology continues to develop quickly, altering social standards and having an impact on every aspect of human life. It might be intimidating to even be aware of the most recent technological advancements, let alone implement them. Compared to other industries, the area of education frequently adjusts to change more slowly, yet it invariably transforms to welcome or accommodate change. In the hands of tech-savvy educators, new tools that were once relegated to the educational periphery frequently find their way into the mainstream paradigm. Once included in this category, the digital delivery of lessons via video conferencing software is now a norm in education.

In future generations, it will be essential to ensure that teachers possess the expertise necessary to integrate VR and AR into their teaching strategies and to offer opportunities for the creation of vital content, including giving teachers and students the tools they need. Policymakers are expected to support programs to extend access to such technologies while also promoting the creation of fresh materials, making the necessary investments in security and effectiveness research, and other actions to promote innovation.

Virtual reality has now started the shift from a cutting-edge technology to one that can be utilized in everyday life. Since VR now is considerably different from VR 5 years ago, many beliefs and presumptions about the invention may not be accurate at all. It would be beneficial for teachers to stay current with technological advancements as they now have clear practical applications in addition to their theoretical value for instructional purposes.

## References

1. Gallup and New Schools Venture Fund, "Education Technology Use in Schools" (New Schools Venture Fund, 2019), http://www.newschools.org/wp-content/ uploads/2019/09/Gallup-Ed-Tech-Use-in-Schools-2.pdf.
2. Fortune Business Insights, "Virtual Realty in Education Market" (Fortune Business Insights, 2019), https://www.fortunebusinessinsights.com/industry-reports/virtual-reality-in-education-market-101696.
3. ABI Research, "Augmented and Virtual Reality Tools Empower Education and Drive AR/VR Market Value to US$700 Million," news release, April 17, 2019, https://www.abiresearch.com/press/augmented-and-virtual-reality-tools-empower-education-and-drive-arvr-market-value-us700-million-2023.

4. David M Markowitz *et al.*, "Immersive Virtual Reality Field Trips Facilitate Learning about Climate (2018), Change," *Front. Psychol.*, 9 (2018), https://doi.org/10.3389/fpsyg.2018.02364.
5. Samsung Electronics, "Survey Finds Teachers Want to Make Virtual Reality a Reality in the Classroom," news release, June 27, 2016, https://www.business-wire.com/news/home/20160627005621/en/Survey-Finds-Teachers-Want-to-Make-Virtual-Reality-a-Reality-in-the-Classroom.
6. Dylan Yamada-Rice *et al.*, "Children and Virtual Reality: Emerging Possibilities and Challenges" (Dubit and DigiLitEY, 2015), http://digilitey.eu/wp-content/ uploads/2015/09/CVR-Final-PDF-reduced-size.pdf.
7. Jennifer Stevens Aubrey *et al.*, "Virtual Reality 101: What You Need to Know About Kids and VR" (Common Sense Media, 2018), https://www.commonsensemedia.org/sites/default/files/uploads/pdfs/csm_vr101_final.pdf.
8. Ben Fineman, "2018 VR/AR in Research and Education Survey" (Internet2, 2018), https://meetings.internet2.edu/media/medialibrary/2018/10/25/2018 1016-fineman-metaverse.pdf.
9. Boost VC, Perkins Coie, and the XR Association, "2020 Augmented and Virtual Reality Survey Report" (Perkins Coie, March 2020), https://www.perkinscoie.com/images/content/2/3/v4/231654/2020-AR-VR-Survey-v3.pdf.
10. Alice Bonasio, "Immersive Experiences in Education: New Places and Spaces for Learning" (Microsoft, 2019), https://edudownloads.azureedge.net/msdownloads/MicrosoftEducation_Immersive_Experiences_Education_2019.pdf.
11. Ashley Deese, "5 Benefits of Gamification," January 8, 2021, https://ssec.si.edu/stemvisions-blog/5-benefits-gamification.
12. Archit Kaushik, "XR for Social Impact: A Landscape Review" (Games for Change, 2020), https://www.gamesforchange.org/refresh2018/wp-content/uploads/2020/10/G4C_XR4C_2020_white_paper_Final.pdf.
13. Barbara Holzapfel, "What Educators Have Learned from Remote Learning Prepares Them for the New School Year," 15, 2020, https://educationblog.microsoft.com/en-us/2020/06/what-educators-have-learned-from-remote-learning-prepares-them-for-the-new-school-year.
14. Ryan Johnston, "VR in Universities a Welcome Addition, but Not Yet 'Plug-and-Play,'" May 26, 2021, https://edscoop.com/virtual-reality-technology-universities.
15. Fineman, "2018 VR/AR in Research and Education Survey".
16. Jennifer Herseim, "How Virtual Reality is Changing the Game of Teacher Training," July 24, 2019, https://districtadministration.com/how-virtual-reality-is-changing-the-game-of-teacher-training.
17. "Project VOISS," accessed August 16, 2021, https://www.projectvoiss.org.
18. Susanne Wish-Baratz *et al.*, "Assessment of Mixed-Reality Technology Use in Remote Online Anatomy Education,"3, no. 9 (September 2020), https://doi.org/10.1001/jamanetworkopen.2020.16271.
19 Vige Barrie, "Literary Dreamscapes Made 'Real' via Virtual Reality," Hamilton College, June 27, 2018, https://www.hamilton.edu/news/story/virtual-reality-technology-and-literary-dreamscapes-intertwined-in-this-classroom.

20. "FE Innovation Partners Employability Training: Transforming Employability Training in the Further Education sector," Bodyswaps, accessed August 16, 2021, https://bodyswaps.co/project/transforming-careers-in-the-education-sector.
21. "Industry Credentials," zSpace, accessed August 16, 2021, https://zspace.com/industrycredentials.
22. Ellysse Dick, "With the Right Investments, AR and VR Can Reduce Education Gaps," 10, 2021, https://itif.org/publications/2021/02/10/right-investments-ar-and-vr-can-reduce-education-gaps.
23. Hu-Au, E., & Lee, J. J. (2018). Virtual reality in education: a tool for learning in theexperience age. *Int. J. Innov. Educ.*, 4(4), 215–226. https://doi.org/10.1504/ijiie.2017.10012691
24. Elmqaddem, N. (2019). Augmented reality and virtual reality in education. Myth orreality? *Int. J. Emerg. Technol. Learn.*, 14(3), 234–242. https://doi.org/10.3991/ijet.v14i03.9289
25. Scavarelli, A., Arya, A., & Teather, R. J. (2020). Virtual reality and augmented reality insocial learning spaces: a literature review. *Virtual Reality*, 0123456789. https://doi.org/10.1007/s10055-020-00444-8.
26. Southgate, E., Buchanan, R., Cividino, C., Saxby, S., Weather, G., Smith, S. P., Bergin, C., Kilham, J., Summerville, D., & Scevak, J. (2018). What teachers should know abouthighly immersive virtual reality: Insights from the vr School Study. *Scan* 37(4). https://education.nsw.gov.au/teaching-and-learning/professional-learning/scan/past-issues/vol-37-2018/research-highly-immersive-virtual-reality

# 5

# Influence of Augmented Reality and Virtual Reality in Special Education in India

**Ravichandran K.**

*Department of Visual Communication and Animation, DR. M. G. R. Educational and Research Institute, Chennai, India*

***Abstract***

This study discusses the benefits of using virtual reality (VR) and augmented reality (AR) technologies for the treatment of autism. These technologies provide controlled virtual environments and facilitate the study of behavioral traits safely. Virtual reality technology can simulate everyday situations and provide early training scenarios tailored to the needs of children with autism, the study found. Augmented reality technology not only focuses on visual and auditory responses but also enhances message delivery through the senses. Personalized therapies using VR and AR help increase engagement and immersion for children with autistic. Virtual reality systems can be used to create virtual characters to interact with autistic children, thereby creating a harmonious environment, reducing anxiety, and practicing social skills through them. Additionally, the integration of AR and VR technologies in the development of smart educational campuses in India improves educational planning and instructional design. It also improves campus efficiency and facilitates three-dimensional digital campus management. The combined use of AR and VR technologies ushers in a new era of transforming digital campuses into smart campuses in India.

***Keywords***: Augmented reality, virtual reality, special education, autistic children and scientific management

*Email*: ravi.news10@yahoo.com

V. Ajantha Devi, Williamjeet Singh and Yogesh Kumar (eds.) Augmented Reality and Virtual Reality in Special Education, (103–120) © 2024 Scrivener Publishing LLC

## List of Symbols and Abbreviations

VR - Virtual Reality
AR - Augmented Reality
ANOVA - Analysis of Variance

## 5.1 Introduction

Augmented reality (AR) and virtual reality (VR) technologies constitute groundbreaking improvements within the digital realm [1]. With AR, digital information is superimposed onto the physical world, enriching our belief and interaction with facts. As an example, using an AR app, users can point their smartphone camera to a particular structure or landmark and instantly have a virtual tour and/or see information about its historical significance, or they could hover over a menu to view pictures of numerous dishes. Then again, the VR era transports customers to entirely new digital environments, immersing them through headsets or comparable gadgets. Its applications span gaming, training, training simulations, medical or surgical demonstrations, and numerous different domain names [2, 3].

### 5.1.1 Increased Usage of AR and VR in Education

The usage of AR and VR technologies has witnessed an enormous surge, particularly within the field of education. These technologies have revolutionized some learning experiences by way of incorporating interactive and immersive solutions that enhance students' comprehension of complex standards [4]. Through AR and VR, college students can visualize abstract thoughts, explore digital environments, and interact with three-dimensional items [5]. Furthermore, these technologies allow the introduction of simulations that mirror real-international eventualities, fostering sensible and attractive studying experiences [6]. Therefore, educators integrate AR and VR more into their coaching methodologies to enhance student engagement and enrich learning outcomes and mastery.

### 5.1.2 The Significance of AR and VR in Special Education

The emergence of AR and VR technologies hold fantastic promise for remodeling special education. These technologies offer college students with disabilities access to more information and gain new knowledge, allowing them to discover new principles inside safe and immersive surroundings [7]. AR and VR also facilitate the introduction of personalized mastering reviews tailored to the individual desires, options, and competencies of each scholar. Substantially, they can play a crucial role in teaching social skills by offering controlled environments for college students with autism spectrum disorder (ASD) to practice social interactions [8].

### 5.1.3 Defining Special Education

Special education encompasses the provision of suitable and individualized educational services to students with disabilities. Its number one goal is to make sure that every college student, no matter their talents or demanding situations, has the right to high-quality education that addresses their unique needs and wishes [9]. Special education services may also encompass personalized instruction, assistive technology, counseling, and other aid services aimed at helping students attain their full potential. The definition of special education has developed alongside society's changing expertise on disabilities. These days, it is often diagnosed as a critical factor in a complete instructional machine that values variety and promotes inclusive learning in diverse environments [10].

### 5.1.4 Overview of Special Education as a Concept

Special education is an academic idea designed to cater to the needs of students with disabilities or special needs. It includes imparting personalized, customized, and individualized preparation to students who require additional help on their learning journey [11, 12]. Special education encompasses specialized services, packages, and instructional techniques tailored to fulfill the precise needs of people with disabilities. Its overarching aim is to ensure that every college student, no matter their abilities or disabilities, is given a chance to have quality education. By adopting this technique, college students with special needs can unlock their full potential and emerge as effective members of society [13].

### 5.1.5 Types of Disabilities Requiring Special Education Services

Special education offerings are designed to address particular wishes of students with disabilities. Various types of disabilities necessitate special training offerings, together with intellectual disabilities, learning disabilities, emotional and behavioral problems, autism spectrum disorders, and physical disabilities [16, 17]. Intellectual disabilities typically impact a scholar's ability to learn and realize new statistics. Learning disabilities may additionally affect a pupil's skills in regions such as studying, writing, and math. Emotional and behavioral problems can pose demanding situations in dealing with emotions within a faculty placing. Autism spectrum disorder impacts social communication abilities and behavioral styles. Physical disabilities, which include blindness or deafness, may also require accommodations to access more educational opportunities [18].

### 5.1.6 Significance of Personalized Learning Plans for Children with Disabilities

Personalized learning plans play an essential role in helping children with disabilities as they deal with particular needs and skills [19, 20]. These plans enable instructors to pick out regions where a toddler can be struggling and design an individualized curriculum that caters to their strengths and demanding situations. Through tailoring the study plan, children with disabilities can study at their own pace, without feeling beaten or left behind [21, 22]. This method fosters a sense of possession over their education mainly to increase self-assurance and motivation. Moreover, customized study plans include parents' involvement in their child's schooling [23].

## 5.2 Review of Literature

### 5.2.1 Use Cases for AR in Special Education

The AR era offers several use cases in special education. It can help college students with learning disabilities visualize and comprehend abstract ideas more effectively. Augmented reality can also provide an attractive and interactive learning experience for college students with autism spectrum disorder, helping them enhance their communication and social abilities [24, 25]. Moreover, AR can be applied to create virtual discipline trips, permitting college students with physical disabilities to explore new environments without leaving the study room. Real-time feedback on college students' development can also be supplied via AR, permitting teachers to modify their teaching strategies for this reason. With its potential to enrich learning experiences and promote inclusivity, AR holds an awesome ability in the discipline of special education [26, 27].

### 5.2.2 Use Cases for VR in Special Education

The VR era can revolutionize special education by imparting immersive and interactive mastering reports tailored to the particular needs of students with disabilities. One use case for VR in special education entails developing virtual environments that simulate real-life scenarios, including social situations or vocational training, where students can also come across demanding situations in their day-to-day lives [28]. Another use case involves imparting visible and sensory stimulation to students with sensory processing problems or autism, helping them learn new abilities and improve their cognitive capabilities. As usual, VR has the capability to enhance conventional classroom coaching methods and create an extra enticing and effective learning [29, 30].

### 5.2.3 VR Supports College Students with ASD during Social–Emotional Development

VR technology can play a massive role in helping students with ASD throughout their social–emotional improvement; it can afford an immersive and secure environment for students to exercise social abilities, including deciphering facial expressions, body language, and tone of voice. It can additionally assist them in learning coping techniques for anxiety and sensory overload in social situations. By utilizing VR generation, teachers and therapists can layout individualized programs that cater to the specific desires of each pupil with ASD [31, 32]. The interactive and customizable nature of VR enables centered interventions and promotes social–emotional growth in a controlled and supportive setting.

## 5.3 Methodology

The methodology employed within the study on the effectiveness of VR and AR in special education applied a quantitative technique. The study that involved 104 members, consisting of 56 men and 48 women, aimed to acquire facts on the effect of VR and AR on learning consequences in special education. Quantitative measures, such as surveys, assessments, and observations, were utilized to collect records from individuals. Surveys were administered to gather records of contributors' perceptions, engagement, and AR technologies. Exams were performed to assess information retention and educational performance before and after using those technologies. Observations were possibly made to examine and report members' behaviors and interactions throughout VR and AR periods.

## 5.4 Results

### 5.4.1 Demographics

In Table 5.1, the demographics are presented, including gender, age, education, and profession. The table presents counts for men and women in each category. Below the gender class, the table shows the number of men and women within specific age ranges. Within the 20–30 years age group, there are 21 men and 20 women. In the 31–40 years age group, there are 26 men and 23 women. Within the 41–50 years and above age group, there are nine men and five women. Shifting to the education class, the table provides the counts of individuals with exclusive tiers of education. Undergraduate education is represented by way of 18 men and 23 women. Postgraduate education is represented by 28 men and 18 women. The "others" class includes 10 men and 7 women. Finally, under the profession class, the table gives statistics of people in teaching and technology fields. In the teaching profession, there are 26 adult men and 27 women. In the technology profession, there are 30 adult men and 21 women. The gender disparity in the technology industry has been a longstanding issue, with women being notably underrepresented in the field. Current information indicates that

**Table 5.1** Demography.

| | | Gender | |
|---|---|---|---|
| | | **Men** | **Women** |
| | | **Count** | **Count** |
| **Age** | 20–30 years | 21 | 20 |
| | 31–40 years | 26 | 23 |
| | 41–50 years and above | 9 | 5 |
| **Education** | Undergraduate | 18 | 23 |
| | Postgraduate | 28 | 18 |
| | Others | 10 | 7 |
| **Profession** | Teaching | 26 | 27 |
| | Technologist | 30 | 21 |

women account for 21% of technology employees, while men make up 30%. This gender gap poses a critical challenge as it restricts the industry's capacity, and it additionally hampers the inclusion of diverse views. One specific region where generation holds huge promise is in special education, specifically in the realm of VR and AR.

Those innovative technologies have proven potential to greatly assist students with disabilities in improving their cognitive skills. By developing immersive environments, VR/AR can facilitate interactive and attractive learning experiences for these children. However, to absolutely harness the ability of these technologies, it is vital to address the issue of range within the enterprise. The challenge is to have more women in the technology sector so they can bring in unique views and novel ideas that can contribute to the emergence of more AR/VR tools. By promoting gender variety and inclusivity, we will foster surroundings that encourage collaboration and innovation in the long run, leading to the development of special education technology and its positive effect on the lives of children with learning disabilities.

### 5.4.2 ANOVA Test

Primarily based on the given ANOVA, Table 5.2 presents the results, enhancing the accessibility of education: The F-value is 0.092, with a corresponding p-value of 0.762. Since the p-value is more than the significant degree of 0.05, we fail to reject the null hypothesis. There is no vast difference among the clusters in terms of improving the accessibility of training.

Using AR and VR in text-to-speech augmenters: The F-value is 0.842, with a corresponding p-value of 0.361. Once more, given that the p-value is greater than 0.05, we fail to reject the null hypothesis. There is no significant distinction between the clusters in terms of the use of AR and VR for text-to-speech augmenters.

Generating physical objects: The F-value is 126.997, with a p-value of 0.000. The p-value is less than 0.05, indicating a significant difference between the clusters regarding generating physical objects.

Illustrating complex concepts: The F-value is 14.038, with a p-value of 0.000. Much like the preceding case, the p-value is less than 0.05, indicating a significant difference among the clusters in terms of illustrating complex concepts.

Adopting AR and VR technology: The F-value is 1.424, with a p-value of 0.235. The p-value is more than 0.05, so we fail to reject the null hypothesis. There is no significant difference among the clusters in terms of adopting AR and VR technology.

**Table 5.2** ANOVA.

| | Cluster | | Error | | | |
|---|---|---|---|---|---|---|
| | **Mean Square** | **df** | **Mean Square** | **df** | **F** | **Sig.** |
| Improving the accessibility of education | .273 | 1 | 2.972 | 102 | .092 | .762 |
| Using AR and VR in text-to-speech augmenters | 2.358 | 1 | 2.802 | 102 | .842 | .361 |
| Generating physical objects | 320.542 | 1 | 2.524 | 102 | 126.997 | .000 |
| Illustrating complex concepts | 23.242 | 1 | 1.656 | 102 | 14.038 | .000 |
| Adopting AR and VR technology | 2.305 | 1 | 1.618 | 102 | 1.424 | .235 |
| Aligning with new age technology | 143.516 | 1 | 3.730 | 102 | 38.475 | .000 |
| Promoting independence and self-confidence | 56.158 | 1 | 3.381 | 102 | 16.609 | .000 |

Aligning with new age technology: The F-value is 38.475, with a p-value of 0.001. The p-value is less than 0.05, indicating a significant difference between the clusters regarding aligning with new age technology.

Promoting independence and self-confidence: The F-value is16.609, with a p-value of 0.001. In addition, the p-value is less than 0.05, indicating a significant difference between the clusters in terms of promoting independence and self-confidence.

There are significant differences among the clusters in generating physical objects, illustrating complex concepts, aligning with new age technology, and promoting independence and self-confidence. However, there are no significant differences in improving accessibility of education and adopting AR and VR technology among the clusters.

### 5.4.3 One-Sample Kolmogorov–Smirnov Test

Table 5.3 and Figure 5.1 provide the outcomes of the one-sample Kolmogorov–Smirnov test for various factors.

Improving accessibility of education: The Kolmogorov–Smirnov Z value is 1.665, with a two-tailed asymptotic importance (p-value) of 0.008. The p-value is much less than 0.05, indicating that there is a significant deviation from the regular distribution for improving accessibility of education.

Using AR and VR in text-to-speech augmenters: The Kolmogorov–Smirnov Z value is 2.157, with a p-value of 0.001. The p-value is less than 0.05, indicating a significant deviation from the ordinary distribution for using AR and VR in text-to-speech augmenters.

Generating physical objects: The Kolmogorov–Smirnov Z value is 1.714, with a p-value of 0.006. Again, the p-value is less than 0.05, indicating a considerable deviation from the regular distribution for generating physical objects.

Illustrating complex concepts: The Kolmogorov–Smirnov Z value is 2.051, with a p-value of 0.001. Further, the p-value is less than 0.05, indicating an enormous deviation from the everyday distribution of illustrating complex concepts.

Adopting AR and VR technology: The Kolmogorov–Smirnov Z value is 1.727, with a p-value of 0.5. The p-value is less than 0.05, indicating a significant deviation from the everyday distribution for adopting AR and VR generation.

Aligning with new age technology: The Kolmogorov–Smirnov Z value is 1.396, with a p-value of 0.041. Yet again, the p-value is much less than 0.05, indicating a huge deviation from the ordinary distribution for aligning with new age generation.

Promoting independence and self-confidence: The Kolmogorov–Smirnov Z value is 2.276, with a p-value of 0.001. Further, the p-value is less than 0.05, indicating a sizable deviation from the normal distribution for promoting independence and self-confidence.

All the variables in the table (improving accessibility of education, AR and VR used in text-to-speech augmenters, generating physical objects, illustrating complex concepts, adopting AR and VR generation, aligning with new age technology, and promoting independence and self-confidence) display large deviations from the ordinary distribution primarily based on the Kolmogorov–Smirnov test.

**Table 5.3** One-Sample Kolmogorov–Smirnov test.

| | N | Normal parameters[a,b] | | Most extreme differences | | | Kolmogorov-Smirnov Z | Asymp. Sig. (2-tailed) | Monte Carlo Sig. (2-tailed) | | |
|---|---|---|---|---|---|---|---|---|---|---|---|
| | | | | | | | | | | 99% confidence interval | |
| | | Mean | Std. deviation | Absolute | Positive | Negative | | | Sig. | Lower bound | Upper bound |
| Improving accessibility of education | 104 | 6.88 | 1.716 | .163 | .163 | -.144 | 1.665 | .008 | .005[c] | .003 | .007 |
| Using AR and VR in text-to-speech augmenters | 104 | 7.37 | 1.672 | .211 | .211 | -.115 | 2.157 | .000 | .000[c] | .000 | .001 |
| Generating physical objects | 104 | 9.49 | 2.369 | .168 | .168 | -.127 | 1.714 | .006 | .004[c] | .002 | .005 |
| Illustrating complex concepts | 104 | 7.87 | 1.366 | .201 | .201 | -.155 | 2.051 | .000 | .001[c] | .000 | .001 |
| Adopting AR and VR technology | 104 | 4.13 | 1.275 | .169 | .169 | -.138 | 1.727 | .005 | .003[c] | .002 | .005 |
| Aligning with new age technology | 104 | 8.74 | 2.256 | .137 | .137 | -.121 | 1.396 | .041 | .036[c] | .031 | .041 |
| Promoting independence and self-confidence | 104 | 10.4038 | 1.97321 | .223 | .223 | -.161 | 2.276 | .000 | .000[c] | .000 | .000 |

a. Test distribution is normal.
b. Calculated from data.
c. Based on 10000 sampled tables with starting seed 2000000.

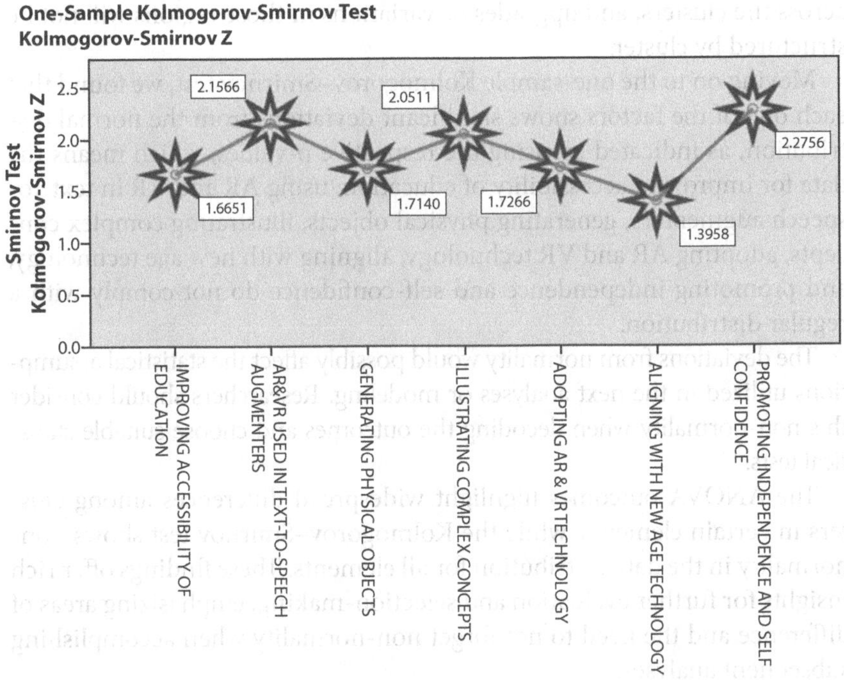


Figure 5.1 One-sample Kolmogorov-Smirnov test.

## 5.5 Discussion

The ANOVA table offers insights into the importance of variations among clusters in various factors, while the one-sample Kolmogorov–Smirnov test assesses the normality of the statistics distribution for each element.

Based on the ANOVA results, significant differences were discovered from most of the clusters in generating physical objects, illustrating complex concepts, aligning with new age technology, and promoting independence and self-confidence. This suggests that there are various stages of overall performance or responses across these factors among the clusters. These differences could indicate capacity regions for improvement or focus on every cluster.

However, for enhancing the accessibility of education and adopting AR and VR technology, the ANOVA results suggest no significant differences between clusters. This shows that these elements are exceedingly regular across the clusters, and upgrades or variations in those regions will not be structured by cluster.

Moving on to the one-sample Kolmogorov–Smirnov test, we found that each one of the factors shows significant deviations from the normal distribution, as indicated by using the respective p-values, which means the data for improving accessibility of education, using AR and VR in text-to-speech augmenters, generating physical objects, illustrating complex concepts, adopting AR and VR technology, aligning with new age technology, and promoting independence and self-confidence do not comply with a regular distribution.

The deviations from normality would possibly affect the statistical assumptions utilized in the next analyses or modeling. Researchers should consider this non-normality when decoding the outcomes and choose suitable statistical tests.

The ANOVA outcomes highlight widespread differences among clusters in certain elements, while the Kolmogorov–Smirnov test shows non-normality in the data distribution for all elements. These findings offer rich insights for further evaluation and selection-making, emphasizing areas of difference and the need to not forget non-normality when accomplishing subsequent analyses.

## 5.6 Findings

Based on the provided ANOVA table and one-sample Kolmogorov–Smirnov test table, the following findings can be summarized:

### 5.6.1 ANOVA Findings

The accessibility of education has been a focus of improvement efforts, and the observed value found no significant difference among clusters in enhancing academic accessibility. The use of AR and VR for text-to-speech augmenters also confirmed no significant difference between clusters. In terms of generating physical objects, a significant difference was found among clusters. A few clusters proved better skill ability in generating physical objects. In terms of illustrating complex concepts, a significant difference was found among clusters. Certain clusters excelled in successfully illustrating complex ideas. The adoption of AR and VR technology showed no significant difference among clusters, indicating a comparable degree of reputation and implementation. Aligning with the new age of technology, a significant difference was found among clusters. A few clusters have been extra proactive in adapting to and incorporating rising technologies. Promoting independence and self-confidence also displayed a significant difference among clusters. Cluster results were more effective in fostering independence and self-confidence among college students.

### 5.6.2 One-Sample Kolmogorov–Smirnov Test Findings

All factors (improving accessibility of education, using AR and VR in text-to-speech augmenters, generating physical objects, illustrating complex concepts, adopting AR and VR technology, aligning with new age technology, and promoting independence and self-confidence) exhibit significant differences from the regular distribution.

Those findings suggest that, while there can be differences between clusters in a few elements, the data distribution for all factors deviate notably from normality. This must be considered when deciphering consequences and choosing appropriate statistical methods for further analysis. These findings offer insights into the variation between clusters and the non-normality of the data distribution, which can guide future evaluation and decision-making methods.

## 5.7 Conclusion

The use of AR and VR technology in education suggests a great possibility to revolutionize learning experiences. These technologies were found to have a significant impact on numerous components, together with enhancing accessibility, helping students with disabilities, generating physical objects, illustrating complex concepts, promoting independence and self-confidence, and aligning with new age technology. The results of ANOVA cluster tests performed on these elements showed significant differences between clusters in terms of generating physical objects, illustrating complex concepts, aligning with new age technology, and promoting independence and self-confidence. These findings highlight the importance of focusing in these areas to enhance overall performance and outcomes. However, no significant variations were found among clusters in enhancing accessibility of education and adopting AR and VR technology.

This shows that those factors are fairly regular across clusters and might not require cluster-precise strategies for improvement. The one-sample Kolmogorov – Smirnov outcomes suggests that the data for all factors significantly deviate from a normal distribution. This emphasizes the need for careful interpretation of the results and attention to alternative statistical techniques. These findings exhibit the transformative capability of AR and VR technology in education. They provide immersive and interactive experiences, which can enhance learning outcomes, offer answers for students with disabilities, and align with modern day-to-day technological inclinations. By way of statistics and leveraging these findings, educators, and decision-makers can create inclusive and powerful learning environments that prepare students for the future.

## Acknowledgments

The DR. M. G. R. Educational and Research Institute, Chennai, provided assistance with this research report. To the students of the Department of Visual Communication and Animation, I would like to thank you.

## Conflict of Interest Statement

The author, Dr. K. Ravichandran, of this work pronounces no conflicts of interest regarding the content material provided in this undertaking. The statistics and references furnished are primarily based on goal analysis and synthesis of present literature. There are no economic or non-public relationships that could affect the objectivity or integrity of the statistics provided. The sole purpose of this work is to offer correct and reliable statistics to the satisfaction of the author's understanding and competencies.

## References

1. İlhan İ, Çeltek E. Mobile marketing: Usage of augmented reality in tourism. *Gaziantep Univ. J. Soc. Sci.*, 2016;15(2):581-599.
2. Styliaras GD. Augmented reality in food promotion and analysis: Review and potentials. *Digital*, 2021;1(4):216-240.
3. Wilkinson N, Ang RP, Goh DH. Online video game therapy for mental health concerns: a review. *Int. J. Soc. Psychiatry*, 2008;54(4):370-382.

4. Petrov PD, Atanasova TV. The Effect of augmented reality on students' learning performance in stem education. *Information*, 2020;11(4):209.
5. Venkatesan M, Mohan H, Ryan JR, Schürch CM, Nolan GP, Frakes DH, Coskun AF. Virtual and augmented reality for biomedical applications. *Cell Rep. Med.*, 2021;2(7):100348.
6. Alanis JM, Pyram RH. From simulations to real-world operations: Virtual reality training for reducing racialized police violence. *Industrial and Organizational Psychology*, 2022;15(4):621-625.
7. Mantovani F. VR learning: Potential and challenges for the use of 3d environments in education and training. *Towards cyberpsychology: mind, cognition, and society in the Internet age*, 2001;2(207).
8. Parsons S, Leonard A, Mitchell P. Virtual environments for social skills training: comments from two adolescents with autistic spectrum disorder. *Comput. Educ.*, 2006;47(2):186-206.
9. Martin EW, Martin R, Terman DL. The legislative and litigation history of special education. *The future of children*, 1996;25-39.
10. Ryndak DL, Jackson L, Billingsley F. Defining school inclusion for students with moderate to severe disabilities: What do experts say?. *Exceptionality*, 2000;8(2):101-116.
11. Al Hazmi AN, Ahmad AC. Universal Design for Learning to Support Access to the General Education Curriculum for Students with Intellectual Disabilities. *World J. Educ.*, 2018;8(2):66-72.
12. Sailor W, Roger B. Rethinking inclusion: Schoolwide applications. *Phi Delta Kappan.*, 2005;86(7):503-509.
13. Dymond SK, Orelove FP. What constitutes effective curricula for students with severe disabilities?. *Exceptionality*, 2001;9(3):109-122.
14. Zigmond NP, Kloo A. General and special education are (and should be) different. In Handbook of special education. *Routledge*, 2017:249-261.
15. Yell ML, Katsiyannis A, Bradley MR. The Individuals with Disabilities Education Act: The evolution of special education law. In *Handbook of special education*, Routledge. 2017:55-70.
16. Bhaumik S, Tyrer FC, McGrother C, Ganghadaran SK. Psychiatric service use and psychiatric disorders in adults with intellectual disability. *J. Intellect. Disabil. Res.*, 2008;52(11):986-995.
17. Autism and Developmental Disabilities Monitoring Network Surveillance Year 2008 Principal Investigators. Prevalence of autism spectrum disorders—autism and developmental disabilities monitoring network, 14 sites, United States, 2008. *Morbidity and Mortality Weekly Report: Surveillance Summaries*. 2012;61(3):1-19.
18. Di Sarro R, Varrucciu N, Di Santantonio A, Natali F, Kaleci S, Bianco A, ... Bertelli MO. Appropriateness of psychopharmacological therapies to psychiatric diagnoses in persons with autism spectrum disorder with or without

intellectual disabilities: a cross-sectional analytic study. *Expert Opin. Drug Saf.*, 2023; just-accepted.

19. Casner-Lotto J, Barrington L. Are they really ready to work? Employers' perspectives on the basic knowledge and applied skills of new entrants to the 21st century US workforce. *Partnership for 21st Century Skills*, 2006. 1 Massachusetts Avenue NW Suite 700, Washington, DC 20001.
20. Palincsar AS. Social constructivist perspectives on teaching and learning. *Annu. Rev. Psychol.*, 1998;49(1):345-375.
21. Huang TK, Yang CH, Hsieh YH, Wang JC, Hung CC. Augmented reality (AR) and virtual reality (VR) applied in dentistry. *The Kaohsiung J. Med. Sci.*, 2018;34(4):243-248.
22. Javaid M, Haleem A. Virtual reality applications toward medical field. *Clin. Epidemiol. Glob. Health*, 2020;8(2):600-605.
23. Labovitz J, Hubbard C. The use of virtual reality in podiatric medical education. *Clin. Podiatr. Med. Sur.*, 2020;37(2):409-420.
24. Cunha P, Brandão J, Vasconcelos J, Soares F, Carvalho V. Augmented reality for cognitive and social skills improvement in children with ASD. In *2016 13th International Conference on Remote Engineering and Virtual Instrumentation (REV)*, IEEE. 2016:334-335.
25. Brandão J, Cunha P, Vasconcelos J, Carvalho V, Soares F. An augmented reality gamebook for children with autism spectrum disorders. In *The International Conference on E-Learning in the Workplace 2015*, 2015:1-6.
26. Papanastasiou G, Drigas A, Skianis C, Lytras M, Papanastasiou E. Virtual and augmented reality effects on K-12, higher and tertiary education students' twenty-first century skills. *Virtual Reality*, 2019;23:425-436.
27. Pellas N, Fotaris P, Kazanidis I, Wells D. Augmenting the learning experience in primary and secondary school education: A systematic review of recent trends in augmented reality game-based learning. *Virtual Reality*, 2019;23(4):329-346.
28. Vasquez E, Nagendran A, Welch GF, Marino MT, Hughes DE, Koch A, Delisio L. Virtual learning environments for students with disabilities: A review and analysis of the empirical literature and two case studies. *Rural Spec. Educ. Q.*, 2015;34(3):26-32.
29. Mallory C, Keehn B. Implications of sensory processing and attentional differences associated with autism in academic settings: an integrative review. *Front. Psychiatry*, 2021;12:695825.
30. Sanz-Cervera P, Pastor-Cerezuela G, González-Sala F, Tárraga-Mínguez R, Fernández-Andrés MI. Sensory processing in children with autism spectrum disorder and/or attention deficit hyperactivity disorder in the home and classroom contexts. *Front. Psychiatry*, 2017;8:1772.

31. Boyd LE, Day K, Stewart N, Abdo K, Lamkin K, Linstead E. Leveling the playing field: Supporting neurodiversity via virtual realities. *Technol. Innovation*, 2018;20(1-2):105-116.
32. Kamińska D, Sapiński T, Wiak S, Tikk T, Haamer RE, Avots E, ... Anbarjafari G. Virtual reality and its applications in education: Survey. *Information*, 2019;10(10):318.

6

# Exploring the Untapped Potential of the Metaverse in Special Education: A Comprehensive Analysis of Applications and AI Integration

**K. B. Priya Iyer[1]* and Ajantha Devi Vairamani[2]**

*[1]Department of Information Technology M.O.P. Vaishnav College for Women (Autonomous), Chennai, TN, India*
*[2]AP3 Solutions, Chennai, TN, India*

***Abstract***
Due to its enormous potential across numerous industries, the metaverse, a ground-breaking technology concept, has attracted a great deal of attention. Educators may have limited awareness of its capabilities and prospective applications because its potential for educational reasons has been largely ignored. By providing a thorough analysis of the metaverse, including its definition, technical specifications, and prospective applications in educational contexts, this research paper seeks to close this knowledge gap. The functions of artificial intelligence (AI) in the metaverse and its possibilities for special education based in the metaverse are also investigated.

The metaverse has the potential to change conventional educational approaches in a variety of ways, from virtual classrooms and simulations to group problem-solving and experiential learning. This paper also identifies important research Important questions related to the incorporation of the metaverse in educational contexts. These problems include pedagogical concerns, technical difficulties, and potential socioeconomic effects. It will be easier for educators and researchers to fully utilize the metaverse are potential while minimizing its limitations if they are aware of and address these study difficulties. Investigating the function of AI in the metaverse is a crucial component of this research. By improving user experiences and building individualized learning pathways for students, AI can serve

**Corresponding author*: drpriyaiyer@gmail.com

V. Ajantha Devi, Williamjeet Singh and Yogesh Kumar (eds.) Augmented Reality and Virtual Reality in Special Education, (121–140) © 2024 Scrivener Publishing LLC

as a facilitator. By adapting educational content to individual requirements and learning preferences, leveraging AI in the metaverse can greatly improve student outcomes.

The study also explores the promising field of special education based on the metaverse. The metaverse holds great promise for students with a variety of learning needs and disabilities by developing inclusive and adaptive learning environments. It will be possible to create a fairer and more inclusive educational environment if we have a better understanding of how the metaverse can accommodate different learning needs. Finally, this study illuminates the underutilized potential of the metaverse in education. Teaching and learning approaches can be completely transformed by embracing this transformative technology if educators and researchers can provide a thorough grasp of the metaverse, its hardware and software requirements, prospective applications, and the role of AI. Additionally, the concept of special education based on the metaverse highlights the significance of developing an inclusive educational ecosystem that meets the various requirements of all students. A dynamic and forward-looking educational environment will be possible through embracing the possibilities of the metaverse in education. This will open new vistas for student participation and the spread of knowledge.

***Keywords***: Metaverse, augmented reality, virtual reality, visually impaired, special education

## 6.1 Introduction

Researchers, technologists, and futurists all share a fascination with the idea of the metaverse as the next evolution in social interaction. The definition, history, and prospective effects of the metaverse on human life are discussed in detail in this study, as well as the convergence of numerous technologies that support it.

The metaverse's primary goal is to create a fully realized virtual reality setting that melds harmoniously with the actual world (Gaudiosi, 2021). Users will be able to engage with virtual things and each other, as well as carry out routine tasks that replicate real-world activities within the metaverse. The metaverse strives to be an all-encompassing platform that extends and improves human life, encompassing work, education, as well as entertainment and socializing.

Several groundbreaking technologies must be incorporated in order for the metaverse to be realized. The core of this technology is virtual reality (VR) and augmented reality (AR), which allow users to fully immerse themselves in digital worlds and interact with virtual objects as if they were physically there (Lee *et al.*, 2019). Additionally, developments in block-chain, cloud computing, and artificial intelligence (AI) help to create a dynamic and interactive metaverse (PwC, 2021).

A reality where individuals can "live" and interact according to predetermined laws set out by its creators is known as the metaverse. It comprises both fully virtual experiences resembling VR devices and partially virtual experiences resembling AR in actual settings. Social engagement in the metaverse can take the form of discourse, cooperative activities, games, experience-based learning, and more. Additionally, especially for kids with disabilities, the metaverse has the power to transform education by providing engaging and authentic learning opportunities outside of the conventional classroom. The concept of the metaverse is discussed in this article along with how it can transform the field of special education.

Users can engage in wholly or partially virtual experiences in the metaverse, a virtual space (Damer, 1998). Augmented reality, where virtual components are superimposed on the real-world environment to enhance the user's perspective, is a prime example of partially virtual experiences. On the other hand, fully virtual experiences use immersive VR technologies that fully immerse users in created surroundings (Snow Crash, 1992).

Users can connect and work together on a variety of projects due to the metaverse's support for various forms of social interaction (Bainbridge, 2007). Users can interact with one another, collaborate on projects, play games, and learn from their triumphs and failures. This feature of the metaverse promotes a dynamic and interactive social environment that transcends geographical limits, offering chances for cross-cultural interactions and communities.

The metaverse has the power to completely transform education, particularly for children with disabilities. The metaverse can expand educational opportunities beyond the traditional classroom by offering open and interesting virtual learning environments (Kharat, 2019). Inclusionary learning opportunities are provided by virtual classrooms that replicate actual educational settings, removing physical obstacles and allowing for remote participation. Students can immerse themselves in dynamic and realistic circumstances through the metaverse, encouraging active learning and memory retention.

There are obstacles to overcome for the metaverse's educational potential to be fully realized. Aspects that are crucial and need attention include ensuring smooth integration, overcoming technical challenges, and taking pedagogical efficacy into account (Devine, 2019).

## 6.2 Pillars of the Metaverse

The "pillars of the metaverse" is a group of essential technologies that make up the metaverse, an expanding digital cosmos. These technologies serve as building blocks for developing compelling, immersive, and interactive virtual experiences for users. These eight crucial technologies that are pertinent to the metaverse are shown in Figure 6.1.

Extended Reality (XR): Virtual reality, AR, and mixed reality are all subsets of the concept known as extended reality (XR). Users of XR technologies can engage with digital objects in their physical environment through a seamless blending of real-world and virtual experiences.

User Interactivity: The goal of user interaction is to enable users to participate actively in the metaverse. Users can interact with virtual objects, environments, and other users through a variety of input devices and interfaces, creating a dynamic and interactive experience.

Artificial Intelligence (AI): AI contributes significantly to the realism and reactivity of the metaverse. To ensure a safe and engaging user experience, AI is utilized to construct realistic avatars, develop lifelike non-player character (NPC) interactions, and monitor servers from a cybersecurity standpoint.

Blockchain: The metaverse is supported by blockchain technology, which offers safe and open data management. It makes it possible to employ

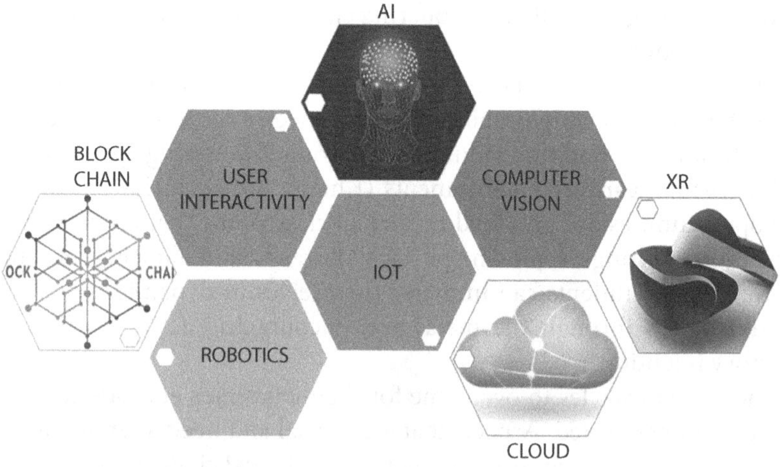


**Figure 6.1** Pillars of the metaverse.

cryptocurrencies, smart contracts, and non-fungible tokens (NFTs), securing the ownership, control, and decentralization of digital assets and data.

Computer Vision: The metaverse can process and decipher visual data from the real world thanks to computer vision technologies. This capacity is essential for AR apps, which use cameras to incorporate digital items into the user's physical environment.

Internet of Things (IoT): By linking gadgets such as speakers, haptic gloves, and VR headsets, the IoT plays a crucial role in the metaverse. The immersion of user experiences is increased by IoT sensors, which enable realistic responses and interactions within the virtual environment.

Robotics: By allowing physical avatars or robotic things to interact in the virtual world, robotics technology can improve the metaverse. Users have control over these avatars, which can mimic their behaviors and motions in the virtual environment.

Edge and Cloud Computing: Edge and Cloud computing are crucial for the seamless transmission and processing of data in the metaverse. Cloud computing offers the resources required for scalable and dispersed virtual experiences, whereas Edge computing enables faster and more effective data processing at the network's edge.

The metaverse develops a huge and interconnected digital universe using these eight essential technologies, allowing users to fully immerse themselves in shared virtual experiences. The metaverse offers a dynamic and transforming platform for social interactions, entertainment, education, and much more, with lifelike avatars, interactive surroundings, secure data management, and real-time interactions. The potential for the metaverse to transform human experiences and relationships is increasing as technology develops.

## 6.3 Importance of Special Education in the Metaverse

Because it promotes inclusion, equity, and individualized instruction for kids with a range of learning needs and disabilities, special education is crucial in the metaverse. The metaverse presents exceptional prospects to revolutionize the educational environment by building open, appealing virtual spaces that are tailored to the individual needs of each learner. To emphasize the significance of special education within the metaverse, this section emphasizes its ability to close learning gaps, promote customized development, and establish an inclusive educational ecosystem.

Accessibility and Inclusivity: In the metaverse, special education ensures that students with impairments are not left out of the classroom. Students can interact with content in a variety of ways using cutting-edge technology like AR and VR, supporting varied learning styles and demands.

Students with visual, auditory, or motor impairments can benefit from and engage in virtual learning experiences, thanks to accessible design and user interfaces (Normand *et al.*, 2019).

Individualized Support and Personalized Learning: In the metaverse, special education offers students individualized learning paths that are based on their individual interests, abilities, and shortcomings. The integration of AI makes it possible to create adaptive learning systems that dynamically modify the content and degree of difficulty, ensuring that students get the support and challenges they need (Kharat, 2019). This individualized method encourages a sense of independence and competence, which raises pupils' self-esteem and learning motivation.

Engaging and Experiential Learning: Students with impairments can benefit greatly from the metaverse's abundance of interactive and experiential learning possibilities. Active inquiry and critical thinking are encouraged by virtual simulations, immersive environments, and interactive learning materials (Guski *et al.*, 2020). Students can learn useful skills, apply knowledge in authentic settings, and obtain a greater comprehension of abstract ideas through these encounters.

Social and Emotional Development: In the metaverse, special education helps students' social and emotional growth in addition to meeting their academic needs. Students can practice social skills, cooperation, and emotional regulation in a safe and controlled setting through virtual social interactions and collaborative tasks.

Virtual support systems can offer therapeutic interventions and compassionate responses, such as AI-powered virtual assistants or emotionally intelligent avatars (Yamada-Rice *et al.*, 2019).

Inclusive Learning Environment: All students can engage in and contribute to learning in the metaverse's inclusive and diverse learning environment. The metaverse establishes a setting where students with impairments can flourish alongside their peers by removing physical barriers and offering personalized learning experiences (Crawford *et al.*, 2017). All students benefit from this inclusive environment's promotion of social cohesiveness, empathy, and understanding.

## 6.4 Inclusion of the Metaverse in Special Education

By incorporating the metaverse into education, it will be much simpler for children and adults with special needs to learn without making any compromises. The notion of immersive gamification boosting the learning process also comes with technology. Education is one of the many domains where the metaverse may be used. The responsibilities of students, instructors, and administrators in schools can be affected by technologies connected to the metaverse. Education in the metaverse can blur the lines between past and present and physical and virtual. It can eliminate the barriers of geography, disabilities, and special needs. It is possible to use the metaverse as a virtual setting to expand the educational options available to students with impairments. It holds the potential to alter education as we know it by extending learning outside the walls of the classroom into engaging, realistic learning experiences. Figure 6.2 shows the companies offering metaverse technologies in education.

No matter where they are in real life, instructors and students with impairments may connect in the virtual world using VR headsets. For individuals prepared to experiment with this very immersive technology, such capabilities can improve education. Sending children with impairments into a virtual environment where they can experiment with things, learn how physics works, reenact various events in history, or do other educational activities has the potential to be fantastic in an accessible metaverse.

It goes one step further with VR learning. A 40% improvement over in-person classroom learning and a 35% improvement over E-learning, PwC discovered that learners educated using VR were prepared to act on what they learned following training. As a result, Figure 6.3 shows the list of popular universities working to create instructional programs that are accessible in VR or AR.

| Company | Website | Features | Applications |
|---|---|---|---|
| ROBLOX | https://roblox.com/ | • Active community<br>• Game creation | • Learning by experience games |
| STRIVR | https://www.strivr.com/ | • 360° VR perspective<br>• Interactive VR | • Enterprise VR training |
| JIG Space | https://www.jig.space/ | • Universal AR<br>• 3D presentation<br>• Mobile application | • Various inteactive 3D models for learning |
| Gather | https://www.gather.town/ | • Video chat platform<br>• Collaborative work | • Virtual school experience |
| XIRANG | https://vr.baidu.com/product/xirang | • Permanent storage<br>• Multi-terminal compatibility | • VR K 12 classroom<br>• VR university laboratory |
| REWORLD | https://www.reworlder.town/ | • 3D physics engine<br>• No-code authoring | • Simulate the regulation of mechanics of real world |

**Figure 6.2** Metaverse education companies.

| University | Platform / Tool | Application |
|---|---|---|
| Stanford University (America) | Self development: The "Virtual Human" course[1] | • Allow all students to break through the space constraints, the " "classroom" can be in a museum, laboratory, under the sea, etc. |
| Embry-Riddle Aeronautical University (America) | Self development: Extended Reality (XR) Lab[2] | • Provide hands-on experiences and augmented learning experiences to serve as supplemental content. |
| Case Western Reserve University (America) | Microsoft: Hololens | • Provide 3D perspective views of parts of the human body.<br>• Enable view perception capabilities. |
| Hong Kong University of Science and Technology (China) | Self development: MetaHKUST | • Provide convenience in notification and administration.<br>• Create your own content freely, such as avatars. NFT |
| University of Cincinnati (America) | Self development UCSIM[2] | • Build a Metaverse learning platform that offers courses in different fields, most notably health care and bioengineering. |
| Soonchunhyang University (South Korea) | SK telecom: Jump VR | • Hold the world's first virtual entrance ceremony this year. |

**Figure 6.3** Metaverse at popular universities.

There are various possible applications for metaverse learning opportunities, which also bring moral and intellectual concerns. For instance, utilizing avatars in a virtual environment can enable students with physical limitations to conceal their impairments. However, if children with physical limitations can use the metaverse to build fully functional avatars, this potential issue could be lessened. Teachers may even instruct students in physics, a topic that is mostly missing from the actual world, using an avatar of Albert Einstein thanks to the metaverse.

The ability to provide an immersive environment for early learning using the metaverse for education is unquestionably advantageous. Students of all skill levels can benefit from using the metaverse as a potent tool to improve their educational experiences. However, because accessibility gear and training are expensive, not everyone can make use of these benefits. Whatever the case, the metaverse may be a potent source of inspiration for both students and teachers if access is made equally available. With the use of realistic events and high-pressure conditions, the metaverse offers immersive, embodied skill-building chances where mistakes can be made without negative repercussions. When done correctly, it blends spatial design, data analytics, and VR to increase learner confidence, engagement, and application. A metaverse learning experience is characterized by visualization and storytelling, both of which are important techniques of communication in teaching and learning.

All learners with impairments will have easier access to education and social opportunities if the metaverse is made more accessible. Young adults with special needs, autism, and social interaction difficulties have the potential to improve their interpersonal and job skills by using the accessible metaverse. These skills may include tasks such as going to the grocery store or mall, stocking shelves in a store, or loading cargo into a truck.

Through VR applications, individuals may engage with others and practice skills in a secure setting without feeling overexcited or anxious. Learning may be improved, and knowledge can be expanded when teachers integrate VR, AR, or other metaverse-type technologies into their courses. According to studies, giving kids the opportunity to really experience a subject rather than just reading about it on a page can help them learn more thoroughly.

## 6.5 Benefits of Metaverse in Special Education

### 6.5.1 Helps Visually Impaired Kids with Sensory Enhancement

It may be very challenging to make visually impaired students feel heard and seen in an online classroom setting since they cannot access movies or concepts that need to be visually explained. As a result, individuals could lag behind their peers, in terms of understanding and grades. The metaverse provides solutions to these challenges through tools like haptic feedback, audio-echo location, and audio-informative menus.

### 6.5.2 Reenacts Social Communication for Kids with Autism

For neurotypical children, having a typical conversation could be easy. Children on the autism spectrum, however, see social interactions as overwhelming and challenging; thus, the opposite is true for them. Frequent practice of these conversations in a secure setting might be the key to overcoming these difficulties.

### 6.5.3 Uses Visual Imagery to Teach Hearing- and Speech-Impaired Students

Children with hearing and speech impairments find it difficult to grasp courses and interact with their peers. By converting gestures into words (and vice versa) and employing a collection of VR visuals that have been put through a program to teach children, metaverse technology can help with communication and understanding issues.

### 6.5.4 Makes Learning Accessible to Everyone

Students all around the world are losing access to top-notch education from prestigious institutions due to prohibitive online tuition fees and rising travel expenses, which has an impact on their mental health and future employment prospects. However, because there are no physical boundaries in the metaverse, students from all over the world may attend classes at an online university, take part in debates, and interact with one another regardless of time zone.

## 6.6 Metaverse vs. Conventional Learning

With effective teaching techniques, learning becomes fun. It provides the educational community with fresh options for experimentation and a wealth of opportunities. Teaching experts concentrate on any technology that might hasten learning results. Realistic social interaction improves problem-solving abilities and fosters collaborative work cultures. Making avatars makes it simple to illustrate the idea by employing a role-playing strategy to simulate real-world situations. The metaverse allows for the creation of many scenarios for real-world circumstances.

It may be quite advantageous to invite notable individuals, such as scientists, physicians, and athletes, and to have students engage with them and benefit from their expertise and experiences. In the metaverse, virtual environments for conferences, symposiums, and lectures can be created. In traditional learning, both the instructor and the student must be present at the same time and same place. The flexibility of learning from any location is made possible via remote learning or screen-based learning. Teachers and students cannot, however, have flexible schedules. With a smart wearable and strong Internet connectivity, the metaverse, on the other hand, offers total flexibility in learning from anywhere at any time. This enables instructors to experiment with brand-new teaching techniques in synchronous and asynchronous learning settings.

Learners interact in person with teachers and classmates in a traditional classroom setting. Screen-based learning poses challenges due to its limitations, which cause disparities, social difficulties, and other issues. The limitations of both teaching strategies are solved by the metaverse. Learners' avatars may communicate with teachers and other students' avatars, allowing for real-time feedback, social interaction, professional assistance with concept learning, individualized guidance, and much more.

In static situations, conventional and screen-based learning typically takes the shape of textbooks, images, videos, and other comparable learning resources. By giving individuals the resources they need to develop and learn through participation in activities, the metaverse provides learners with realistic learning scenarios. Assessments in traditional and screen-based learning can be done primarily in a summative fashion in the form of tests and grades. Giving useful real-time input becomes difficult with these techniques.

Budget restrictions can be addressed by educational institutions and students with the aid of the metaverse. Online learning has decreased the expenses needed for the maintenance of physical structures and colleges. Virtual classrooms may be built and maintained for a significantly lower price than traditional classes. By incorporating education into the metaverse, the school may save money by reducing the cost of building up physical study tools while still providing essential study materials. As an alternative to dissecting a real cadaver, students can practice in a virtual cadaver's simulated environment, which is less expensive.

The metaverse enables teachers and students to communicate freely and more effectively, personalizing the learning process. Educational institutions can transport students to various lifelike settings so they can participate in activities and then talk about their learning and discoveries. This virtual environment enables students to acquire practical skills without endangering themselves or others. The metaverse is changing the way that education is traditionally done by encouraging students to hone their abilities and get ready for real-world tasks. Within the metaverse, students can practice intricate procedures or risky experiments without endangering anyone's life.

## 6.7 Accessibility Features in the Metaverse

The metaverse's capacity to turn the universe into a school is another benefit. Teachers can aid students in applying theory and remembering information by giving them the opportunity to experience an immersive setting. Simulators and video games that mimic real-world scenarios can also help students become more interested. Students may learn ideas and theories in a pleasant and engaging way with the aid of 3D representations. A potent learning resource for educators is the metaverse. A benefit of the metaverse for education is that it will enable teachers to design immersive learning environments for young children.

- Students who are blind or visually challenged require screen reading software and flawless audio descriptions.
- Input devices that people with hand movement challenges use to access a computer readily transferable to the metaverse can be used with high-performance voice activation systems for students with motor and dexterity limitations.

- To connect it to previously learned material, they can also employ metaverse learning. The metaverse is a new means to inspire learning and advance knowledge, not a replacement for instructors.
- Teachers can assist students with impairments in overcoming social and academic problems by incorporating accessible metaverse-based teaching with class activities.

To provide students the freedom to learn at their own speed and in their own style, the metaverse may also be utilized to design a personalized learning experience.

## 6.8 Risks of Metaverse in Special Education

The main issues at hand are user addiction and inappropriate social media use. Social media, video games, and Internet addiction all have long-term mental and physical effects including depression, anxiety, and other sedentary lifestyle-related problems, like an increased risk for obesity and cardiovascular disease. Experts are also concerned that, similar to current Internet technologies, the metaverse may be exploited as an "escape" from reality.

Sex abuse, child grooming, and other types of virtual criminality pose serious problems on VR social platforms now, and they could be just as common in the metaverse. Despite the minimum age limit of 13 years, investigations by BBC News and The Washington Post in February 2022 revealed that children were participating in adult behaviors in programs like VRChat and Horizon Worlds.

## 6.9 AI Integration in the Metaverse for Special Education

With the ability to provide tailored and inclusive learning experiences for kids with a range of learning needs and disabilities, the integration of AI into the metaverse has the potential to completely transform special education. Applications in the metaverse that are AI-powered improve realism, adaptivity, and support while accommodating different learning preferences and promoting overall development. This section explores many facets of AI integration for special education in the metaverse, emphasizing its revolutionary effects on avatars, learning pathways, evaluation, and cybersecurity.

AI-Generated Avatars for Realistic Interactions:
AI is used in the metaverse to build sophisticated, lifelike avatars that represent individual learners (Bailenson *et al.*, 2008). These avatars may mimic students' voices, movements, and facial expressions, allowing for realistic and empathic interactions in virtual learning environments. Students' sense of presence and social connectivity is increased by AI-generated avatars, which encourages motivation and involvement in the learning process.

Pathways for Adaptive Learning and Personalized Support:
According to Kharat (2019), AI integration in the metaverse enables adaptive learning systems that modify content and exercises to each student's abilities and progress. Artificial intelligence algorithms examine performance information and learner choices to dynamically change the level of a lesson's complexity and tempo. This individualized approach gives students the freedom to learn at their own speed, developing confidence and independence throughout their academic career.

AI-Based Assessment and Progress Monitoring:
By offering real-time and data-driven insights into students' learning outcomes, AI in the metaverse improves assessment methods (Baek *et al.*, 2021). Artificial intelligence algorithms can evaluate performance data, monitor development, and pinpoint areas for improvement. By using these data, educators and teachers may decide on interventions and instructional practices with confidence, ensuring that children get the help and resources they need.

Virtual Assistants with AI for Educators and Students:
Within the metaverse, virtual assistants with AI skills can offer helpful assistance to both teachers and pupils (Desselle *et al.*, 2021). Teachers can manage virtual classrooms, receive automated feedback on students' projects, and manage administrative work with the help of AI-powered virtual assistants. Personalized learning recommendations, questions, and guidance can all be given to students by virtual assistants throughout virtual learning events.

AI in Virtual Environment Cybersecurity:
In the metaverse, AI is essential for maintaining data privacy and cybersecurity (Chou *et al.*, 2020). Virtual environments may be continuously

monitored by AI algorithms, allowing for the detection and prevention of potential security breaches. Artificial intelligence-driven cybersecurity solutions safeguard private student information to provide a secure learning environment online.

## 6.10 Challenges and Considerations

Although the metaverse has enormous potential to transform special education, there are a number of issues and problems that must be taken into account before it can be implemented. This section outlines some of the major obstacles and factors to be considered while using the metaverse for special education, from practical difficulties to moral and educational ramifications.

Technical Difficulties and Infrastructure Needs: To produce smooth and engaging virtual experiences, the metaverse requires a robust technical infrastructure. Real-time interactions and seamless user experiences depend on high-performance computation, dependable Internet access, and low-latency networks (Crawford *et al.*, 2017). It can be extremely difficult to guarantee that educational institutions and students have access to essential technology and software, especially for those who live in underserved areas.

The integration of the metaverse into special education necessitates rigorous pedagogical preparation, as well as awareness of its ethical ramifications (Devine, 2019). To enhance learning outcomes, educators must establish a balance between the use of virtual technologies and conventional teaching techniques. To safeguard vulnerable students in virtual environments, ethical issues with data privacy, student consent, and digital safety must also be addressed.

Accessibility and Inclusivity in the Metaverse: According to Normand *et al.* (2019), ensuring accessibility and inclusivity inside the metaverse is a crucial factor in special education. To meet the needs of all learners, virtual learning resources, interfaces, and interactions must be created using Universal Design for Learning principles. This entails offering alternate content forms, adaptable engagement techniques, and assistance for students with disabilities.

Data Privacy and Security Issues: According to Chou *et al.* (2020), the collection and use of student data within the metaverse raise issues with data privacy and security. Protecting sensitive student data and preventing unwanted access require special consideration. Building confidence among students, teachers, and parents requires the implementation of effective cybersecurity measures and adherence to pertinent data protection laws.

Training and Professional Development: Educators must have enough training in using virtual technologies and successfully integrating them into their teaching methods before introducing the metaverse to special education (Baek *et al.*, 2021). Teachers' expertise and confidence in utilizing the metaverse for inclusive and effective teaching can be increased by offering them thorough professional development opportunities and assistance.

Digital Divide and Equity: According to Sung *et al.* (2021), utilizing the metaverse for special education is still hampered by the digital divide. The lack of equal access to the required technology among pupils can worsen already-existing educational disparities. To guarantee that all students may profit from the metaverse, efforts must be made to close the digital gap and offer fair access to online learning possibilities.

## 6.11 Future Directions and Potential Impact

A world of intriguing possibilities and prospective effects on the educational environment is made possible by the incorporation of the metaverse in special education. The metaverse holds the potential to revolutionize how students with a range of learning needs and disabilities access education as technology and research in this area evolve. This section examines potential outcomes and future paths, highlighting important areas of advancement and the profound impact that the metaverse can have on special education.

Improved Online Learning Experiences:
The metaverse is projected to provide students with impairments with progressively more advanced and immersive virtual learning experiences as technology progresses. More realistic and interesting interactions with virtual worlds will be made possible by improvements in XR technology, such as enhanced haptic feedback and 3D audio (Bailenson *et al.*, 2021). The distinction between real life and VR will become even more hazy because of these improvements, increasing the opportunity for hands-on learning and the development of useful skills.

Effortless Virtual Learning and AI Integration:
The integration of AI-powered features in the metaverse will become more seamless and organic as a result of future breakthroughs in AI. The ability to recognize students' emotional states and learning requirements will improve with the development of advanced AI algorithms (Desselle *et al.*, 2021). Virtual assistants and avatars powered by AI will improve

their responsiveness and provide students with timely, adaptable support throughout their academic careers.

Collaborative Learning and Social Interaction:
Students with impairments can benefit from the collaborative learning and social contact that the metaverse can promote. Beyond physical bounds, cross-cultural partnerships, virtual group projects, and shared virtual spaces are all possible (Sung *et al.*, 2021). Students from all backgrounds will be encouraged to communicate, work together, and show empathy through these collaborative activities, which will improve their social and interpersonal abilities.

Improvements in Accessibility and Inclusive Design: The metaverse's virtual learning environments will become more accessible as inclusive design principles continue to be prioritized. A larger spectrum of disabilities will be catered for by advances in user interfaces, assistive technology, and sensory feedback, ensuring that all students have fair access to educational resources (Normand *et al.*, 2019). The metaverse will consequently develop into a more inclusive and varied learning ecosystem.

Research and Evidence-Based Practices: Ongoing research and evidence-based practices will serve as a roadmap for future directions in the metaverse's impact on special education. To investigate best practices, find efficient interventions, and comprehend how virtual learning affects kids' academic and socioemotional growth, researchers and educators will work together (Guski *et al.*, 2020). The design and execution of virtual learning experiences will be guided by this research-driven methodology, assuring their efficacy and relevance.

The metaverse has the potential to have a significant and far-reaching impact on special education. The metaverse has the potential to dismantle obstacles and revolutionize educational possibilities for students with disabilities by offering individualized, inclusive, and exciting learning experiences. It can close knowledge gaps, boost motivation and self-efficacy, and provide a sense of community in an encouraging online setting. Additionally, the metaverse has the potential to have an impact on educational policies, teacher preparation programs, and the future of inclusive education, in addition to having an impact on children with special needs specific kids.

## 6.12 Conclusion

The metaverse has enormous potential to revolutionize special education by changing how students with various learning difficulties and needs can access, participate in, and profit from educational experiences. The metaverse provides personalized, inclusive, and immersive learning environments that are tailored to individual skills, needs, and preferences through the seamless integration of XR, AI, and other essential technologies. This transformative strategy has the potential to dismantle obstacles, close knowledge gaps, and build a more just and liberating educational ecosystem.

It is impossible to overestimate the significance of the metaverse in special education. The use of AI-generated avatars, adaptive learning systems, and virtual simulations in special education can give students real-world learning experiences that will help them develop their skills and gain confidence. Additionally, the metaverse supports inclusive learning environments where all students, regardless of their skills or location, can succeed and collaborate.

However, utilizing the metaverse to its full potential in special education has its own set of difficulties and concerns. Making a sustainable and productive virtual learning environment requires addressing the needs for technical infrastructure, maintaining accessibility and data privacy, and providing proper training for instructors. To protect vulnerable students and foster trust among all stakeholders, the implementation process must prioritize ethical issues related to AI use and student data security. The metaverse's potential future paths and positive effects on special education are encouraging. Virtual learning experiences will continue to be improved by developments in XR technology and the incorporation of AI, making them more realistic, adaptive, and supportive. The creation of efficient solutions and best practices will be guided by ongoing research and evidence-based procedures, ensuring that the metaverse meets the particular requirements of students with disabilities.

In conclusion, the metaverse offers special education a revolutionary chance that will catapult the discipline into a new era of individualized, inclusive, and exciting learning experiences. Educators, academics, and legislators can create an educational environment where all students can succeed and realize their full potential by embracing the metaverse and tackling its problems.

## References

1. Baek, Y., Seo, J., & Lee, J. (2021). An AI-Based Adaptive Learning System to Improve Student Learning Outcomes in Virtual Reality Learning Environments. *Educ. Sci.*, 11(2), 61.

2. Bailenson, J. N., Blascovich, J., Beall, A. C., & Loomis, J. M. (2001). Equilibrium Theory Revisited: Mutual Gaze and Personal Space in Virtual Environments. *Presence: Teleoperators and Virtual Environ.*, 10(6), 583-598.
3. Bailenson, J. N., Yee, N., Blascovich, J., Beall, A. C., Lundblad, N., & Jin, M. (2008). The Use of Immersive Virtual Reality in the Learning Sciences: Digital Transformations of Teachers, Students, and Social Context. *J. Learn. Sci.*, 17(1), 102-141.
4. Bainbridge, W. S. (2007). The Scientific Research Potential of Virtual Worlds. *Science*, 317(5837), 472-476.
5. Chou, T. C., Lee, Y. W., & Lin, C. P. (2020). The Challenges of Cybersecurity Education in the Artificial Intelligence (AI) Era. *Information*, 11(4), 176.
6. Crawford, C., Hancock, J., O'Sullivan, A., & Hill, A. (2017). Reclaiming the 'Special' in Special Education: A Virtual Reality Approach. In *Proceedings of the International Conference on Human-Computer Interaction with Mobile Devices and Services (MobileHCI '17)*, Article 63.
7. Crawford, C., Hancock, J., O'Sullivan, A., & Hill, A. (2017). Reclaiming the 'Special' in Special Education: A Virtual Reality Approach. In *Proceedings of the International Conference on Human-Computer Interaction with Mobile Devices and Services (MobileHCI '17)*, Article 63.
8. Damer, B. (1998). *Avatars! Exploring and Building Virtual Worlds on the Internet*. Peachpit Press.
9. Desselle, A. S., Boote, A. M., & Nersessian, N. J. (2021). Towards Conversational Virtual Agents in Science Education: Exploring Students' Reactions to Human– AI Interaction in Dialogues About Computational Modeling. *Int. J. Artif. Intell. Educ.*, 31, 116-140.
10. Devine, A. (2019). Immersive Technology in Education: VR, AR, MR, and Beyond. *Educause Review*. Retrieved from https://er.educause.edu/articles/2019/8/immersive-technology-in-education-vr-ar-mr-and-beyond
11. Gaudiosi, J. (2021, March 24). What Is The Metaverse? How It Could Impact the Future of Virtual Reality. *Forbes*. Retrieved from https://www.forbes.com/sites/johngaudiosi/2021/03/24/what-is-the-metaverse-how-it-could-impact-the-future-of-virtual-reality/?sh=27e779967a4e
12. Guski, R., Böhm, C., Jochems, N., & Köppen, J. (2020). Simulating Inclusion – A Review on Virtual Reality and Augmented Reality Applications for Persons with Disabilities in Educational Contexts. In *Proceedings of the International Conference on Computers Helping People with Special Needs (ICCHP '20)*, 47-54.
13. Kharat, S. (2019). Augmented Reality in Special Education: A Scoping Review. *J. Educ. Technol. Syst.*, 47(4), 492-508.
14. Lee, J., Xu, J., Ooi, K. T., & Lee, B. S. (2019). An Overview of Augmented Reality Technology: Characteristics, Applications, and Limitations. *Proceedings of the International Conference on Industrial Engineering and Operations Management*. Retrieved from https://www.researchgate.net/publication/

334472685_An_Overview_of_Augmented_Reality_Technology_Characteristics_Applications_and_Limitations.
15. Normand, J. M., Banville, F., & Moussa, M. B. (2019). Inclusive Design for Augmented Reality and Virtual Reality Learning Experiences. In *Proceedings of the 18th International Conference on Interaction Design and Children (IDC '19)*, 498-505.
16. PwC. (2021). Seeing is Believing: PwC's Virtual Reality Predictions. *PwC US*. Retrieved from https://www.pwc.com/us/en/services/consulting/library/consumer-intelligence-series/virtual-reality-predictions.html
17. Sung, Y. T., Wang, H. Y., Chang, K. E., Liu, T. C., Yang, J. M., & Tsai, C. C. (2021). Immersive Virtual Reality for Remote Online Science Laboratory Activities: The Effects of LabSpace on Learning Performances, Cognitive Load, and Situational Interest. *Journal of Educational Technology & Society*, 24(1), 78-91.
18. Yamada-Rice, D., Walshe, N., Eleftheriou, D., Green, L., & Donelly, D. (2019). Developing a Virtual Reality Augmented Social Communication System for Users with Complex Communication Needs. *Disabil. Rehabil.: Assist. Technol.*, 14(7), 704-713.

7

# Fostering and Integrating Augmented Reality/Virtual Reality Experiences for Learners with Autism Spectrum Disorders (ASDs)

**Usha Nandhini R.*** **and P. Senthamizh Pavai**

*Faculty of Education, Dr. M.G.R. Educational and Research Institute, Chennai, India*

***Abstract***

Education is one of the pillars of our society. It is about effective knowledge exchange and expansion, and we may use new technologies in the process of being education. Education is a serious matter, and some problems remain, including a shortage of skilled staff and a shortage of readily available educational facilities. In addition, there is an issue concerning education for those with developmental disabilities. For all these reasons, we believe that integrating augmented reality (AR) and virtual reality (VR) technologies into the educational system is a great idea for children with autism. Henceforth, we discussed the needs of special education learners to cope with the dynamic society and become socially capable and able to achieve their goals achieving its goals. Virtual and augmented reality is the obvious next development step for the educational system. A lot of responsibility must be assumed to create high-quality AR/VR educational content that will effectively advance its cause. Making educational content is a considerably more complex, time-consuming process that needs close coordination and adaptability, especially when working with children. For example, creating an engaging VR educational process for a science activity involves more than just producing a beautiful replica of the human body, its parts, and functions, students' abilities and level of comprehension should be considered accordingly. In this chapter, we further discussed the integration of AR/VR technology, its benefits, handling/engaging the learners, and challenges faced in implementation for learners with developmental disabilities.

**Corresponding author*: nandhini.sahana@gmail.com

V. Ajantha Devi, Williamjeet Singh and Yogesh Kumar (eds.) Augmented Reality and Virtual Reality in Special Education, (141–160) © 2024 Scrivener Publishing LLC

***Keywords:*** Virtual reality, augmented reality, developmental disabilities, learners experience, special needs, knowledge expansion

## List of Abbreviations

| | |
|---|---|
| AR | Augmented Reality |
| ASC | Autism Spectrum Conditions |
| ASD | Autism Spectrum Disorder |
| BPS | Brain Power System |
| EV | Educational Video |
| HMD | Head-Mounted Display |
| URL | Universal Resource Locator |
| VE | Virtual Environment |
| VR | Virtual Reality |

## 7.1 Introduction

One of the many innovations emerging today to help connect the lapse between the digital and real world is the use of digital environments (augmented reality [AR]/virtual reality [VR]). Through them, we can interact with appealing information and content visually. This is in the same way that we interact with the world around us in a tactile manner. To simplify our lives, we can make use of AR by adding it to everyday activities such as finding information, shopping, and expressing ourselves. This will make our lives easier, and it is a way to exercise what it would be like to be anywhere in the world, from the front row of a concert to the far reaches of space, using VR.

There are several different types of autism spectrum disorders (ASDs) that are categorized by an inability to comprehend the emotions of others. There is proven evidence that children with ASD identify the central traits. This may result in them ignoring non-oral gestures and societal indications, such as facial expressions, which are typically used to aid cooperativeness and sociability among children with these types of disabilities. They find difficulty in altering and swapping their attentional focus. Therefore, we utilize nonverbal social cues by implementing AR/VR technology to reinforce and grab the attention of young kids. AR/VR serves several purposes: For example, in a storybook, it builds on the common aspects of a story and also focuses on certain information to catch learners' attention [1].

With the help of this emerging technology, we can pave the way for children with this disorder and make their learning more fun, and tasks can be done more easily and in an effective manner instead of traditional approaches. It was found that the intervention system had a significant effect on assisting children in maintaining their attention on the self-motivated graphic videos and demonstrative expressions of the cast in it, as well as in helping them make better opinions about other people's facial expressions when they watched the videos. During the project, it triggered the children's motivation to learn using nonverbal social signals, and it helped them become more socially aware. It would be beneficial to include research concerning AR/VR technology and a greater number of participants with ASD of all ages to pinpoint the focus of the research. Furthermore, we hope that it analyzes how visual media can be reinvented to increase their capability to grasp and ability to recognize inarticulate sensitive indications in communal circumstances by reinventing visual media.

The integration of digital information with the real world is referred to as AR. The marker used in this technology points at a picture and prompts the message to play a graphical animated motion picture (Example: brushing one's teeth). When AR was introduced to the classroom, the students were able to learn to do that task by looking at the video on their own without any assistance as they practice several times. The implications of incorporating new technologies in teaching such children with disorders help them identify the behavior properly.

## 7.2 Augmented Reality (AR) in Learning

The implementation of AR allows a device to assist in people's or learners' day-to-day activities by allowing them to interact with digital content the same way they interact with their surroundings. The digital world combines the virtual world and physical elements to create a virtual environment that users can experience. The AR technology can also be used as search tools for finding things visually, for example, by pointing a camera at them. By superimposing graphical, interactive substances onto a real environment, users or learners can find answers to certain questions using an AR tool to share the accurate information needed.

The possibilities of AR are almost endless. It has been years now that smartphone-based AR software has recognized environments and provided additional information about what it sees, such as live translation of text or pop-up reviews about restaurants on your phone as you look at them. As a result, dedicated AR headsets, such as the HoloLens, can do even more, such as the ability to place different apps around the user in the form of floating windows.

Augmented reality allows you to augment reality with metaphors, typescripts, and extra simulated data using equipment including electronic gadgets, tablets, smart eyewear, and AR glasses that add visuals, messages, and other simulated data to the factual world. It can be used for something other than entertainment [2].

### 7.2.1 Status of AR from the Beginning to the Present

Figure 7.1 illustrates the status of AR from 1980 to 2016.

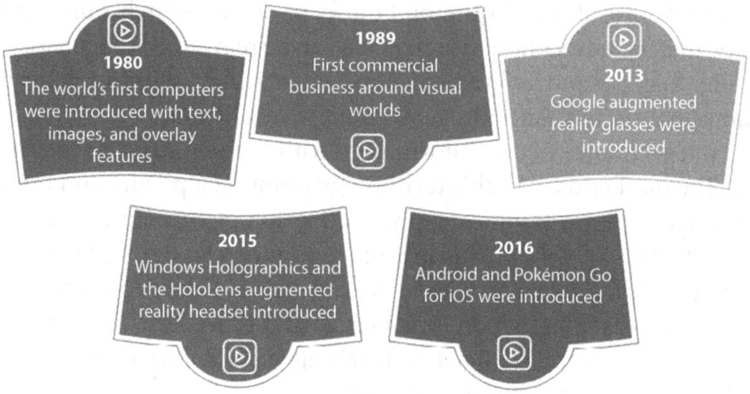


**Figure 7.1** Status of AR from the beginning to the present.

### 7.2.2 Learning with AR in Special Education

A digital platform combines online information with the physical world in AR. With AR, we can show data such as images, text, or video within a live, physical environment using a device's camera. Augmented reality can display digital information (videos, pictures, etc.) by scanning a trigger image, such as a paragraph to read. The dimensions can also be measured using a smartphone digital ruler.

Interventions founded on AR have been used to support people with disabilities, and are proven to advance learning and societal, physical and life skills of children with various disabilities, according to a recent meta-analysis. Individuals with disabilities have also found AR technology effective at improving independence and learning opportunities. After adopting AR-based task suggestions, these children were able to enhance their routine during regular activity. An AR system improved learners' feedback period in spotting letters, numerals after being used by children with ASD. Students with ASD can benefit from AR in their theoretical studies, especially in scientific skills, text identification, and interpretation.

### 7.2.3 How Does AR Support Special Education?

There is an emerging demand in AR applications among learners in special education, such as those with logical disabilities, ASD, and physical disabilities. In this study, AR applications will be examined in further detail to determine whether they improve knowledge and expert acquisition among these learners with special needs. In terms of learning aids, AR had the most significant impact, followed by communal, kinesthetic, and life skills. In this chapter, we can learn how augmented reality can be used successfully as a tool in special education in promoting academic and functional skills in people with disabilities. Adolescents with special needs, some of them ASD with analytical and logical disabilities, are also provided with research-based guidance. Symbolic thinking is impaired or delayed in children with ASD. Pretend play is habitually absent in early childhood. They cannot maintain a psychological illustration of pretense fixed with instantaneous certainty. Children with autism spectrum conditions (ASCs) have impaired social interaction, communication, and imagination [3]. Additionally, it is thought that pretend play is intimately tied to the capacity for mental understanding of others, which is illustrated by AR technology. Studies conducted on 4- to 7-year-old children with ASD have shown that pretend-to-play leveraging an AR system is significantly better than pretend play without the use of a computer. Our study found distinct alterations, exchanges of knowledge, and boundaries of the projected structure [4].

By meaningfully integrating reality with a virtual material, AR technologies enable users to better understand their environment. This expertise inspired us to investigate whether AR can create such an environment for pretend play to the real environment in a virtual manner [5]. Figure 7.2 shows how AR could help with a logical illustration of presenting the replication of the real environment by swapping out a wooden block with a toy car. A child can manage fictitious worlds that are also visibly depicted by moving the block about the scene as the augmented vehicle tracks its location. It is like an invisible fantasy [5].

Lack of creativity is one of the many symptoms of autism, and various individuals with autism exhibit varying degrees of deferred progress. In light of this, the "one treatment for all" strategy is practically unfeasible. However, examining individual performance variance shows an improved description of the group that benefited from the AR system designed to enhance one's creativity or imagination.

Augmented reality applications reflect images by passing data from the physical domain through an imaging device and transferring them to reality.

**Figure 7.2** In reality, the child holds a block in his hand. In the AR display, an imaginary car overlays on the block.

It is an essential task to monitor, sense, image, and interact in AR applications to create reality. This application uses a visual pointer code or a physical object that the AR system can detect. The AR program displays the enhanced simulation using the information it obtains from the precise indicator. Even some of the books have been built with AR on the screen [6].

### 7.2.4 Benefits of AR

1. It aids in the teaching of science experiments that are expensive and challenging to perform in the physical domain.
2. Augmented reality enhances student–teacher and student–student collaboration by facilitating collective tasks.
3. It promotes the growth of students' creativity and imagination.
4. Augmented reality can be used to increase students' communication with the physical domain for education, entertainment, or didactic playoffs [6].
5. In AR applications that use a virtual trainer at their own pace, students can receive individualized instruction.
6. It is effective in teaching concrete concepts, as well as developing students' abilities for critical analysis and problem-solving [6].
7. It effectively raises learners' interest and curiosity about the subject [6].
8. According to research, the efficacy and accuracy of learning are directly linked to the content's lifelikeness. In other words, the degree to which the curriculum is analogous to and related to real-world situations determines the efficiency and effectiveness of teaching [6].

### 7.2.5 Issues with AR

- Because of the inward/outward reversal of the mirrored image, children must devote considerable time comprehending the spatial link to properly match things with the 3D virtual objects placed in a setting, for example, on a table.
- Whenever AR and non-AR items share the same play space, it can become extremely crowded. In these usability considerations, there are trade-offs between outstanding monitoring precision, preventing diffraction while setting a pointer on the surface, and better convergence reliability.
- We could improve things by placing a real marker like a blotch placed on the table to represent the virtual objects in extensive training.
- Most children with autism have relatively few interests. As a result, having their favorite play theme available might be a key motivation.
- Among the AR props submitted by children and parents were superheroes, dinosaurs, humans, infants, cops, automobiles, sailboats, pets, emergency crews, and personalities from popular digital media shows.
- Identifying modifications to this reality may allow youngsters to acquire not only simple concepts about how to imagine, but to actively make assumptions.
- For the visual effect, a phasing out technique focused on one of the prompting techniques typically employed in the integrated behavioral approach might be used to progressively connect the imaginary play experiences from the AR environment to real-life circumstances.

## 7.3 VR in Learning

Virtual Reality is a form of computer-generated simulation of an alternate world or reality. This type of technology is used in 3D cinemas and audiovisual games with the help of computers and physical devices like headsets and gloves. It is possible to create experiments of reality and allow the viewer to actively engage in them. Many organizations, such as those in the fields of defense, design and engineering, medicine, academia, and others industries use VR in their daily operations. In VR, people can experience a trip to a location even before taking flight;

toddlers would know how to walk on the moon via a virtual (but almost real) stroll; and troops can prepare for combat situations.

### 7.3.1 Status of VR from the Beginning to the Present

Figure 7.3 illustrates the status of VR from the 1965 to 2007.

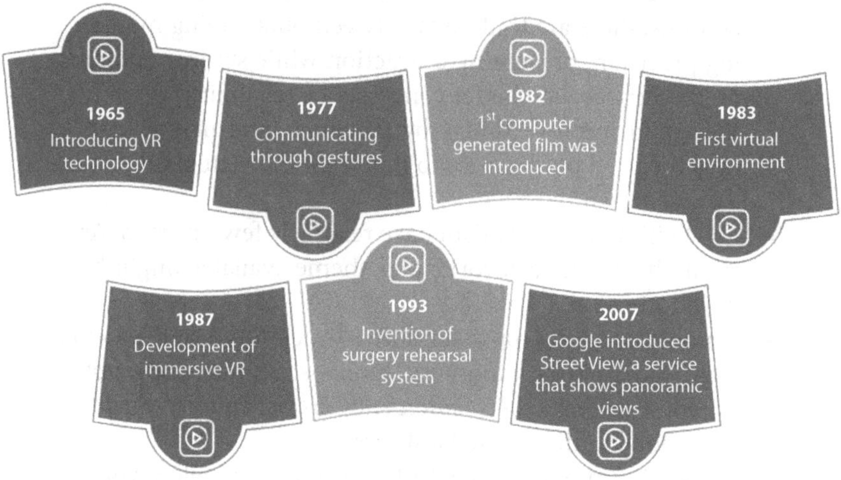


**Figure 7.3** Status of VR from the beginning to the present.

### 7.3.2 Learning with VR in Special Education

Through VR, schoolchildren can receive thorough safety training in a monitored setting under the direction of a special educator [4]. Virtual reality has evolved from a bi-dimensional digital model that students use to exercise their learned concepts in the bidirectional and photo-realistic environment and relate with roles that project on the screen, which completely immerse children in tailor-made settings, or by buying from outsourcing agencies through VR headsets to visualize the panoramic digital environment. It is possible to provide virtual environments at three distinct categories of immersion by displaying them on a computer monitor with a constrained viewpoint and concentrating on just one sense. The high absorption experience engages multiple sensory techniques such as acoustic, observable, structural, and physical [7].

An extended view on a large screen can facilitate sensible involvement with one to two sensory techniques. Virtual reality offers various degrees of immersion: virtual environments (like Second Life), panoramic views, or simulated environments, which could be seen on some electronic gadgets. Immersion-based VR interventions can improve social skills, emotional adaptability, and physical activities for students with disabilities. It is possible to improve students' abilities to acquire skills through VR-based interventions in a structured and safe environment using avatars, simulating virtual scenarios, and creating authentic environments. Improved social interactions and increased social cognition are facilitated by VR interventions. Social skills, including nonverbal communication and social initiation, improved in children with ASD, aged between 10 and 13 years old. Young adults with autism who undergo VR training can also improve emotional recognition and theory of mind [7].

### 7.3.3 What is the Impact of Integrating VR Technology into Special Education?

In special education, VR describes technology tools, such as head-mounted displays (HMDs), haptic gloves, and motion-sensing controllers for VR games [8]. It features a collection of technologies and methods and also an immersive dimension to it [9]. As a student interacts with a VR system via hardware and software equipment, he or she will be participating in a technical recreation, often three-dimensional based models. When used in an educational setting, VR gives students the impression that they are actually in a real world; students feel as though they are witnessing and communicating in a real setting. Virtual fieldtrips are one of the best examples for exploring the world over simulations that could reflect real environments [9].

Because technology is constantly evolving, the potential of VR technologies has grown and improved quickly over time. An HMD has motion sensors to present immersive experiences using VR hardware. The following are the three main categories of VR [9].

#### *7.3.3.1 Non-Immersive*

The user cannot feel completely involved in the virtual world because VR is frequently computer-generated.

#### 7.3.3.2 *Semi-Immersive*

It facilitates children's interaction with a photorealistic virtual world while remaining conscious of their real immediate environment, although the real world is important in this learning experience, which includes more than just the real-world surroundings.

#### 7.3.3.3 *Fully Immersive*

Users can only see, hear, and interact with the virtual world. The user gets the sense that they are "there," or present, in the virtual environment, thanks to this immersion. A crucial component of full immersion is visual material [9].

### 7.3.4 Benefits of VR in Special Education

1. Broadens the knowledge base.
2. Active experience as opposed to passive information.
3. Aids in the comprehension of complex concepts, subjects, or theories.
4. No distractions while studying.
5. Increases students' creativity.
6. Increases students' ability to learn.
7. Increases interest in subjects that some children may find boring or less engaging.
8. Students' understanding is improved.
9. Improves teachers' teaching skills by providing a deep level of knowledge through VR.
10. Improves memory power by linking emotions and education.
11. Understanding of very complex topics takes very little time.
12. With VR, a lesson or course syllabus can be evaluated and then simulations can be created and used for virtual learning environments
13. Fun, virtual tour and existing game-based learning
14. Enhances a student's imagination

### 7.3.5 Issues with VR

- A shortage of material is one of the most fundamental issues that VR in education confronts. The fact is that developing additional material may be quite expensive; not every education system can afford to employ a software development business to help them with content creation.

- Though several students can afford expensive VR headsets, there are those who cannot. As a result, they are unable to profit from VR-based learning. The issue that needs to be addressed is the provision of VR headsets to all pupils.
- Many individuals are unaware that cyber-sickness exists. It is comparable to dizziness and can impair learning. The best part is that as technology progresses, cyber-sickness becomes less prevalent.

## 7.4 Variance between AR and VR

Table 7.1 illustrates the difference between augmented reality and virtual reality and its environment.

**Table 7.1** Augmented reality vs. virtual reality.

| Augmented reality | Virtual reality |
|---|---|
| • Augmented reality adds data to what you have been already perceiving, creating the illusion of reality. | • Virtual reality technology can replace reality by transporting you somewhere else. |
| • Images are projected onto screens or viewers from real-life views (such as phone cameras) and then inserted into the experience at various points. | • It immerses people in experiences, often using very expensive technology, such as headsets, and it focuses on the experience. |
| • In AR, the real world can be seen through digitally enhanced lenses. | • It is presented with a completely simulated picture, not just simply augmented. |
| • It refers to the placement of realistic digital virtual goods as an addition to actual environment. | • It replaces the actual environment with the 3D virtual world. |
| • It creates an interactive sequence of digital elements based on markers and the location of users that can be detected. | • It creates an interactive sequence of digital elements with predefined elements, and there is no need for markers or the need to know the location of users to present the content. |

## 7.5 AR/VR Enhancement in Children with Autism

Brain Power System (BPS) is a device made of smart glasses-based interactive aid intended to improve one's degree of understanding, besides self-restraint in children with ASD. BPS comprises hardware and software add-ons that enable smart glasses to be integrated into wide-range platforms and to be used to extend their functionality [10]. Throughout this report, the physical characteristics of the BPS are described. This device will allow them to access the gamified strategies that will facilitate concurrent data collection among a variety of experiences such as movements and sensitivity. Concurrent tracking of eye movements and directions is possible with smart glasses, thanks to their integrated gyroscopes and accelerometers. Besides providing users with visual feedback through a small screen overhead (above the right eye) and an earphone behind the right ear, BPS can also provide them with auditory feedback. This application can enhance the communal and cognitive abilities of learners with ASD [11, 12]. Using gamified BPS apps such as the AutisMate, Choiceworks, Pictello, My PlayHome can enhance children's abilities to participate, which will help them improve their ability to properly recognize facial expressions and develop socio-emotional skills.

Face-recognizing game apps can become essential tools to support social evidence and help users accurately discern certain emotions, thereby improving how they pay close attention to facial expressions. Compared to their typically developing peers, people with ASD may have altered facial patterns and reduced attention to other people's faces. To explain the decrease in eye contact in autism, two main theories have been put forward: these are the look of disgust and the look of indifference. Many theory advocates claim that children with ASD avoid eye contact because the action is aggressive or fear-inducing, or because of excessive physiological stimulation. In contrast, gaze apathy underpinning its idea, which decreases eye interaction in ASD, may be a submissive singularity in which a person fails to perceive another's gaze as interesting or relevant.

Figure 7.4 shows the Brain Power System used for children with ASD.

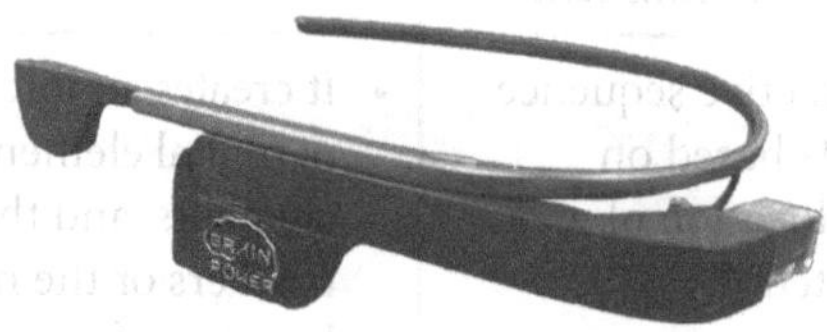


**Figure 7.4** Brain power system.

By using Face Game, users can overcome gaze apathy and aversion while visually processing other people's faces. In Face Game, gamut AR tackles gaze apathy, in addition to meeting various obstacles described in this theory. By using this app, children can participate in interactive video games and experience the reality. There are several levels in the Face Game, and while real-world interactions remain subtle, the digital elements do not become more important (*Frontiers* n.d.).

## 7.6 The Plan and Expansion of an AR/VR Application for Children with ASD

Learners with ASD may be exposed, under the control of their respective parents, to intricate, self-motivated, collaborative AR/VR apps simultaneously in three dimensions in which they can participate. As a result of these applications, cognitive, behavioral, and functional outcomes can be obtained, allowing children to be introduced to possible actions that are roughly equivalent to reality and allowing, in this way, to improve the assessment of the child's symptoms and treatment. It is therefore evident that the use of emerging and challenging technologies can underlie the development of environments that support diagnosis, treatment, and therapy. It should be noted that the use of the trending digital environment has so far been primarily considered in the areas related to phobia, autism, and rehabilitation, among others.

Implementation requires a more integrative and thoughtful approach in collaborating in the experimental requirements of some diseases and the detailed competencies of other individuals. Based on the requirements needed in terms of children's level of progress, AR/VR apps should be designed to accomplish learning objectives. To create such designs, we need to ask the basic questions as follows:

1. Is the child with ASD exposed to stimuli simply or directly? Is the child hyperactive?
2. Can we apply sensory facets?
3. The position of the teacher (What will their role be?)
4. How will the participant's progress be evaluated? Who will manage the session's progression?
5. Variables and performance must be recorded (What terms are needed to measure success?)

6. Once these reflections have been made, we can focus on the simulations to be created. The created simulations must be navigable. Experiments and measurements to evaluate the created simulations can be used.
7. Finally, interactive boundaries need to be set and constructed to make them work as naturally as possible. The specifications (resolution, image field) are to be determined by the targeted children with ASD. The next step is to model the EVs of the different elements. EV designs must be approved by designers at various stages.

## 7.7 Setup Requirements for AR/VR

AR/VR engineering can satisfy all requirements. When placed in a familiar setting, AR/VR allows delivery of response stimuli in a more sustainable manner (in a classroom or a store). Using these realities, distractions are managed, stimuli can be made complex, and these variables are dynamically changed based on the child's actions. A more precise analysis can be performed by collecting other specifications of the responses [13].

The digital checking-out setting and the usefulness of incentives can lessen the range of conventional assessment. Furthermore, it may enhance validity with the aid of permitting greater targeted and well-specialized behavioral surveys and with the aid of measuring its ecological individuality. Persons with ASD often have attentional difficulties. In children with ASD, attentional skills are crucial for all cognitive functions; evaluating and rehabilitating attentional skills are essential:

1. During educational activities, anticipate possible concerns.
2. Measure outcomes and performance, determine tasks in special education, and perform certain treatments.
3. Additionally, rehabilitation should address the easiest and the best way to enhance one's intellectual faculties, such as remembrance, dimensional and observable competencies, and managerial and analytical skills.

Virtual reality or AR techniques provide a greater level of experiments that facilitate improvements in the evaluation and rehabilitation of attention span. Thus, measurement and treatment can be more accurate.

## 7.8 Suggestions to Address Technical Problems Encountered in AR/VR Applications

- Use a designed environment to help children with specific educational requirements so that their overall knowledge and technical or computer skills grow.
- Boost the number of AR/VR environments for diverse subjects for special-needs students.
- In special education institutions, schools with structural components such as tablet devices and projection devices, as well as AR instructional materials, can be designed and distributed.
- The employment of AR applications with upcoming technology such as vision glasses, as well as pedagogical results, should be explored to evaluate possible advantages.
- The potential of AR might be further enhanced by creating it for use with varied groups like children with special needs, early education, and independent thinkers.
- Proposed solutions to problems should be extensively evaluated when they pertain to student involvement with the outside world in location-based AR apps.
- To further comprehend the advantages of AR in academic settings, additional studies might be aimed at student happiness, enthusiasm, connections, and involvement.

## 7.9 Experimental Implementation for Autistic Children Based on Research Articles

### 7.9.1 Experiment 1: Virtual Public Speaking

This experiment focuses on individuals with autism during socially constructed situations; researchers developed this experiment and conducted research on it, and the same was published on May 20, 2013 [14]. The researcher can conduct this experiment several times in different laboratories in the same circumstances for children between 8 and16 years old. In these settings, the child looks at the screen, which shows seven virtual individuals who look like their peers. Here, the researchers question the child and encourage him/her to answer to all virtual peers. One virtual participant is directly placed in front of the participant and the rest of them are placed far from others, and they all respond to the participant by blinking their eyes and nodding their head. The child is provided with a headgear by the researcher to track the individual that the child is looking at and the child's attention span. They found that many of the children were looking at the virtual participant placed in the middle rather than at the back and on either side. They had symptoms of social anxiety and show lower intelligence quotient values. At the same time, children spent less time once the images of virtual participants were replaced with some spheres. Hence, it could mean that children do not have an aversion to communicating with people, the researchers say.

### 7.9.2 Experiment 2: Stimming—Repetitive Behaviors

This experiment attempts to identify the function of behavior that is confusing or restricting an autistic individual from actively engaging in school and perhaps other activities. If an autistic child's anxiety is relieved by spinning in circles in class, her doctor may try to find ways to reduce the fear or suggest another calming behavior that is less disruptive. In the case of unusual behaviors, autistic people may require assistance in developing and implementing strategies to postpone engaging in those behaviors until they are alone or surrounded by nonjudgmental people, or it could simply be that society, not autistic people, needs to change [15].

## 7.10 Challenges and Solutions

- It is very difficult for students to adapt to and use this reality. It needs extensive user interaction. It can be used only with the support and guidance of a teacher or an instructor.
- Users may encounter technical and application-related issues. Though the teacher is present, he/she cannot handle this issue on his/her own. There is a need for technical assistance.
- There is an increased workload for teachers because they need to cater to individual differences. They need to create several assessment patterns depending on the learner.
- Stress among teachers can be seen because of continuous repetition in teaching the concepts several times. It requires teachers' patience and full-fledged efforts.
- Without prior planning of lessons, teachers should not start with the process. Also, planning educational content using

this technology is difficult because teachers need to record the past behaviors of learners and their academic success.

- Teachers should be highly confident in adapting this technique. The pros and cons must be recorded and the teaching strategy should be improvised.
- Teachers should be open to learning new things and upgrading their technical knowledge to cope with advancements in teaching techniques.
- Some special schools may lack the capacity in setting up this technology due to lack of funds, non-availability of resources, and support from the management. Hence, the management should take it as a serious issue and help teachers by providing them with resources they need.
- In some schools, we have found that resources are unused and idle due to a lack of knowledge in using the technology, an inability to learn, dodging to learn, and lack of interest in learning new things, among others. Some may feel that the traditional method was better to implement, and the result may also be better. Hence, they may not adopt the new one. They may also think that AR/VR may lead to confusion among these learners while learning. In such a case, we can go ahead with what suits the learner best, according to individual differences.

## 7.11 Discussion

- Augmented reality/VR promotes extended pretend play among autistic children, which creates an influential environment through AR/VR systems with 3D visual indications. It shows that the quantity of pretend play is continued.
- Researchers say that learner engagement was high while using this immersive technology. It becomes the prime motivational factor among autistic learners.
- On the other hand, in the case of autistic learners, "one approach for all" never works. Learners show different levels of developmental progress and sense of imagination. We cannot say that they think and develop the same attitude. So, teachers need to adapt to several teaching strategies based on their understanding.

- Lagging and falling behind technology upgrade and teachers' knowledge may lead to the failure of this system.
- Teachers should have more patience in handling and implementing this system for autistic learners because the expectation of results is always a slow process among these learners, and sometimes, it shows no effect too. Therefore, teachers should not be solely result-oriented.

## 7.12 Conclusion

To conclude, AR/VR technology can help individuals with developmental disabilities acquire new skills, recall knowledge for extended periods, find competitive work, and live independently. Augmented reality teaching resources were reasonable and successful in terms of aiding a child's development with specific learning needs through the availability of simulations of real-life experiences. Additionally, in the application of AR/VR tools, learners have always been more motivated and teachers concerned about the content delivery and ensure whether it satisfies the intended purpose. Commitment and dedication of special educators have increased in recent days by presenting interesting topics to the autistic learners, which makes them completely involved and probably answer questions accurately. According to the findings, the use of this designed technology-based environment to establish support for healthy and safe learning in children with ASD is beneficial.

In a nutshell, we propose that AR/VR be used to help autistic learners with their psychosocial, logical, and academic demands. It was also discovered that AR/VR might be used to improve good social qualities, which include an emotional understanding of interactions, especially among those with ASD. This would help people grasp basic nonverbal interactions, which are important for the development of individual constructive social relationships. This perception also highlighted the possibility of employing AR/VR to educate people on basic life skills for accomplishing daily tasks with minimal human help. AR/VR has been demonstrated to boost their capacity to autonomously undertake self-care chores, providing children with considerable self-directed learning.

## Acknowledgments

Usha Nandhini expresses deepest gratitude to Dr. P. Senthamizh Pavai, research supervisor and co-author of this chapter. Her suggestions and encouragement helped with the development and completion of this study. Without her contributions, this work would not have been possible.

## Conflict of Interest Statement

The authors have no conflicts of interest to declare. There is also no financial interest to report. Both authors have agreed to the contents of this chapter and certify that the submission is an original work and is not under review at any other publication.

## References

1. Chen CH, Lee IJ, Lin LY. Augmented reality-based video-modeling story-book of nonverbal facial cues for children with autism spectrum disorder to improve their perceptions and judgments of facial expressions and emotions. *Comput. Human Behav.*, 2016;55:477-485. doi:10.1016/J.CHB.2015.09.033
2. Forbes. https://www.forbes.com/?sh=246c91812254. Accessed December 8, 2022.
3. Bai Z, Blackwell AF, Coulouris G. Using augmented reality to elicit pretend play for children with autism. *IEEE Trans. Vis. Comput. Graph.*, 2015;21(5):598-610. doi:10.1109/TVCG.2014.2385092
4. Rizzo AA, Schultheis M, Kerns KA, Mateer C. Analysis of assets for virtual reality applications in neuropsychology. *Neuropsychol. Rehabil.*, 2004;14(1-2 SPEC. ISS.):207-239. doi:10.1080/09602010343000183
5. Bai Z, Blackwell AF, Coulouris G. Through the looking glass: Pretend play for children with autism. *2013 IEEE Int Symp Mix Augment Reality, ISMAR 2013*. 2013:49-58. doi:10.1109/ISMAR.2013.6671763
6. Cakir R, Korkmaz O. The effectiveness of augmented reality environments on individuals with special education needs. *Educ. Inf. Technol.*, 2019;24(2):1631-1659. doi:10.1007/S10639-018-9848-6
7. Yakubova G, Kellems RO, Chen BB, Cusworth Z. Practitioners' Attitudes and Perceptions Toward the Use of Augmented and Virtual Reality Technologies

in the Education of Students With Disabilities. *J. Spec. Educ. Technol.*, 2021. doi:10.1177/01626434211004445

8. Lecture Notes in Computer Science | Book series home. https://www.pringer.com/series/558. Accessed December 9, 2022.
9. Carreon A, Smith SJ, Mosher M, Rao K, Rowland A. A Review of Virtual Reality Intervention Research for Students With Disabilities in K–12 Settings. *https://doi.org/101177/0162643420962011*. 2020; 37(1):82-99. doi:10.1177/0162643420962011
10. Liu R, Salisbury JP, Vahabzadeh A, Sahin NT. Feasibility of an autism-focused augmented reality smartglasses system for social communication and behavioral coaching. *Front. Pediatr.*, 2017;5(June):1-8. doi:10.3389/fped.2017.00145
11. Home - Springer. https://link.springer.com/. Accessed December 8, 2022.
12. Sahin NT, Keshav NU, Salisbury JP, Vahabzadeh A. Safety and Lack of Negative Effects of Wearable Augmented-Reality Social Communication Aid for Children and Adults with Autism. *J. Clin. Med.*, 2018;7(8). doi:10.3390/JCM7080188
13. Fridhi A, Benzarti F, Frihida A, Amiri H. Application of Virtual Reality and Augmented Reality in Psychiatry and Neuropsychology, in Particular in the Case of Autistic Spectrum Disorder (ASD). *Neurophysiol.*, 2018;50(3):222-228. doi:10.1007/s11062-018-9741-3
14. Wright BYJ. *Virtual public speaking assesses social attention in autism.* 2013:1-2.
15. Deweerdt S. Repetitive behaviors and 'stimming' in autism, explained. *Spectr.*, 2020:1-4. doi:10.53053/wszv77551

# 8

# Impact of AR/VR in the Learning Process of Children with Dyslexia

**C.V. Suresh Babu*** **and Vinutha S.**†

*Department of Information Technology, Hindustan Institute of Technology and Science, Padur, Chennai, India*

***Abstract***

Around 15% of people worldwide have a disability of some kind, including dyslexia, and 2%–4% of them struggle significantly to function. Education is important for people with disabilities, especially individualized instruction as it enables them to build confidence and realize their full potential. It is crucial that all kids with special needs obtain quality education for them to develop personally. Emotional, mental, physical, or developmental disabilities may be present. In this study, the interview results revealed 15 issues, of which the top five, in order of importance, were (1) emotional disturbance and lack of concentration; (2) an unfavorable learning environment in the classroom; (3) communication issues; (4) low cognitive level; and (5) a lack of specialized instructional tools. Teaching children to perform new skills productively and effectively has become very challenging. Augmented reality (AR) and virtual reality (VR) are unique in their display as they are implemented in such a way that they have to be viewed at a very close range. Any deformities or absence of clearness in the display can be extremely self-evident. Furthermore, display execution issues, for example, slow frame rate, slow pixel refresh rate, or mutilation can adversely affect the children's learning experience. After evaluating the learning difficulties introduced by AR/VR, four primary disruptive issues are found when contrasted with face-to-face guidance: the absence of social communication, decreased children's commitment and concentration, diminished understanding and data retention, and the absence of adaptable and adjustable training resources. A large part of the current examination looking at AR/VR and student assessment does not address the benefits, difficulties, or the cycle of having educators plan evaluations efficiently when working together with

**Corresponding author*: pt.cvsuresh.hindustanuniv.ac.in

†*Corresponding author*: vinuthas707@gmail.com

V. Ajantha Devi, Williamjeet Singh and Yogesh Kumar (eds.) Augmented Reality and Virtual Reality in Special Education, (161–188) © 2024 Scrivener Publishing LLC

this technology. However, as AR/VR is an intrinsically captivating innovation, trainers should be aware that there is no misleading in children's commitment with improved learning. This research will help teachers and trainers to further think about the worth, as well as the intricacy, of arising technologies such as AR/VR in the learning area and introducing assessments to evaluate children's learning with those innovations.

***Keywords***: Smart learning, convenience aid, fault identification, user experience, innovation

## 8.1 Introduction

Dyslexia is a neurodevelopmental condition that affects the way the brain processes written and spoken language. Individuals with dyslexia often struggle with reading fluency, comprehension, and accurate word recognition. Traditional teaching methods and interventions have proven beneficial, but virtual reality (VR) technology introduces an innovative approach that enhances engagement and facilitates a multisensory learning experience.

A special learning challenge in fundamental reading abilities is linked to dyslexia. Students with dyslexia may experience difficulties with spelling, doing other related tasks, and reading. Using written language, several students and People with dyslexia have trouble distinguishing the different speech sounds inside a word and learning how each letter represents a sound. The IQ or learning capacity of a pupil with a desire to study is unaffected by dyslexia. These are the key traits of students with dyslexia, along with poor word recognition, spelling, and decoding abilities. These problems are typically caused by phonological language impairments, which are frequently unanticipated in light of other cognitive abilities and the efficacy of classroom instruction. The indirect impacts of reading comprehension problems and a limited reading experience may hinder the development of one's vocabulary and background knowledge (International Dyslexia Association Board of Directors, November 12, 2002).

It is unclear exactly what are the causes of dyslexia. However, research on brain imaging reveals notable variations in the growth and operation of a dyslexic child's brain (Shaywitz, *et al.*, 2001). The distinct neurobiological characteristics of a dyslexic student show that dyslexia typically results from neurological issues that are inherited in origin. They likely face challenges throughout their lives. According to the National Centre for Learning Disabilities (NCLD), 15*–20% of the population, or one in five people, has a learning disability [1, 2]. Around 70% to 80% of the pupils have reading deficiencies with symptoms varying in severity. Dyslexia Help at the University of Michigan shows that both boys and girls experience dyslexia at similar rates. However, the difference can be seen in the test results, which is higher for men.

According to recent studies, the ability of augmented reality (AR) and virtual reality (VR) to give pupils immersive real-world experiences that could improve learning's long-term effects is one of their greatest advantages. But can VR improve a dyslexic child's reading experience? Based on case studies from many users and in-depth classroom sessions, in both teaching and observing children's experiences of learning through VR, the leaders of the Lyfta digital platform have concluded that educational content presented in a VR format is more intuitive and memorable for learners.

When studying phenomena in a context-specific setting, teachers have found that "children are able to make factual connections above their typical level," according to educators Serdar Ferit and Katri Meriläinen in a recent interview with C.M. Rubin, the founder of CMRubinWorld. In collaboration with two Finnish institutions, to fully comprehend the potential of VR for dyslexic youngsters, Lyfta is doing academic research. According to preliminary findings, dyslexic children's reading experiences can be greatly enhanced by a specially created VR environment.

Virtual reality refers to an immersive computer-generated environment that simulates real-world experiences. This technology combines interactive visuals, sounds, and sometimes even haptic feedback to create a multi-sensory experience. Its applications span various industries, including entertainment, training, therapy, and education. In recent years, VR has shown great potential in supporting individuals with dyslexia, offering a unique and engaging platform to enhance learning and overcome reading difficulties. This article aims to explore how VR technology can be beneficial for individuals with dyslexia, highlighting its key advantages and potential applications. By leveraging the immersive and interactive nature of VR, we can create tailored experiences that address the specific needs of individuals with dyslexia, ultimately promoting their literacy skills and overall learning outcomes.

Multi-Sensory Engagement: VR offers a multi-sensory learning environment that can be very helpful for those with dyslexia. It can engage several senses concurrently by mixing visual, aural, and occasionally, touch stimuli, which helps reinforce learning and memory retention. This multimodal method aids dyslexic people in better understanding and processing information, improving their reading comprehension and language abilities.

Personalized Learning Experiences: VR enables the development of adaptable learning activities that are tailored to the particular requirements of people with dyslexia. Learning materials can be presented in a variety of ways, allowing students to interact with the information at their own pace and according to their preferences for learning. Examples of these formats include interactive games, 3D simulations, and virtual storytelling. Personalized feedback and adaptive features can improve learning even more by offering prompt guidance and motivation [3].

Safe and Calm Environment: For those with dyslexia, traditional school settings can be stressful, resulting in anxiety and lowered self-esteem. Virtual reality provides a secure and regulated environment where students can hone their language, reading, and writing skills without worrying about criticism or unfavorable outcomes; it offers a good learning experience by lowering stress and anxiety and promoting self-esteem and motivation in dyslexics.

Multi-Sensory Reading Interventions: By utilizing VR technology's immersive features, creative reading interventions can be created. Reading may be made more interesting and enjoyable in virtual settings by presenting text in dynamic and interactive ways. Individuals with dyslexia can enhance their decoding, word identification, and tracking abilities by integrating strategies like color-coding, interactive word highlighting, and visual aids into VR experiences.

Virtual reality holds tremendous promise as a tool to support individuals with dyslexia in their learning journey. By providing a multi-sensory, personalized, and low-stress environment, VR technology can enhance reading, writing, and language skills, while boosting self-confidence and motivation. Continued research and development in this field have the potential to revolutionize dyslexia interventions, making education more inclusive and empowering for individuals with dyslexia.

Moreover, VR interventions can address specific difficulties experienced by individuals with dyslexia. For instance, some dyslexic individuals struggle with visual tracking, the ability to smoothly follow text on a page. Virtual reality can simulate reading exercises that require tracking moving text or objects, helping to improve eye movements and visual attention. Additionally, VR can offer multisensory experiences by combining visual and auditory cues, reinforcing reading skills and facilitating better language processing [4].

Beyond reading skills, VR technology can also support dyslexic individuals in other areas. It can enhance spatial awareness and visual processing, which are often areas of strength for dyslexic learners. Virtual reality simulations can provide interactive experiences that promote problem-solving,

**Figure 8.1** Virtual reality in education.

critical thinking, and creativity, fostering overall cognitive development and boosting self-confidence.

## 8.2 Background of the Study

One of dyslexia's most prevalent challenges is learning to read. It has an impact on a child's capacity to identify and control language sounds. Dyslexic children have trouble deciphering new words or breaking them down into manageable parts that they can subsequently sound out. As a result, reading, writing, and spelling become challenging. While they can make up for this by learning words by heart, they may struggle to comprehend unfamiliar words and take longer to recall even those they are already familiar with. Dyslexia is seen as a gap between a child's ability and achievement rather than a reflection of their intelligence. With a little assistance, some dyslexic children, at least in the early grades, may catch up to their peers.

In the third grade, however, when students are required to read quickly and fluently to keep up with their work, they begin to experience problems. With the correct assistance and coping skills for their decoding difficulties, dyslexic students are capable of learning to read and achieving academic success. Dyslexia, on the other hand, is a disorder that cannot be cured. Dyslexia affects up to one in five children, and it is estimated that 80%–90% of children with learning challenges also have the disorder. Sally Shaywitz, MD, the co-director of the Yale Center for Dyslexia and Creativity, notes that many children go untreated because academic challenges are incorrectly attributed to intelligence, level of effort, or environmental factors [5]. Although experts traditionally claimed that dyslexia more frequently affects males than females, recent evidence shows that both genders are equally affected.

Dyslexia is a common learning disorder that affects approximately 10% of the global population. It is characterized by difficulties in reading, writing, and spelling, despite normal intelligence levels and adequate educational opportunities. While various traditional interventions exist for dyslexia, the emergence of AR and VR technologies has opened new possibilities for supporting individuals with dyslexia. AR and VR technologies offer immersive and interactive experiences that can create multisensory learning environments, catering to the specific needs of dyslexic individuals. These technologies provide real-time feedback, personalized instruction, and engaging visual and auditory stimuli, making learning more enjoyable and effective. As a result, researchers and educators have begun exploring the potential of AR/VR interventions for dyslexia.

Several studies have investigated the impact of AR/VR on dyslexia and have shown promising results. For example, researchers have utilized AR/VR to enhance reading skills by presenting text in dynamic and interactive ways, such as moving or floating words, thereby improving visual tracking and attention. These interventions have demonstrated improvements in reading accuracy, speed, and comprehension among dyslexic individuals.

Additionally, AR/VR technologies have been used to address phonological awareness, a key difficulty for many dyslexic individuals. Phonological awareness refers to the ability to recognize and manipulate the sounds of language. By incorporating interactive games and exercises within AR/VR environments, researchers have successfully targeted and improved phonological skills, which are crucial for reading and spelling proficiency. Furthermore, AR/VR interventions have the potential to strengthen cognitive abilities associated with dyslexia. Spatial awareness, working memory, and executive functions are areas where dyslexic individuals may face challenges. AR/VR applications can provide engaging activities and simulations that enhance these cognitive skills, leading to overall academic and cognitive improvements.

It is important to note that while the initial findings are promising, the field of AR/VR in dyslexia is still relatively new, and more research is needed to fully understand the effectiveness, optimal implementation, and long-term benefits of these interventions. Ongoing studies aim to explore the specific mechanisms through which AR/VR impacts dyslexia and to refine the design of interventions for maximum impact. The integration of AR/VR technologies into dyslexia interventions offers a promising avenue for supporting individuals with dyslexia. These immersive and interactive technologies have the potential to enhance reading skills, address specific difficulties, and improve overall cognitive abilities. As research in this field continues to advance, AR/VR interventions may play a vital role in empowering dyslexic individuals and transforming their learning experiences [6].

### 8.2.1 Statement of the Problem

A child with dyslexia might have difficulty memorizing even basic rhymes, have a speech problem, be unable to adhere to instructions, repeat or omit shorter words like *and*, *the*, and *but*, and have trouble distinguishing between left and right. Dr. Cruger claims that several programs can be useful and may include attributes such as teaching students how to decode through a variety of senses, repetition, and skill review; being pulled out of class more frequently than once a week for additional support; or individual or small-group instruction, the intensity of which can be increased, maximizing the potential benefits, developing their decoding skills, practicing sight words, and learning comprehension strategies. But still, the struggle with reading is inevitable. Due to difficulties of doing things that appear to come readily to others, dyslexia can cause frustration, discomfort, avoidance, and low self-esteem.

Other measures that could benefit a dyslexic child include listening to audiobooks rather than reading, and using apps that make studying entertaining by turning decoding into a game rather than writing on a computer or tablet. With the aid of a ruler, children can read in a straight line, which can aid in maintaining their attention on that line [7].

Efficacy and Effectiveness: There is a lack of comprehensive studies examining the efficacy and effectiveness of AR/VR interventions specifically designed for dyslexic individuals. Further research is needed to determine the impact of AR/VR interventions on improving reading skills, phonological awareness, and overall academic performance in dyslexic learners.

Individualized Approach: Dyslexia is a heterogeneous condition, and there is a need for personalized interventions that cater to the specific needs and strengths of each dyslexic individual. Research is required to explore how AR/VR technologies can be customized and adapted to address the unique challenges faced by different individuals with dyslexia.

Long-Term Benefits: While initial studies have shown short-term improvements in reading skills, it is crucial to investigate the long-term benefits of AR/VR interventions in dyslexia. Longitudinal studies are needed to assess whether the gains made through AR/VR interventions are sustained over time and translate into improved academic performance and quality of life for dyslexic individuals.

Implementation Challenges: AR/VR interventions require specialized equipment and training, which may pose implementation challenges in educational settings. Research is necessary to identify the barriers and facilitators of integrating AR/VR technologies into existing dyslexia intervention programs, including considerations of cost, accessibility, and feasibility.

User Experience and Acceptance: Understanding the user experience and acceptance of AR/VR interventions among dyslexic individuals is crucial for their successful implementation. Research should explore the perceptions, attitudes, and preferences of dyslexic learners, educators, and parents regarding the use of AR/VR technologies in dyslexia interventions.

## 8.3 Medical Background

In 1877, a German physician named Adolph Kussmaul originally proposed the idea of "word blindness" as a distinct disorder. Oswald Berkhan first recognized the condition in 1881, and in the same year, Rudolf Berlin, an ophthalmologist working in Stuttgart, Germany, subsequently created the word "dyslexia" to describe a patient's limited reading ability. Although the young child in question was just averagely intellectually and physically gifted in all other areas, reading and writing were very difficult for him to learn. The situation was described by him using the word. Berlin used the word "dyslexia" to describe this situation.

In a study for the British Medical Journal, a British doctor called W. Pringle Morgan from Seaford, East Sussex, described a learning disorder that only impacts reading using the term "Congenital Word Blindness," [8, 9]. The study focused on a 14-year-old child who had not yet mastered reading but had average intelligence and was usually skilled in other areas typical for his age. The child could read and write every letter of the alphabet, but he had trouble reading simple monosyllabic words. The child's handwriting and spelling were dreadful. Word suffixes (such as "winder" for "winding") and the letters inside the words (such as "Precy" for Percy) were transposed by him. The boy had no difficulty reading multi-digit numbers and accurately solving equations like (a + x) (a - x) = (a2 - x2). Thus, Morgan concluded that reading disabilities are congenital and that the left angular gyrus of the brain was not properly developed as a result.

Neurobiological Basis of Dyslexia: Dyslexia is believed to have a neurobiological basis, primarily affecting areas of the brain involved in language processing, such as the left temporoparietal region and the inferior frontal gyrus. Studies using neuroimaging techniques have identified differences in brain activation patterns and structural connectivity in dyslexic individuals, suggesting atypical neural processing of written language.

Phonological Processing Deficits: One of the core difficulties in dyslexia is impaired phonological processing, the ability to recognize and manipulate the sounds of language. Dyslexic individuals often struggle with phonological awareness, phonological memory, and the ability to map sounds to letters. These deficits can significantly impact reading and spelling abilities.

Visual Processing Challenges: Dyslexia is also associated with visual processing difficulties, such as problems with visual tracking, visual attention, and visual–spatial processing. These challenges can affect the smooth and accurate movement of the eyes during reading, making it harder for dyslexic individuals to track and decode text.

Multisensory Integration: Dyslexia interventions often utilize a multisensory approach, capitalizing on the brain's ability to integrate information from multiple sensory modalities. AR/VR interventions can provide a multisensory learning experience by combining visual, auditory, and kinesthetic elements. This approach aims to enhance reading skills by engaging multiple neural pathways and facilitating better language processing.

Individualized Interventions: Dyslexia is a highly heterogeneous condition, and there is significant individual variation in the specific challenges and strengths exhibited by dyslexic individuals. AR/VR interventions have the potential to be tailored to each individual's needs, providing personalized and adaptive learning experiences. This individualized approach can target specific deficits and optimize the effectiveness of the intervention.

Cognitive Skills Development: AR/VR interventions in dyslexia can also target cognitive skills associated with dyslexia, such as working memory, executive functions, and spatial awareness. By providing interactive and engaging activities, these interventions can strengthen cognitive abilities that are essential to successful reading and learning.

### 8.3.1 Significance of the Study

This study attempts to explore the possible solutions for dyslexic people using AR/VR technology to increase accessibility and interactivity. Using VR technology, the wearer enters a computer-generated environment using a head-mounted device, enabling an immersive experience. The wearer may even be able to move about the environment as if they are being transferred to another place and time, thanks to this cutting-edge technology. Additional wearable gear, such as VR-compatible gloves, can improve the experience even further. These "peripheral" devices offer haptic feedback, allowing for the reception of tactile information. The wearer can use this function to touch, feel, and engage with the virtual world in addition to the audiovisual simulation [10].

Virtual reality technology provides layouts, font styles, and backdrop colors that may be changed to match the needs of dyslexic pupils, in contrast to traditional textbooks. While dyslexic individuals are intelligent in many areas, they frequently get distracted by unnecessary details in their study materials. They have more trouble deciphering words if this occurs. Because a dyslexic reader's reading experience can be impacted by font faces and spacing, the structure of the study materials is crucial to their learning.

The study focusing on the use of AR and VR in dyslexia interventions holds significant importance due to the following reasons:

Enhanced Engagement and Motivation: AR/VR technologies offer immersive and interactive experiences that captivate and engage dyslexic learners. By providing a stimulating and engaging learning environment, AR/VR interventions can increase motivation and interest in reading, making the learning process more enjoyable and effective.

Personalized and Adaptive Learning: Dyslexia is a heterogeneous condition, and each individual has unique strengths and weaknesses. AR/VR interventions can be customized and tailored to the specific needs of dyslexic learners, allowing for personalized and adaptive learning experiences. This individualized approach can optimize intervention outcomes and cater to the diverse learning styles of dyslexic individuals.

Multisensory Learning Experience: Dyslexia often involves difficulties in both visual and auditory processing. AR/VR interventions can provide a multisensory learning experience by combining visual, auditory, and kinesthetic elements. This multisensory approach can enhance language

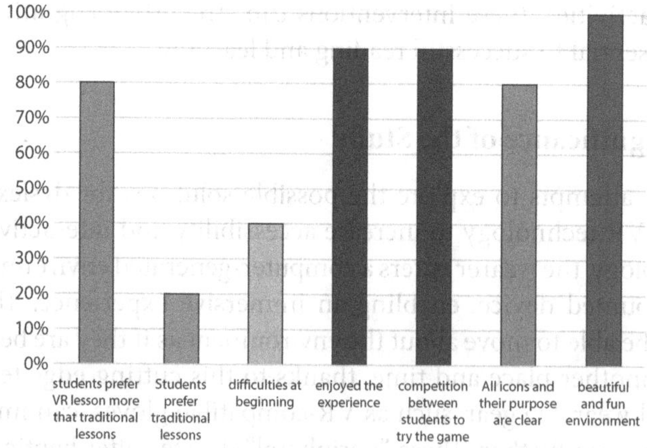


**Figure 8.2** Using virtual reality in teaching students with dyslexia.

processing, improve phonological awareness, and reinforce reading skills in dyslexic learners.

Targeted Intervention for Specific Challenges: AR/VR interventions can specifically target the challenges faced by dyslexic individuals, such as visual tracking difficulties and phonological processing deficits. By creating dynamic and interactive environments, AR/VR technologies can address these challenges in a controlled and supportive manner, providing targeted intervention and support.

Transferable Skills: AR/VR interventions can promote the development of skills beyond reading, such as problem-solving, critical thinking, and spatial awareness. These skills have practical applications beyond the classroom, empowering dyslexic individuals to succeed in various aspects of their lives [11].

Technological Advancement: Conducting research on AR/VR in dyslexia contributes to the advancement of educational technology and its application in the field of learning disabilities. By exploring the potential of these emerging technologies, researchers can push the boundaries of intervention approaches and develop innovative tools to support dyslexic individuals.

Improved Quality of Life: Dyslexia can significantly impact an individual's self-esteem, academic performance, and overall quality of life. AR/VR interventions have the potential to improve reading skills, enhance academic achievements, and boost self-confidence in dyslexic individuals. Ultimately, these interventions can contribute to a better quality of life for individuals with dyslexia.

Studies in AR/VR and dyslexia hold great significance as they offer innovative approaches to support dyslexic individuals, providing enhanced engagement, personalized interventions, targeted support, and the development of transferable skills. By harnessing the power of AR/VR technologies, researchers can make a positive impact on the lives of dyslexic individuals, empowering them to overcome reading challenges and reach their full potential.

### 8.3.2 Suitable Alternative

Dyslexic people have a significantly enhanced reading experience, thanks to the technological developments that led to the creation of electronic readers, often known as e-readers. These gadgets, which come in a variety of designs, are useful for enhancing reading comprehension in patients with this disorder. Readers may stay focused on reading with the help of dedicated e-readers since they have no games, advertisements, notifications, or other distractions.

**Figure 8.3** Text-to-speech feature.

#### *8.3.2.1 Text-to-Speech Feature*

A text-to-speech feature is also available on some e-readers. People who have trouble reading may now listen to the content without having to read it, thanks to this addition. Particularly for dyslexic people with significant reading difficulties, this is a comfort. Websites, workplace papers, emails, and portable document format (PD) may all be read aloud by text-to-speech software in natural-sounding voices [12]. Additionally, they enable dyslexic people to review their work in the workplace and at school to look for spelling or grammar mistakes.

#### *8.3.2.2 Audiobooks*

Another technological advancement that is highly beneficial to those with dyslexia is audiobooks. It can take dyslexic students substantially longer to finish assignments or read from a textbook, especially if they have reading difficulties. Thankfully, we live in a time where almost all books can be found in audio format. As a result, you may choose to listen to the information, which is simple to comprehend, rather than read the text directly.

The books that are for sale are even accessible in audio format on online stores like Amazon.

## 8.4 Research Aim, Objectives, and Hypothesis

### 8.4.1 Research on Dyslexia Bars

Examples of stimuli and experimental paradigm are illustrated in Figure 8.4. A visual representation of one trial's chronology is shown in Figure 8.4a. By hitting the space bar, participants could control the entire paradigm. A drift correction circle, which is smaller than it seems in the illustration, points the participant's attention in the direction of the text's beginning [13]. Participants

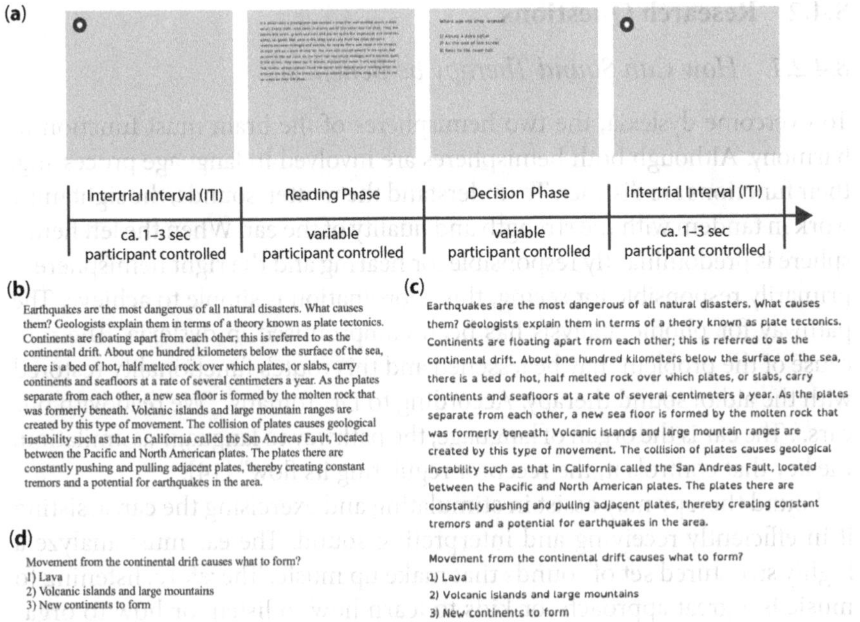


**Figure 8.4** Stimuli and experimental paradigm examples.

focus on it and press the space bar to bring up a text that is then silently read once. Following the reading portion, participants are given a brief multiple-choice attention question about the material of the previous text to complete without being rushed. This process is carried out ten times. An example of one text (Figure 8.4b) and its corresponding attention question (Figure 8.4d) is displayed in Times New Roman font.

It should be noted that this text is not delivered; rather, it serves as a representative example of the texts from the commercial reading assessment (IReST). The initial texts are safeguarded. Figure 8.4c shows an illustration of the identical text and associated multiple-choice questions in Open Dyslexic font, and Figure 8.4d shows an illustration of the multiple-choice attention questions that go along with the sentences in panels b and c. Questions about one's attention are always displayed in the same font as the materials that come before them.

### 8.4.2 Research Questions

#### *8.4.2.1 How Can Sound Therapy be Beneficial?*

To overcome dyslexia, the two hemispheres of the brain must function in harmony. Although both hemispheres are involved in language processing, their functions are distinct. To understand the written sounds, the sight must work in tandem with the strength and quality of the ear. When the left hemisphere is predominantly responsible for hearing and the right hemisphere is primarily responsible for seeing, this coordination is simple to achieve. The pathway for phonic analysis has been compromised in dyslexia. The root cause of the problem may be lessened and this route's functionality restored with the aid of sound therapy. According to Dr. Tomatis, "We read with our ears... The ear is the organ of language, the pathway to language assimilation, the key that controls it, the receptor regulating its flow" [14].

Sound therapy may assist in stimulating and exercising the ear, assisting it in efficiently receiving and interpreting sound. The ear must analyze a highly structured set of sounds that make up music. Therefore, listening to music is a great approach for kids to learn how to listen, or how to organize their perception of sounds. All sound therapy recordings intentionally boost the level of sound going to the right ear, which encourages the right ear to take on the role of the directing ear. The issue of reversal is likely to go away after the right ear has gained control.

#### *8.4.2.2 What Benefits does AR Offer?*

Augmented reality is the ability to overlay information on the actual world as seen through a mobile device's camera. Users can now enjoy a more interesting and interactive experience. According to studies, improved realism raises consumers' perceptions of an item or brand's worth. Additionally, innovative businesses that successfully use AR activity exhibit inventiveness and adaptability.

**Figure 8.5** Overcoming dyslexia bars with AR.

Enhanced User Experience: AR enriches the user experience by overlaying digital content onto the real world, creating a blended environment. This interactive and immersive experience provides users with a more engaging and captivating interaction with their surroundings [15].

Real-Time Information and Contextual Guidance: AR provides real-time information and contextual guidance by overlaying digital information onto the user's physical environment. This can be particularly beneficial in areas such as navigation, training, maintenance, and education, where users can receive relevant information and instructions directly in their field of view.

Improved Learning and Training: AR offers unique opportunities for learning and training. By overlaying digital content, such as interactive 3D models, animations, and instructions, onto real-world objects, AR enhances understanding, engagement, and retention of information. This technology is particularly effective in complex subjects, hands-on training, and skill development.

Visualization and Spatial Understanding: AR enables users to visualize and understand spatial relationships and complex data more easily. By placing virtual objects and data within the real-world environment, AR helps users perceive and interact with information in a more intuitive and natural way. This is valuable in fields like architecture, engineering, design, and data visualization.

Remote Collaboration and Communication: AR facilitates remote collaboration and communication by allowing users to share their augmented view with others in real-time. This technology enables teams to work together, regardless of their physical location, by overlaying annotations, instructions, and virtual objects onto the shared augmented environment.

Increased Efficiency and Productivity: AR can improve efficiency and productivity in various industries. By providing contextual information, step-by-step instructions, and real-time feedback, AR can streamline complex tasks, reduce errors, and optimize workflow processes. This can lead to improved productivity, cost savings, and enhanced operational efficiency.

Entertainment and Gaming: AR offers new and immersive experiences in the realm of entertainment and gaming. Users can interact with virtual characters and objects in their real-world environment, creating a highly interactive and entertaining experience. Augmented reality gaming experiences often blend physical and digital elements, enhancing the enjoyment and excitement for players.

Marketing and Advertising: AR presents new possibilities for marketing and advertising. Brands can leverage AR to create interactive and engaging campaigns that allow users to visualize products, try virtual try-ons, or experience immersive storytelling. Augmented reality experiences can capture users' attention and create memorable brand interactions.

Accessibility and Inclusivity: AR has the potential to enhance accessibility and inclusivity by providing additional support and accommodations. For example, AR can assist individuals with visual impairments by overlaying auditory cues or tactile feedback onto their surroundings, enabling them to navigate and interact with the world more independently.

#### *8.4.2.3 What is the Situation of the Healthcare AR and VR Market Right Now?*

Emerging technologies in the healthcare sector include AR and VR. Both could be applied in a variety of contexts, such as doctor training, patient care, and hospital administration. The North American healthcare stated that the AR and VR market was worth $477 million as of 2018. That is anticipated to rise sharply to $4.64 billion by 2025.

#### *8.4.2.4 Despite Its Many Drawbacks, Is VR Still Worthwhile?*

Yes. Due to existing technology, its uses are constrained, but that does not imply that it is dangerous. For the industries in which it is commonly employed, VR is a ground-breaking innovation. Virtual reality will be used in both gaming and healthcare in the future. The underdog of modern technology is VR. You can never entirely tell when it will decide to leave everything behind. The big moment for VR is just a matter of time [12].

### 8.4.3 Hypothesis on AR/VR

Virtual reality has been widely applied in learning settings. The use of AR technology for general usage is increasing as it becomes more widely available. While VR is typically thought of as a three-dimensional computer-generated environment that is immersive, AR is the overlaying of virtual components over the real world. Virtual reality is a three-dimensional environment that may either replicate the actual world or operate as an alternate universe [16]. Virtual environments may accommodate the auditory, haptic, olfactory, and even taste senses, but most of them focus on the visual sense. Virtual reality is frequently used as a research, educational, and entertaining tool. Since virtual environments may be tailored to the needs of the researcher, they provide a broad range of possibilities and opportunities for conducting research, especially in the study of human behavior.

AR has been developed as a subset of VR. While AR enables the overlaying of virtual components onto the real world, VR entirely submerges the user in a computer-generated environment where they are unable to relate to it. As a combination of virtual and real worlds, AR enhances reality rather than replaces it. Given the similarity and overlap of some features between these two interfaces (AR and VR), it is imperative to determine whether they have benefits or drawbacks for application in a particular area.

### 8.4.4 Objectives of the Solution

Both AR and VR have been found to improve short-term memory, foster engagement, boost motivation, and make lessons more entertaining. The biggest impact is on communication skills, especially for hearing-impaired pupils [17]. Virtual reality seems to make social contact easier for kids with autism.

Virtual reality and augmented reality have frequently been utilized to help children with impairments. Veronica Lewis, a teacher, uses Google Chromecast to expand images for persons who are blind or visually challenged. She uses the alternate text in the photographs and videos, as well as VR screen readers like Voiceover and Talkback, to narrate the environment. Morehead State University researcher Sue Parton has proven how Google Glass, in addition to video and 2D barcode camera phone scanning, benefits deaf students. Teachers at The Deaf and Dumb School in Gujarat, India help students who occasionally have problems recalling their own names by using VR images that have been modified with a program called Foton. Numerous studies have demonstrated how VR and AR can enhance social skills and help persons on the autistic spectrum perceive facial emotions.

For those with learning difficulties, AR can increase vocabulary through gamification. Teachers in India created an interactive textbook that explains text using 3D images, audio clips, and movies [18]. Various disorders, such as Down syndrome, dyslexia, attention deficit hyperactivity disorder (ADHD), physical or motor impairment, and social anxiety have been successfully treated using VR, according to additional research.

For field trips at the 53rd St. School, Milwaukee special needs teacher Megan Rierdon uses Google Earth VR. According to Rierdon, who was quoted by the Milwaukee Journal Sentinel, "The youngsters sat down on a chair, put on a virtual reality headpiece, and witnessed a tour strolling around an entire greenhouse." They stooped to touch the ground and were waving to the people they saw.

Students who participate in Molly Porter's AI-based Training are better prepared to talk about their limitations during interviews.

### 8.4.5 Delimitations of the Study

Studies show that AR poses several, previously unheard-of health issues, even though its limitations are still up for debate. The immersion of AR gadget users in virtual content could lead to behavioral changes, hearing loss, and eye and/or hearing damage.

People may wrongly believe a virtual environment to be real, according to a new Google Daydream study, which may alter how they take in and process information. Such thinking or perception could lead to PTSD and other mental health problems. In AR technologies, the real environment is covered with a virtual layer. It can be used in a variety of contexts, such as gaming and entertainment. There has previously been AR [19].

They have only lately experienced significant technological breakthroughs that have contributed to their increased popularity, with smartphones and tablets providing users with AR experiences at an affordable price. With AR, privacy or security issues could surface. This is brought on by the fact that AR makes it challenging to distinguish between actual and unreal situations, which breeds a dread of being "tricked" by an attack. Social media users, for example, may be more likely to accept incorrect information if they feel their friends have posted it on Facebook.

Some common delimitations of AR: Limitations of the hardware used to deliver AR experiences, such as smartphones, tablets, smart glasses, or headsets, are significant. The quality and complexity of AR applications may be constrained by the performance and capabilities of these devices. The whole AR experience can be impacted by processor speed, battery life, and display resolution limitations.

Field of View (FOV): Most AR devices have a constrained field of view, which means that while wearing the device, users can only see augmented content in a particular area. Users may need to frequently alter their eyes to interact with virtual items, which can cause a mismatch between the digital and physical environments.

Accurate tracking is crucial to AR's ability to smoothly overlay virtual content since it allows for precise tracking of the user's position and the environment around them. However, it might be difficult to achieve accurate tracking in real-time across many lighting scenarios and surroundings. The user experience may be impacted by inaccurate tracking if it leads to misalignments or unsteady augmentation [20].

Environmental Constraints: The physical environment can have an impact on AR experiences. Object detection, tracking, and augmentation can be affected by elements including lighting, reflective surfaces, and occlusions. Augmented reality systems may find it difficult to read and overlay digital content accurately in chaotic or highly dynamic surroundings.

Limitations of Interaction: When using handheld devices, interactivity with augmented items can be restricted. It is possible that tangible things provide a higher level of natural engagement and intuition than touchscreens and gestures. Additionally, the lack of tactile feedback while engaging with virtual things in AR may reduce the impression of realism and immersion.

Content Development and Adaptation: Producing top-notch AR content calls for specialized knowledge and resources. It can take a long time and money to make realistic 3D models, animations, and textures. Due to the differences in technology, screen sizes, and input techniques, it can be difficult to adapt AR experiences to various platforms and devices.

Societal Acceptance and Privacy Issues: The widespread use of AR technology brings up issues with societal acceptance, data security, and privacy. If done improperly, superimposing digital content on the actual world might violate people's privacy. Additionally, the use of AR in public places could lead to social and ethical issues like the invasion of privacy or distraction in high-stakes situations.

### 8.4.6 Limitations of Using AR/VR

- Price of VR equipment:

As with any breakthrough, the initial costs for new technologies are relatively high. Even inferior VR technology is expensive. This trend is expected to continue for the next 10 years unless we can find a way to reduce the price of VR-capable hardware.

With its Google Cardboard VR headset, Google did play quite an astute game with VR. But it is really just a cardboard smartphone assembly, not a full-fledged VR gear. However, it does the job. Users can enjoy VR at a much lower cost, thanks to it. Having said that, its use is restricted in the broadest sense of technology even though it is useful for education [21].

When it comes to actual VR equipment, the majority of gadgets range in price from $300 to $800. The devices will advance as VR's capabilities increase, much like PCs do. Most consumer VR technology now available on the market interacts with other systems. For instance, popular "VR" devices like the Oculus connect to your PC and then run the program. Oculus is now a VR device, as well as a computer add-on. True VR sets with their own assemblies are still in motion due to the high cost of production.

- Software in VR's size:

The software for VR is much larger than the devices themselves, a less-discussed component of VR technology. Additional programming will undoubtedly be required for VR devices to offer an immersive experience. Virtual reality software consumes a lot of storage space and processing power in comparison to other devices. This is one of the reasons why commercial VR software often looks worse than comparable PC software. Although it is not very difficult to compress software, it will take some time for VR software to become smaller. However, the initial expenses of VR will go up as a result of this compression.

- Movement sickness:

Virtual reality successfully mimics the illusion of reality by placing it near your visual field, but it is also the very thing that can cause the illusion that VR is trying to create to be shattered. Instead of using the user's actual motions, VR systems continue to simulate movement using joysticks and in-built game/software mechanisms. A condition called locomotor sickness is the result of this.

In medical terms, when you move around in a virtual environment, your eyes see that your body is moving and tell your brain as much. However, the fluids in your ears maintain the equilibrium and inertia of your body. Your brain receives a confusing signal since your ear fluids are not moving, which causes discomfort, nausea, and in worst cases, dizziness.

- Weight of VR equipment:

With the exception of Google Cardboard, all VR devices are fairly heavy, and extended use may cause headaches and neck strain. There are ways to reduce this weight with sturdy yet lightweight materials, but doing so will probably result in a considerable price increase for VR gear. This explains why consumers have only a slight preference for AR. Augmented reality often solves the aforementioned problem.

- The inability to see the surroundings:

In actuality, once you put on a VR device, you are unable to see anything around you. This is not quite a deal-breaker; this is a serious drawback when using a VR device at home because the loss of eyesight can result in expensive accidents. Several videos on the internet prove the same.

• Addiction potential:

When considering VR, this problem is one that many psychologists are concerned about. Virtual reality causes people to become more removed from reality, which is never really a healthy thing. As a result of its limited graphical capabilities, VR currently falls short in the realism sector.

However, VR addiction is a very real prospect with improved graphics and compelling, immersive content. Videogame addiction is already a widespread issue, but due to the total immersion that VR technology offers, addiction to the VR experience will be more pronounced.

• Graphic limitations:

It has been over 10 years since the invention of VR. Its graphical user interface is somewhat limited for such an old piece of software. Virtual reality experiences are well supported by 360-degree cameras, but their primary application in the game industry has been absolutely underwhelming thus far.

Most VR graphics are substantially worse and seem to be at least 10 years old when compared to all current systems. Game physics is practically nonexistent on VR platforms. From an economic perspective, VR is waging a losing battle since the size of the software is a drawback in and of itself.

• Conflict between vergence and possible eye damage:

Potential eye damage is at the top of the list of serious VR risks. Virtual reality is essentially just a screen that is placed right in front of your eyes. This has a considerable impact on eyesight, and eye injury is a major source of worry. Our dependence on computers has resulted in a brand-new problem known as computer vision syndrome. There is compelling evidence that the use of computers, televisions, and cell phones has led to a rise in eye problems worldwide. Despite the high-quality display panels used in VR, this is a major drawback that, if things go out of hand, might prompt government involvement.

There is also the vergence conflict to consider with VR. Under normal vision, the focal length and vergence length are essentially equal. Simply said, this period enables us to focus. When a VR screen is present, the object's focal length is cut in half from its vergence length. This interferes with our ability to focus and makes our eyes work harder, which severely exhausts them. The cost of VR software is increased by the usage of complex solutions to this problem. But most VR hardware still do not offer a fix for this problem.

- Lack of comprehension:

Virtual reality is still a novel concept. Despite the seeming breadth of its applications, every technology has a drawback that cannot be fixed. Up until now, VR has dealt with severe setbacks. How useful is it? Apart from a few niche usages in the gaming, healthcare, and education industries, there are no real-world applications for VR in major organizations.

In large businesses, VR has no practical uses. There are certainly creative applications for VR, but its close relative AR is the exact opposite, benefiting almost every significant industry. Due to the lack of applications, investing in VR is not profitable, which is never a good thing. With that out of the way, VR is the technology that will develop over time because of how important its use in the aforementioned industries is. Play VR games now compared to five years ago.

## 8.5 Proposed Methodology

According to studies, the demand for effective learning tactics and techniques grows as the number of dyslexic students climbs. For kids with learning difficulties, in general, and dyslexic students, in particular, there are not enough technological resources to facilitate learning. This issue, which impacts students with learning difficulties, also affects parents and teachers. Dyslexic students have trouble processing information and remembering it, which makes learning more challenging and time-consuming for them, especially when learning basics like the alphabet. A teaching methodology has been developed that combines instruction with enjoyment and creates an effective manner of teaching to aid parents, teachers, and students in the learning process.

The proposed application requires students to trace the letters in their beginning, middle, and final forms while giving them instructions on how to pronounce each letter and teaching them the alphabet. It uses a friendly VR environment [22]. Virtual reality is one of the most modern techniques that has been shown to be effective in both entertainment and instruction. It motivates pupils to learn and converse and enhances the efficacy of the educational process.

It is shown that 3.5% of students in contemporary educational institutions experience reading difficulties. One of the most prevalent learning disabilities among students is dyslexia. It makes reading and language in general extremely challenging, necessitating specialist training. Since ICTs are now used in classrooms, it will be simpler to include them in dyslexic students' education. Incorporating diverse virtual items into the actual world without distorting the sense of reality, AR allows people to view and experience it [23]. This tool can help dyslexic children and their teachers since it can make learning more interesting and enjoyable.

Progress Monitoring and Assessment: Implement mechanisms to track and assess individual progress throughout the AR/VR intervention. Utilize data analytics and assessment tools to measure improvements in reading skills, identify areas for further development, and guide instructional adjustments.Regularly evaluate the effectiveness of the AR/VR intervention through standardized assessments and user feedback.

Goal Setting: Set clear goals and objectives for the AR/VR intervention based on the needs assessment findings. These goals could include improving reading fluency, enhancing phonological awareness, or increasing reading comprehension.

Content Development: Design or select AR/VR content that aligns with the identified goals. This could involve creating virtual environments, simulations, or interactive experiences that engage users in reading-related activities. Consider incorporating elements such as visual cues, interactive text, audio feedback, and multisensory stimuli to enhance learning and engagement [24].

User Interface and Experience Design: Pay careful attention to the user interface (UI) and user experience (UX) design. Ensure that the AR/VR application is intuitive, user-friendly, and accessible for individuals with dyslexia. Consider font styles, colors, contrast levels, text size, and other design elements that can optimize readability and reduce cognitive load.

Integration with Traditional Interventions: AR/VR interventions should be seen as a complementary tool rather than a standalone solution. Integrate the use of AR/VR with traditional dyslexia interventions such as structured literacy programs, tutoring, and classroom instruction. Collaborate with educators, therapists, and parents to create a holistic approach that combines the strengths of various interventions.

Long-Term Follow-Up and Support: Establish a long-term support system to ensure the continued success and maintenance of reading skills gained through AR/VR interventions. Provide resources, recommendations, and ongoing access to AR/VR tools to reinforce and generalize learning outcomes in real-world reading contexts.

### 8.5.1 Implementation of AR/VR for Dyslexia Bars

By using AR/VR, we can solve such issues and make the children read effectively. The use of VR headset with a microphone is necessary to make this happen. At first, using a microphone, the words read by the children will be listened to in the background. Then those words would be recognized on the page and will be highlighted in a bold font along with the next two words on the page.

Other words on the page will be in a normal font. So, when a child with dyslexia starts reading the words on the page, the words currently read by the child and the next two words will be highlighted as they read. This will make children effectively recognize the words within large paragraphs without confusion. Also, visual images will be displayed according to the sentence they read. It is an easier and less time-consuming way for treating children with dyslexia.

Needs Assessment: Conduct a thorough needs assessment to identify the specific challenges and needs of dyslexic learners. This assessment should consider the range of reading difficulties, cognitive skills deficits, and individual strengths of the target population. Understanding these needs will guide the development and customization of AR/VR interventions [26].

Collaboration with Experts: Collaborate with dyslexia specialists, educators, and researchers who have expertise in dyslexia interventions. Their input and insights will help ensure that the AR/VR interventions align with evidence-based practices and are designed to address the specific needs of dyslexic learners.

Development of AR/VR Content: Work with developers, instructional designers, and content creators to design and develop AR/VR content specifically tailored for dyslexic learners. This content should incorporate multisensory elements, dynamic visuals, interactive activities, and targeted exercises that address specific reading and cognitive difficulties.

Access to AR/VR Technology: Ensure that dyslexic learners have access to the necessary AR/VR equipment and technology. This may involve securing funding, obtaining the required hardware and software, and ensuring the compatibility of the technology with the dyslexia interventions. Device availability, affordability, and technical support should be considered [27].

Training and Support: Provide training and support to educators, therapists, and other professionals involved in implementing AR/VR interventions for dyslexia. They should be familiar with the technology, understand the goals and objectives of the interventions, and be proficient in facilitating the AR/VR experiences for dyslexic learners. Ongoing support and professional development opportunities should be provided to ensure effective implementation.

Integration into Existing Programs: Integrate AR/VR interventions into existing dyslexia intervention programs and educational curricula. Collaborate with schools, educational institutions, and relevant stakeholders to align the interventions with the existing educational framework. This integration should ensure continuity and consistency in the learning experiences of dyslexic learners.

Monitoring and Evaluation: Establish mechanisms for monitoring and evaluating the effectiveness of the AR/VR interventions. Collect data on reading progress, cognitive skills development, engagement levels, and user satisfaction. Use such data to refine and improve the interventions over time, ensuring continuous enhancement and optimization.

Ethical Considerations: Consider ethical guidelines and privacy concerns when implementing AR/VR interventions for dyslexia. Ensure the protection of personal information and obtain informed consent from participants and their parents/guardians. Safeguarding the well-being and rights of dyslexic learners should be a priority throughout the implementation process.

Collaboration and Knowledge Sharing: Foster collaboration and knowledge sharing among researchers, educators, and professionals working in the field of AR/VR and dyslexia interventions. Share best practices, experiences, and research findings to advance the field and promote the widespread implementation of effective AR/VR interventions for dyslexia.

### 8.5.2 Comparisons

Reading together with an audiobook can substantially help kids with dyslexia bridge the gap between word decoding and meaning assignment. Having access to information both visually and audibly improves word recognition, fluency, and advanced comprehension abilities, making learning more effective by listening. It can be difficult for students to keep up with the growing amount of reading as they advance in their studies. Students who read slowly can benefit from audiobooks since they can focus on understanding what they are reading rather than trying to decipher the words on the page. Generally, a dyslexic may be better at understanding spoken language than reading. These children can access materials that may be above by listening to text [28].

Touch typing has been shown to be helpful for kids who struggle with dyslexia in terms of enhancing other abilities such as spelling, memory, vocabulary, and reading. Regardless of whether they have dyslexia, students who acquired touch typing at a young age typically outperformed their peers on examinations that required these abilities. Importantly, typing offers dyslexic pupils with an additional method of learning. As a result of the muscle memory required for touch typing, transposing or misspelling words becomes a little more than a series of patterns on the keyboard.

Students with dyslexia frequently experience difficulties with handwriting. Due to the difficulty of correcting mistakes in handwritten texts, papers frequently contain crossed-out words and eraser marks, as students struggle with spelling without the aid of spellcheck [29, 30]. Touch typing is typically a lot faster, more effective, and simpler for students to do their work, regardless of whether they have dyslexia. Additionally, because typing gives the learner more freedom to experiment with writing styles, touch typing has been demonstrated to improve handwriting skills in dyslexic individuals. Learners will be able to progress on both skills at the same time by learning touch typing, not just by replacing one with the other.

Dyslexics often find it simpler to write down their ideas on paper or a computer screen first, then rearrange and structure the information later due to brain processes that are unique to people with this disability.

## 8.6 Conclusion

Teaching students with dyslexia necessitates a more specialized educational model that has been demonstrated. Augmented reality is a technology tool that can improve student learning and make it easier for dyslexic kids to learn. The Distribution of the Solutions Definitely Agree No Disagreement Strongly Object. The inclusion of kids with dyslexia in the educational process may be aided by the development of supplementary materials based on prescribed school texts. Applications like the one described in this research have the potential to completely alter how dyslexic kids are taught in the classroom and enhance the learning environment. The application's instructor evaluation revealed a favorable attitude toward the use of AR in dyslexic pupils' education. The provision of supplemental materials for ages 6 to 18 and for subjects like history in other academic programs may be the topic of future studies. Small advances have been made toward the implementation of AR in the education of dyslexics, but these steps could serve as the cornerstone of a future educational system that treats learning disorders like dyslexia with respect and care.

This research will help children with dyslexia to learn and gain new skills and also help teachers and trainers to consider the worth, as well as the intricacy, of arising technologies such as AR/VR in the learning area and introducing assessments to evaluate children with dyslexia in learning with these innovations.

## References


1. Gill, the insignificance of null hypothesis significance testing. *Polit. Res. Q.*, 52, 647–674 (1999).
2. Bannatyne, A.D. (1971) *Language, Reading and Learning Disabilities*, Springfield, IL, Thomas.
3. Wadsworth, S.J., Knopik, V.S. and DeFries, J.C. (2000) 'Reading disability in boys and girls: no evidence for a differential genetic etiology', *Reading and Writing: An Interdisciplinary Journal*, vol. 13, pp.133–45.
4. Everatt, J. (1997) 'The abilities and disabilities associated with adult developmental dyslexia', *J. Res. Read.*, vol. 20, pp. 13–21.
5. Faludy, A. (1998) 'How I faced the bullies and won', *The Guardian*, 29th August 1998, p.
6. Francis, M., Taylor, S. and Sawyer, C. (1992) 'Colored lenses and the Dex frame: new issues', *Support for Learning*, vol. 7, pp.2 5–7.
7. Bradley, L. and Bryant, P.E. (1978) 'Difficulties in auditory organization as a possible cause of reading backwardness', *Nature*, pp. 271 and 746–7.
8. Everatt, J. (1999) (ed.) *Reading and Dyslexia: Visual and Attentional Processes*, London, Routledge.
9. Stein, J. (1994) 'Developmental dyslexia, neural timing and hemispheric lateralization', *Int. J. Psychophysiol.*, vol.18, pp. 241–9.
10. Firth, U. (1985) 'Beneath the surface of developmental dyslexia', in Patterson, K., Marshall, J.C. and Coltheart, M. (eds) *Surface Dyslexia: Neuropsychological and Cognitive Studies of Phonological Reading*, London, Laurence Erlbaum Associates.
11. Dancey, C.P. and Reidy, J. (2002) *Statistics Without Math's for Psychology* (2nd edn), Harlow, Pearson Education.
12. Snow, C.E. (1991) *Unfulfilled Expectations: Home and School Influences on Literacy*, Cambridge, MA, Harvard University Press.
13. Stein, J. and Walsh, V. (1997) 'To see but not to read: the magnocellular theory of dyslexia', *Trends Neurosci.*, vol. 20, pp. 147–52.
14. J.N. Rouder, P.L. Speckman, D. Sun, R.D. Morey, G. Iverson, Bayesian t tests for accepting and rejecting the null hypothesis. *Psychon. Bull. Rev.*, 16, 225–237 (2009).
15. P.E. Tressoldi, G. Stella, M. Faggella, the development of reading speed in Italians with dyslexia: A longitudinal study. *J. Learn. Disabil.*, 34, 414–417 (2001).
16. M. Perea, V. Panadero, C. Moret-Tatay, P. Gomez, The effects of inter-letter spacing in visual-word recognition: Evidence with young normal readers and developmental dyslexics. *Learn. Instr.*, 2012.
17. Anderson, R., Hiebert, E., Scott, J. and Wilkinson, I. (1985) *Becoming a Nation of Readers: The Report of the Commission on Reading*, Champaign, IL, Center for the Study of Reading.

18 Baker, S.M. (1985) 'A biochemical approach to the problem of dyslexia', *J. Learn. Disabil.*, vol. 18, no. 10, pp. 581–4.
19. Chall, J.S. (1996) *Learning to Read: The Great Debate* (3rd edn), Fort Worth, TX, Harcourt Brace College Publishers.
20. Clay, M.M. (1990) 'Learning to be learning disabled', *ERS Spectrum*, vol. 8, pp. 3–8.
21. Courcy, A., Béland, R. and Pitchford, N.J. (2000) *Phonological Awareness in Preliterate French-Speaking Children, Paper presented at the Society for the Scientific Study of Reading Annual Conference*, Stockholm, July 2000.
22. Critchley, M. (1970) *The Dyslexic Child*, London, Heinemann.
23. Eglington, E. and Annett, M. (1994) 'Handedness and dyslexia: a meta-analysis', *Percept. Mot. Ski.*, vol. 79, pp. 1611–6.
24. Seymour, P.H.K. (1986) *Cognitive Analysis of Dyslexia*, London, Routledge and Kegan Paul.
25. Skinner, B.F. (1953) *Science and Human Behavior*, New York, Macmillan.
26. Spear-Swerling, L. and Sternberg, R.J. (1998) *Off Track: When Poor Readers Become Learning Disabled*', Boulder, CO, Westview Press.
27. Stanovich, K.E. (1991) 'The theoretical and practical consequences of discrepancy definitions of dyslexia', in Snowling, M.J. and Thomson, M.E. (eds) *Dyslexia: Integrating Theory and Practice*, London, Whurr.
28. Stein, J., Richardson, A.J. and Fowler, M.S. (2000) 'Monocular occlusion can improve binocular control and reading in developmental dyslexics', *Brain*, vol.123, pp. 164–70.
29. Stoll, A.L., Severus, Eland Freeman, M.P. (1999) 'Omega-3 fatty acids in bipolar disorder: a preliminary double-blind, placebo-controlled trial', *Arch. Gen. Psychiatry*, vol. 56, pp. 407–12.
30. Vinegrad, M. (1994) A Revised Dyslexia Checklist, *Edu care*, no. 48, March 1994, British Dyslexia Association.
31. West, T.G. (1997) 'Slow words, quick images – dyslexia as an advantage in tomorrow's workplace', in Gerber, J. and Brown, D.S. (eds) *Learning Disabilities and Employment*, Austin, TX, Pro-Ed.

# 9

# Immersive Experience in the Education of Special Kids Using the Metaverse Platform

**Magesh Kasthuri**

*Distinguished Member of Technical Staff, Wipro Limited, Bengaluru, India*

***Abstract***
The education of special kids is always challenging as the mindset and reactions from kids with special needs are different and unpredictable. It requires special expertise to attract the attention of these kids to enable an effective education mechanism. The metaverse platform provides an immersive user experience using virtual avatars, and special kids' education can be disruptive in a metaverse experience. With machine learning-based customized experience built into the platform, it can provide new experiences to special kids and improve the learning process. This chapter explains how to build a metaverse platform-based solution for special kids and how it can accelerate their education using a digital transformation experience.

***Keywords***: Metaverse, special kids' education, augmented reality (AR), virtual reality (VR), mixed reality (MR)

## 9.1 Introduction

New ways of learning are always experimental, and emerging technologies aid the growth of the educational system in many ways, especially in terms of special education, to provide customized, interactive, and at the same time rich, educational, and captivating experiences for students with disabilities. It is always challenging to educate students with special needs because it requires a customized focus and concern to make them get into the customer centric of the educational system.

*Email*: magesh.kasthuri@wipro.com

V. Ajantha Devi, Williamjeet Singh and Yogesh Kumar (eds.) Augmented Reality and Virtual Reality in Special Education, (189–208) © 2024 Scrivener Publishing LLC

The metaverse is still in the infant stage and not completely matured as per the Gartner research report, as it classifies the metaverse maturity into stages: Emerging stage, Advanced stage, and Mature stage as shown in the figure.

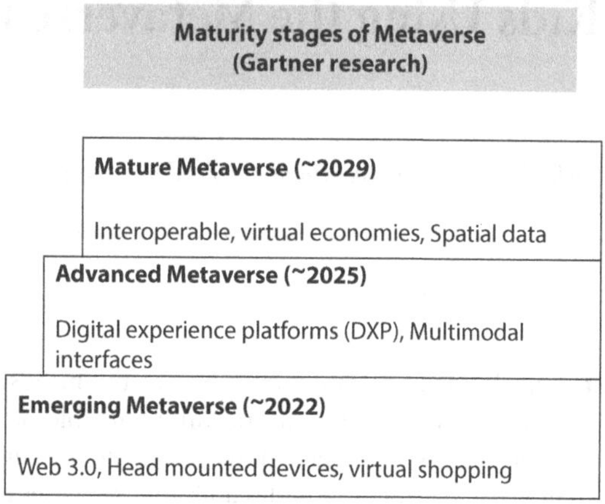


**Figure 9.1** Metaverse maturity stages in various industrial usage.

In recent years, there has been rapid growth in the use of various technologies in special education, especially with the interactive and immersive experience kind of facilities in cutting edge technologies like the metaverse and augmented reality (AR). The metaverse is more promising compared to other learning experiences for students with disabilities because it helps them immerse into the virtual world, and in the process, they learn more.

## 9.2 Technologies Used in Special Education

### 9.2.1 Artificial Intelligence

Artificial intelligence (AI) has been an emerging and ever-growing technology for the past two decades in that it has the potential to revolutionize special education by providing various personalized and rich user experiences in instruction to attract the attention of students. In addition to that, AI can facilitate machine learning and data analytics to analyze student data including interests, hobbies, and focus. This analysis can help identify areas for improvement in preparing customized learning objectives for individuals. Various studies and research have shown that the use of AI in developing facilities for special education can improve student learning outcomes and increase student engagement (Hwang *et al.* 2019).

### 9.2.2 Virtual Reality

Virtual reality (VR) is also a fast-growing and emerging technology that has been used in special education to create simulated virtual experiences and create immersive and engaging learning environments. It can simulate real-world experiences using special head-mounted gears, such as visiting historical or tourism sites, exploring scientific concepts, or discovering the underwater world, and it can also be used for immersive quiz contests to test the knowledge of students. Various research and studies have shown that experience-based studies using VR can enhance learning outcomes and increase engagement among students with disabilities (Chen *et al.* 2020). Virtual reality can also create cost-effective study facilities in safe and controlled environments for students with disabilities to practice subject learning and skills development in a realistic setting.

Virtual reality has been experimented with in the development of special education facilities to teach social and scientific development skills to children requiring special care such as those with autism spectrum disorders (ASD). Based on the technical feasibility and scientific research conducted by M. Woltering *et al.* (2011) on immersive experiences in the social education field, VR can be attractive option in implementing teaching social skills like color identification using cubes, learning directions using puzzles, turn-taking using gamification, and joint attention exercises for children with ASD to help them focus on learning. Research has unveiled that children who had undergone VR-based social skills training have shown significant interest and improvements in their social communication skills as compared to regular education modes.

Another application of VR in special education for kids is bringing improvisation to cognitive and social skills in kids with learning disabilities including mental ailments, and vision or hearing problems. One of the pioneering studies by J. D. Westwood *et al.* (1999) found that learning with virtual environments can be used to improve focus and attention and cognitive and social skills for children with learning disabilities, such as poor attention span, memory, problem-solving skills, and social skills.

### 9.2.3 Augmented Reality

Augmented reality is yet another immersive technology that has been used in providing experience-based learning for kids with special education needs. AR can be used to build an infrastructure that overlays digital information onto the real-world environment by enabling real-world integration in the digital world, providing students with a more interactive and engaging learning experience. Studies have shown that special education using AR devices can improve student engagement and motivation (Klopfer *et al.* 2014). Augmented reality can also provide an experience-based learning facility through visual, haptic, and auditory cues, which can aid kids with disabilities to concentrate, learn, and interact with the world around them and improve their knowledge.

Augmented reality technology has been tremendously popular in improving reading skills in children with reading problems like dyslexia. Based on a recent study by M. Maekawa *et al.* (2017), AR-based learning experiences for reading interventions can help children with problems like dyslexia to improvise and focus on reading accuracy, memorizing information, and fluency in reading speed. This research also mentions that children who have experienced AR-based reading interventions have shown gradual and significant improvements in gaining reading skills compared to typical children in the control group. Augmented reality has also been helpful in creating teaching kits about social skills for children with difficulties like ASD by customizing features based on psychological reactions in recognizing human emotions and understanding facial expressions (J. M. Santos *et al.* 2017).

Gamification in preparing educational kits and materials is the art of integrating game design elements in a non-game context, such as creating contextual education features or educational avatars in a virtual platform. Gamification has been used as a medium for special education in creating interactive, customizable, and engaging learning experiences for students and that can motivate special attention-seeking students to develop learning skills and knowledge in a fun and interactive way. Many recent research studies using new-age technologies have shown that gamification can improve attention, student interaction, engagement, and user experience development for special kids. It also improves problem-solving skills and knowledge mining through new ways of mind map games (Kapp, 2012).

### 9.2.4 Robotics

Robotics is another popular technology that needs heavy physical infrastructure development such as robots and robotic devices. It has been engaged in special education formation to provide personalized user interaction and instruction in developing customized learning facilities that support students who need special attention. Various research and academic studies have implied that robots can help develop experience-building facilities, which improve student engagement and motivation, and aid students in developing social and emotional skills through a new-age creative learning process (Mubin *et al.* 2013).

### 9.2.5 Gamification Using Gadgets

Gamification is the use of game-like elements in building non-game contexts, such as learning and education. Gamification has been used in developing special education frameworks to create engaging and interactive learning experiences. Recent studies and surveys have shown that gamification has been instrumental in improving student engagement and motivation, and it also helps students to develop problem-solving skills (Kapp, 2012).

### 9.2.6 Metaverse Platforms

The metaverse platform is the development of immersive experiences within a virtual world that enables users to interact in a digitally simulated environment using advanced new-age technologies like VR and AR, or simply extended reality (XR), which amalgamates VR, AR, and mixed reality (MR). The metaverse, in the context of learning and development, has a wide range of usage and applications, including special education aids. In developing special education, the metaverse can provide unique, immersive, and engaging learning experiences for students, which can be more interactive than traditional classroom instruction for community development.

The metaverse also offers various benefits in the development of special education, which can enhance the learning and development of students to improve their learning experience. These benefits include the development of immersive learning experiences, the creation of personalized learning, access to inaccessible environments through digital media, and the enhancement of social skills.

Immersive learning experiences using new-age technologies such as the development of metaverse platforms can provide students with a virtualized and simulated learning environment, which is more engaging and interactive than creating experiences with legacy and traditional classroom instruction. This is called the phygital environment, a new-age concept that combines physical or real-world objects with digital or virtual-world objects to create an immersive virtual experience. This approach allows students to learn in a way that is customized to their individual needs and preferences, resulting in more effective instruction.

The metaverse also provides access to real-world (physical) environments that might be inaccessible or unsafe for students with disabilities. This allows them to learn and explore within a safe and controlled setting using virtual environments, promoting their mental development and understanding of the world around them through digital realities.

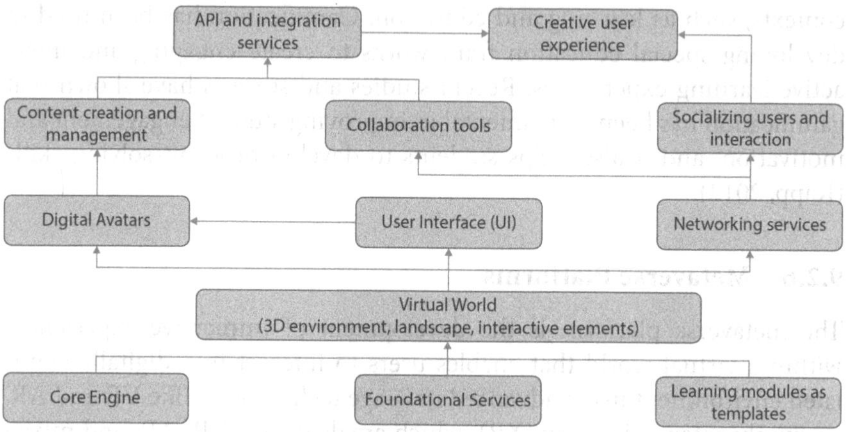


**Figure 9.2** Component architecture of the metaverse in learning and development.

The development of metaverse-based solutions offers various opportunities for students with disabilities and their teachers to interact and collaborate with their peers and other student communities, promoting the development of social skills, community building, and communication abilities.

To determine which metaverse-based solution is most suitable for certain learning objectives or student populations, forward-thinking educators and technology professionals should consider the features, security needs, benefits, limitations, and typical applications of each technology. By doing so, they can make customized and informed decisions about which type of metaverse solution or tools to use to support the learning and development of students with disabilities.

## 9.3 Component View of the Metaverse in Special Education

The component architecture of metaverse services in special education typically includes several key components as explained below. Some of them can be used to create customized interactive platforms that can be used for

**Table 9.1** Technologies and features in special education.

| Technology | Features | Benefits | Limitations | Example applications |
|---|---|---|---|---|
| **Virtual reality** | Immersive, interactive, simulate real-world environments | Enhance learning, increase engagement | High-cost equipment and setup requirements | Simulated field trips, sensory integration therapy |
| **Augmented reality** | Overlay digital content onto the real world | Enhance learning, improve access to information | Limited field of view, may be distracting | Providing visual supports, enhancing instruction |
| **Mixed reality** | Blend of virtual and real worlds, allowing interaction with both | Enhance learning, promote creativity | Limited availability and high cost | Creating personalized learning experiences |
| **Gamification with gadgets** | Use of game-like elements in educational activities | Increase engagement, promote motivation | May not be appropriate for all students | Reinforcing learning objectives, building social skills |
| **Robotics** | Use of physical robots for teaching and learning | Promote social and emotional development, enhance STEM skills | High cost, may require specialized training | Social skills training, programming, and engineering education |
| **3D printing** | Create physical objects from digital designs | Enhance creativity, promote problem-solving skills | High cost of equipment and materials | Creating tactile and visual learning aids, building models |

other learning and development solutions such as competitive examination training and simulated practical learning.

User interface: This is the underlying core component that serves as the base factor of the platform. It provides a physical or digital interface through which platform users, such as students with special educational needs, can interact with the metaverse service directly for a customized experience. This may include a variety of standardized visual and auditory elements, such as the development of digital avatars, 3D environments, and sound effects.

Content creation tools: These are second-layer services on top of the core platform services that aid creative tools to enable platform users to create and develop customized content for the metaverse service. These tools help reuse services as needed for enhancing the future design of the platform. This may include designing and developing theme-based virtual environments through digital services, developing and customizing interactive activities for user experience, and creating digital learning resources such as whiteboarding activities that can be reused across various platforms.

Virtual world engine: This is the digital or virtual component and it is responsible for developing the special user experience by rendering and displaying the virtual world through a digital canvas and its elements. This may include the development of physical multimedia engines, animation tools or avatars, and other digital features to create a realistic and engaging user experience.

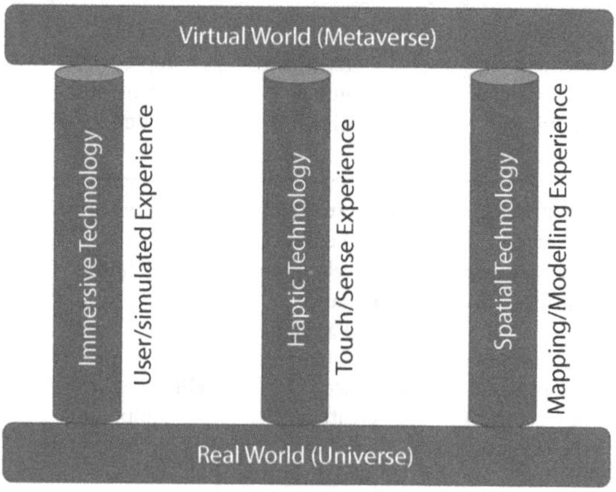


Figure 9.3 Building blocks of the metaverse solution.

Communication and collaboration tools: These are peripheral tools for the platform that enable users to develop communication facilities with different components and collaborate on learning or educational activities using a customized learning platform. This kind of facility may include various services like text chat, voice chat or messages, video conferencing, visual aids, and other features.

Analytics and tracking tools: These tools are heavy data-intensive services that enable users, educators, and platform developers, including platform administrators, to record and track user engagement, record platform usage patterns and application performance, monitor learning progress, and make conscious, data-driven decisions about instruction and support.

Access and security controls: These services create controls that ensure users have appropriate identity and access management (IAM) to the metaverse platform service and its features that aid in developing sensitive information protected from unauthorized access. This may include login authentication, user roles and permissions, and encryption of data.

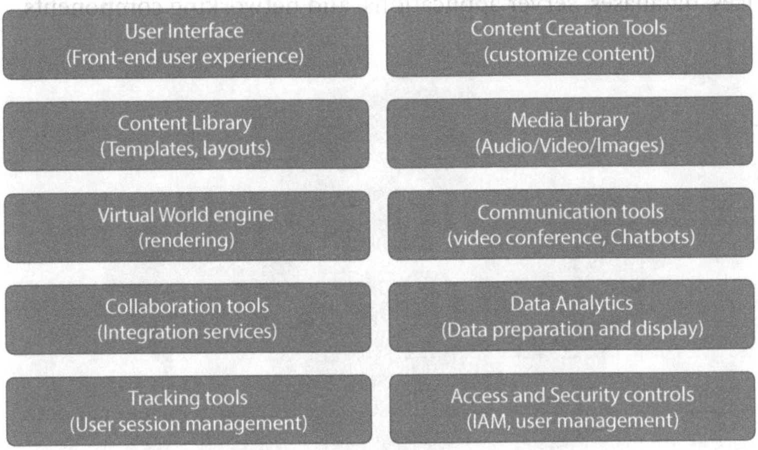


**Figure 9.4** Component view of the metaverse in special education.

By leveraging the latest technologies and tools, metaverse services can offer innovative and effective solutions for addressing the diverse needs and challenges of learners with disabilities. The component architecture of metaverse services in the learning and development industry, such as platform development for special education, caters to support immersive and interactive learning experiences, with a focus on engagement, accessibility, and customization.

## 9.4 System Architecture of Metaverse in Special Education

Though there is no fixed design model for metaverse solutions in special education as they are still in their early stage of development, based on component level services explained above, there are some mandatory system services or components required for the development of metaverse-based special education applications. These components are listed below.

Client-side services: These include the device used by the user to access the metaverse application, such as a computer, tablet, or smartphone through a browser or dedicated software or apps. The client-side also includes the head-mounted VR headset or AR glasses if the application supports those technologies.

Server-side services: The server-side consists of the backend infrastructure that runs in a centralized system and manages the application's data and communication between users. The server-side may include security services, databases, server applications, and networking components.

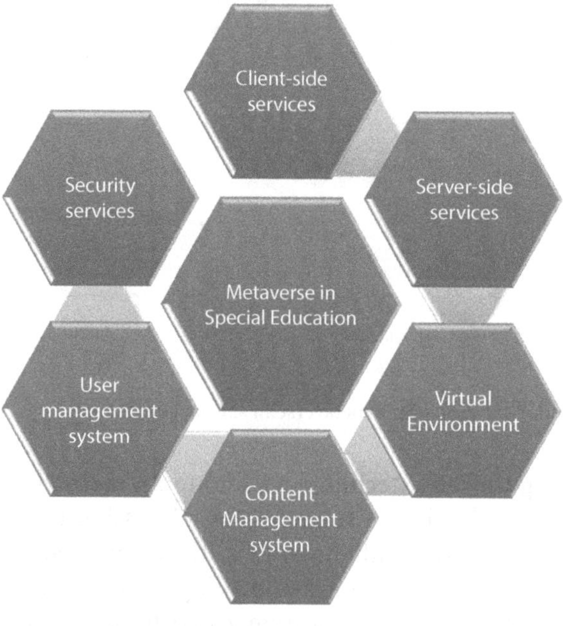


**Figure 9.5** System view of the metaverse in special education.

Virtual environment: The virtual environment or digital service in the digital space is created by the metaverse application that runs on a virtual platform. It can be designed to simulate a learning space such as a classroom, a laboratory, or any other environment that supports the learning objectives of the application.

Content management system: The content management system is the tool or component used by educators or metaverse designers to design and manage the content within the virtual environment as creative digital assets. It may include pre-built learning modules, assessment tools, and customization options.

User management system: The user management system is responsible for handling users for the platform in creating and managing user accounts within the metaverse application. It may include features for user authentication, access control, and user data management.

Security services: Since efficient data management, data privacy, compliance, and data protection are the most important expectations in this development, security services play a vital role in developing compliance, roles, and principles for the domain services.

## 9.5 Recent Studies on Trends in Special Education

Several studies have shown the potential benefits of the metaverse in special education. For example, a study by M. Woltering *et al.* (2011) found that VR can be used to teach social skills to children with ASDs. Another study by J. D. Westwood *et al.* (1999) found that virtual environments can be used to improve cognitive and social skills in children with learning disabilities.

Research analysts has also highlighted the potential of the metaverse in special education. According to a report by MarketsandMarkets (2021), the global VR and AR in the education market is expected to reach $9.3 billion by 2026, with a compound annual growth rate of 29.6% from 2021 to 2026. This research report points out that the development of VR and AR technologies can help develop customized and immersive learning experiences for students, including those with special needs through interactive experience.

Another research report by Technavio (2021) on new-age technologies in special education highlights the use of XR-based technology in special education. This research report also provides statistical notes that VR can be used to develop safe and controlled environments for students with special cases like autism, allowing these students to practice and develop social and communication skills in a realistic setting. This research report also provides insights that can be used to improve skills in students with physical disabilities, as well as to create immersive and engaging learning experiences for all students in different age groups.

The metaverse platform has the potential to develop and transform needs for special education by providing facilities to customize immersive learning environments, which cater to the unique needs of each student through custom experience. Research analysts suggest that VR/AR technologies can be used to provide safe and engaging interactive learning experiences to students of different age groups, including those with special needs in learning. As technology continues to develop advanced facilities, more educational institutes such as schools and universities experiment with special needs using virtual learning environments, the use of the metaverse platforms in developing special education is expected to grow and become more immersive significantly in the future.

## 9.6 Why Use Metaverse in Special Education?

The metaverse-based platform development and experience building refer to the development of a virtual digital world with avatars and realistic experiences where various users can use this digital environment to interact with fellow students and teachers using digital objects within a fully- or semi-immersive environment. By using the metaverse platform, administrators and educators can develop custom learning environments that can cater to the needs of students with disabilities and provide them with a safe and inclusive space to learn and develop knowledge. This kind of technology has the potential to elevate and revolutionize educational needs, especially for special education students as they tend to face unique challenges in traditional classroom settings.

It is a business model and concept that has been around for decades in learning and the development system, but recent technological advancements have made it more friendly, agile, accessible, and realistic. The metaverse platform solution has the potential to develop and revolutionize the education industry in the future, especially for special education students who often face unique and complex challenges in developing and customizing traditional classroom settings. Metaverse platforms refer to virtual spaces and immersive experiences where users can interact with each other and digital objects in a fully or semi-immersive environment.

Metaverse platforms also provide safe and inclusive virtual spaces for students with disabilities who may feel marginalized, pacified, or excluded in traditional classroom settings or feature development. One of the key advantages of metaverse platforms in the special education system provide custom learning environments that cater to the needs of each student within the classroom community. For example, a student with dyslexia could benefit from an immersive virtual environment that uses text-to-speech technology to interact with other students, while a student with autism might benefit from a more sensory-focused environment.

The metaverse platform in special education development is different from other applications due to several factors such as:

Personalization: The metaverse platform allows the development of high-level customized views in developing a personalization and immersive experience development, which is always critical in meeting the individual user needs and preferences of students with disabilities or special attention. For example, metaverse platforms can be customized to provide various types of personalized advice, feedback facilities, support services, and pacing for each student, allowing them to learn and interact at their own pace and in their own way.

Immersive learning: The metaverse platform creates immersive and engaging learning experiences that can aid students with disabilities in developing unique experiences for understanding complex concepts and ideas for learning. For example, the metaverse platform can create a simulated real-world environment through digital services and situations by providing students with a customized hands-on experience that they may not be able to access in the physical world.

Accessible learning: The metaverse platform can provide access to inaccessible learning environments for students with disabilities, such as field trips or going to historical sites through a virtual immersive experience. These experiences might not be practically feasible, cost-effective, or safe for students with disabilities. This will lead to developing new opportunities in learning and education needs and can help bridge the gap between students with and without disabilities.

Social interaction: The metaverse platform can provide business model developments for students with disabilities to immerse, interact, and collaborate with other users or peers, which is highly critical in the development of social skills and communication abilities. For example, metaverse platforms can help develop simulated group projects and team-based activities, providing students with disabilities with an immersive, safe, and supportive environment to practice their interpersonal skills.

Multi-sensory learning: The metaverse platform can support multi-sensory learning which is essential for students with disabilities who may have challenges and difficulties in processing information through traditional modes of learning instruction. For example, the metaverse platform can incorporate visual, immersive, auditory, and tactile elements to create a more engaging and accessible learning and educational experience.

The metaverse platform in special education development provides a unique and customizable set of benefits and features, which are specifically customized to the needs and challenges of students with disabilities. While other industrial applications may offer some similar features and facilities, the metaverse platform is uniquely developed and positioned to provide cost-effective, immersive, accessible, and customizable/personalized learning experiences, which can help improve outcomes for students with disabilities.

**Table 9.2** Pros and cons of embracing metaverse in special education.

| Pros | Cons |
|---|---|
| Enhances student engagement and motivation | Requires access to technology and the Internet |
| Promotes collaborative and interactive learning | May require additional training and support for teachers |
| Provides opportunities for personalized and adaptive learning | Privacy and security concerns for student data |
| Offers a range of sensory experiences for students with disabilities | Risk of perpetuating existing inequalities and biases |
| Facilitates remote learning and reduces geographic barriers | Can be costly to implement and maintain |
| Creates more inclusive and equitable learning environments | Requires ongoing evaluation and assessment of effectiveness |
| Provides opportunities for students to develop digital literacy skills | Can be challenging to ensure accessibility and usability for all students |

It is always important to keep in mind that while there are potential advantages and benefits of embracing the metaverse platform in the development of special education, there are also significant challenges that must be addressed in the future. These challenges include access to new-age technology, privacy/compliance and security concerns, and equity and inclusion issues, and they also make the costs associated with implementation and maintenance cheaper. It is essential that these challenges are carefully considered and addressed to ensure that metaverse technologies are used effectively with technical needs and ethically in special education contexts.

## 9.7 Challenges of the Metaverse in Special Education

While the metaverse platform has the potential to develop and revolutionize the special education system, there are also several important challenges in the learning and development field that must be addressed to successfully engage and embrace these new-age adaptive technologies. Despite its many benefits and flexibility to adapt, the metaverse platform also poses several critical challenges in the development of special education needs. Some of the main challenges include:

High cost or investment: The metaverse platform can be expensive in its current context, but it is expected to be more mature and cost-effective in the future for the development, engagement, and implementation of services, making it less accessible for institutions and schools with limited budgets.

Technical expertise or engineering capability: The metaverse platform always requires specialized technical expertise in integrating services, which may be technically difficult for administrators and educators to acquire.

Equipment and infrastructure requirements for virtual environments: The metaverse platform often requires costly specialized hardware and infrastructure, which may not be available in the market or may not be feasible in some educational settings.

Safety and privacy concerns for security needs: The metaverse platform raises serious concerns about safety and privacy/compliance, particularly for students with disabilities who may be more vulnerable to exploitation or harassment in virtual environments through an immersive experience.

Access to technology to cater to platform development: One of the key technical challenges faced in the embracing the metaverse platform in developing special education is the issue of access to technology features. Various students with disabilities may not have access to the necessary digital hardware, software, or internet connections to fully participate in metaverse activities and training facilities. This can create a digital platform to divide and limit the potential benefits of these technologies.

Training and support for customer service: Another key challenge is the need for training and support for teachers and other educators or any users. Many teachers may not be familiar with the metaverse or other new technologies and may require additional training and support to effectively integrate these tools into their teaching practices.

Data privacy and security for data protection: As with any digital technology, privacy and security are important and a major concern when it comes to the metaverse in special education for compliance and efficient data management. There is a need to ensure that student data and personal information are protected and that appropriate safeguards are in place to prevent unauthorized access or data breaches.

Inclusion and equality to develop sustainable solutions: While the metaverse platform has the potential to create a social impact to be more inclusive and equitable in virtual and immersive learning environments, there is also a potential risk that these kinds of technologies could perpetuate existing inequalities and reinforce biases in learning and development. It is important to ensure that metaverse-based technology is designed and implemented in a way that promotes equity and inclusion for all students.

Large-scale implementation: Implementing a metaverse-based solution for virtual experiences in special education can also be costly and poorly secured due to its infrastructure or resource needs, particularly when taking into multi-fold development of large-scale services for various schools and educational institutions across the city. Institutes like schools or districts are required to procure new infrastructure, which requires high capital expenditure, software, or other VR-based devices like head-mounted devices. There may also be ongoing costs associated with training, maintenance, and support.

In summary, the features of the metaverse platform in the development of special education are designed to provide customizable, immersive, accessible, and personalized learning and development experiences, which can help improve outcomes for students with disabilities. Addressing these kinds of key technical challenges will be highly critical to ensuring the successful acceptance and practical implementation of the metaverse platform in the development of special education. This will also require a cost-effective, collaborative, and multi-disciplinary approach, involving educators, technology developers, policymakers, and other stakeholders.

## 9.8 Future Potential of the Metaverse in Special Education

Even though there are many roadblocks in the development of the metaverse platform, including practical and technical challenges, such as difficulties in using OpenSource or commercial metaverse platforms in the implementation of special education, the metaverse platform has significant potential to interact, elevate, or transform students with special education needs in the future. As technology continues to mature and become more agile, affordable, and accessible, it may become a potentially attractive mainstream platform for supporting the learning and development of students with disabilities. Some key potential areas for future development are listed below.

Expansion of applications for future needs: Metaverse platforms may be used for a practically customizable and wider range of educational applications within the metaverse-based platform, including vocational training development and language learning facilities.

Integration with other technologies or development of combinational technology: The metaverse platform may be technically integrated with other new-age technologies, such as artificial intelligence and machine learning, to develop integrated combinational services that can create more sophisticated and effective learning experiences.

Improved accessibility and experience: Metaverse platforms may become more flexible and accessible to students with disabilities, with the development of new features/tools to support and implement their unique needs and requirements.

Metaverse platforms have significant potential to enhance, elevate, and transform special education needs for students by providing agile, immersive, engaging, and personalized learning experiences. While there are practical challenges, obstacles, and special concerns that are associated with this technology, the benefits outweigh the drawbacks in implementing these technologies. As technology continues to grow and develop, it may become an attractive, mainstream tool to support the diverse needs and challenges of students and learners with disabilities.

The concept of developing a metaverse platform solution has been gaining momentum over the past few years, which can disrupt various industries. Its practical and potential applications in various fields, including special education, are being explored. The metaverse platform is a collective virtual shared space or development of new-age services within a Phygital system that is created by the convergence of the physical and virtual worlds and their digital assets. It also offers a range of possibilities for meeting educational needs, such as developing interactive or immersive learning environments, aiding collaboration among students or teachers, and developing personalized or customized learning opportunities for the future.

## 9.9 Conclusion

The metaverse platform is an experience-based facility in a virtual world where students and various users can immerse themselves and interact with each other as a community using digital objects, such as virtual avatars within a fully immersive environment. It has the potential to develop and transform the learning and educational experience, especially for special education students who face unique roadblocks in traditional and legacy classroom-based educational systems. By using the metaverse technology-based platform, students and educators create custom and unique learning and educational services within a virtual environment, which cater to the needs of every student, providing them with a safe and inclusive space to learn.

The future of the metaverse in special education looks highly promising for the development of new-age business models for learning and development. In the United States, during the COVID-19 lockdown when remote learning started, several schools and universities have already started experimenting with virtual learning environments, and the use of VR and AR in education is expected to grow significantly in the coming years. In Europe, several countries have launched trailblazer initiatives to incorporate VR technology into their education systems, and in Asia, the use of VR and AR is already widespread through various government initiatives.

The metaverse has the potential to transform special education by providing customized learning environments that cater to the unique needs of each student. However, several concerns need to be addressed before it is widely embraced. As technology continues to advance and more schools and universities experiment with virtual learning environments, the future of the metaverse in special education looks promising.

## Acknowledgments

The author would like to acknowledge Wipro Limited for providing the opportunity to learn, research, explore new-age technologies, and gain expertise in technologies, which helped in preparing the idea and framework discussed in this chapter.

## Conflict of Interest Statement

The author would like to clarify that the content shared in this chapter only reflects the views of the author and does not express the views of his organization. The author shares his knowledge in this chapter and does not share any confidential or proprietary information of his organization.

## References

1. Chen, J. A., Chang, C. Y., Wu, Y. H., & Liang, C. Y. (2020). Effects of virtual reality on learning outcomes for students with disabilities: A meta-analysis. *Educ. Res. Rev.*, 29, 100308.

2. Klopfer, E., Sheldon, J., Perry, J., & Scheintaub, H. (2014). Augmenting your own reality: Student authoring of science-based augmented reality games. *New Dir. Youth Dev.*, 2014(144), 85-94.
3. Mubin, O., Stevens, C. J., Shahid, S., Al Mahmud, A., & Dong, J. J. (2013). Robotics for education and therapy of children with autism spectrum disorder. *J. Med. Syst.*, 37(6), 9941.
4. Hwang, G. J., Lai, C. L., & Wang, S. Y. (2019). Seamless flipped learning: A mobile technology-enhanced flipped classroom with effective learning strategies. *J. Educ. Techno. Soc.*, 22(2), 37-50.
5. Kapp, K. M. (2012). *The gamification of learning and instruction: Game-based methods and strategies for training and education.* John Wiley & Sons.
6. Meichenbaum, D. (1996). A cognitive-behavioral approach to intervention with students with learning disabilities. *J. Learn. Disabil.*, 29(5), 551-563.
7. Semrud-Clikeman, M., & Harder, L. (2013). Technology-based interventions for students with attention-deficit/hyperactivity disorder: A review of the literature. *Child Youth Care Forum*, 42(2), 103-121.
8. Neshatian, K., AleAhmad, M., & Ghasemi, M. (2020). A review of technology-enhanced interventions for students with intellectual disability. *Int. J. Dev. Disabil.*, 66(5), 310-328.
9. Kramarski, B., & Mizrachi, N. (2006). Online discussion and metacognitive knowledge: Learning assisted by the type of social and cognitive guidance. *J. Educ. Comput. Res.*, 35(3), 285-312.
10. Blamires, M., & Watson, J. (2012). *Technology and special needs.* Routledge.
11. Butler, D. L., & Sellbom, M. (2019). Opportunities and challenges for augmented reality in education: A systematic review of the literature. *Educ. Res. Rev.*, 27, 180-195.
12. Liu, P. L., & Chen, C. H. (2021). Applications of augmented reality and virtual reality in special education: A review of the literature. *Comput. Educ.*, 169, 104143.
13. Patnaik, A., & Singh, R. (2021). Applications of virtual and augmented reality in special education: A literature review. *Int. J. Educ. Technol. High. Educ.*, 18(1), 1-22.
14. Sultana, M. S., Mustapha, R., & Baharudin, H. (2019). A systematic review on virtual reality in education: A tool to promote engagement and learning among students with disabilities. *Int. J. Emerg. Technol. Learn.*, 14(22), 5-22.
15. Ternier, S., Tabuenca, B., Drachsler, H., & Specht, M. (2020). Augmented and virtual reality applications in special education: A systematic review. *Educ. Technol. Soc.*, 23(1), 1-15.
16. Wang, X., & Gu, X. (2018). A systematic review of research on augmented reality in education from 2005 to 2016. *Int. J. Distance Educ. Technol.*, 16(3), 1-19.
17. Wu, Y. H., Chen, J. A., & Liang, C. Y. (2020). Effects of virtual reality on learning outcomes for students with disabilities: A systematic review and meta-analysis. *Comput. Educ.*, 149, 103806.

18. Boletsis, C., & McCallum, S. (2017). Virtual reality and special needs. In *Virtual, augmented and mixed reality* (pp. 229-243). Springer.
19. Chen, J. A., Chang, C. Y., Wu, Y. H., & Liang, C. Y. (2020). Effects of virtual reality on learning outcomes for students with disabilities: A meta-analysis. *Educ. Res. Rev.*, 29, 100308.
20. Devlin-Scherer, R., & Eaton, J. (2018). VR for inclusive special education: A systematic review of design principles and applications. *J. Educ. Techno. Soc.*, 21(4), 188-204.
21. Hsiao, Y. P., Chen, C. H., & Chen, Y. L. (2020). Learning with augmented reality: Empirical study on cognitive and affective gains in students with disabilities. *Comput. Educ.*, 147, 103780.
22. Kuo, Y. C., & Chuang, T. Y. (2020). Augmented reality-based science learning: A review of recent studies. *J. Educ. Techno. Soc.*, 23(2), 157-172.
23. Mubin, O., Stevens, C. J., Shahid, S., Al Mahmud, A., & Dong, J. J. (2013). Robotics for education and therapy of children with autism spectrum disorder. *J. Med. Syst.*, 37(6), 9941.
24. Sánchez, J., & Cortés, U. (2019). Virtual and augmented reality-based tools for special education: A systematic review. *Multimodal Technol. Interact.*, 3(4), 69.
25. Ternier, S., Tabuenca, B., Drachsler, H., & Specht, M. (2020). Augmented and virtual reality applications in special education: A systematic review. *J. Educ. Techno. Soc.*, 23(1), 1-15.

10

# Privacy and Security Concerns with Augmented Reality/Virtual Reality: A Systematic Review

**Sukhpreet Kaur[1], Saumya Rajvanshi[1,2]* and Gurleen Kaur[2]**

[1]*Department of Computer Science & Engineering, Chandigarh Engineering College, CGC Landran, Mohali, Punjab, India*

[2]*Department of Computer Science & Engineering, CGC-COE Landran, Mohali, Punjab, India*

***Abstract***

Extended reality (XR), which includes augmented reality (AR) and virtual reality (VR) has made significant progress in the field of education, both theoretically and practically. With the advancement of immersive technology, professionals in well-known fields like flight simulation, design, humanities, medicine and vocational training, have been using AR/VR extensively. The channel of adoption of such technologies in the sphere of education has attracted a lot of interest due to its primary use in training. With the development of AR and VR, many new opportunities for teaching and learning open, and these opportunities have been widely recognized as advantageous by educational academics since millions of children around the world who have disabilities have no access or have limited access to education. It has been demonstrated that emerging technologies like AR and VR greatly benefit such young people. By adding information to the real environment, AR has the extra benefit of serving as a support for impaired senses. Furthermore, AR may be used both indoors and outdoors because its fundamental benefit is interaction with the real environment. People with Down syndrome, attention deficit hyperactivity disorder (ADHD), linguistic impairments, and social anxiety can benefit from VR. Although there are many benefits to such technology, using AR and VR in the classroom poses privacy and security risks. The integration of educational technology with the desired learning outcomes is difficult when using AR in teaching and learning. The security privacy and safety (SPS) threat

**Corresponding author*: saumyar25@gmail.com

V. Ajantha Devi, Williamjeet Singh and Yogesh Kumar (eds.) Augmented Reality and Virtual Reality in Special Education, (209–232) © 2024 Scrivener Publishing LLC

scan has a negative effect on instructional user experience and makes it more difficult to present VR content. An invader can record videos or data of a potential victim entering a password on a screen while pretending they are playing. This chapter's main goal is to undertake a comprehensive analysis of various security risks and threats and how to mitigate them. The many security risks posed by AR/VR devices are covered in this chapter, along with the techniques used to mitigate those risks. This chapter's introduction, motivation, and work history make up Sections 10.1 and 10.2. The benefits of AR/VR and numerous security threats are covered in Sections 10.3 and 10.4. Section 10.5 highlights reported works that detail the researchers' in-depth analysis and the methods they employed to eliminate hazards. The comparative analysis and conclusion are in Sections 10.5.1 and 10.6. It analyzes the work of many researchers who have made security less secure by introducing various parameters including attacks on passwords.

***Keywords:*** Extended reality, social virtual reality-based learning environments, artificial intelligence

## List of Abbreviations

| | |
|---|---|
| AR | Augmented Reality |
| VR | Virtual Reality |
| ADHD | Attention Deficit Hyperactivity Disorder |
| VLE | Virtual Learning Environment |
| VE | Virtual Environment |
| IoT | Internet Of Things |
| WoW | Window On World |

## 10.1 Introduction

A major real-world environment is seen in improved reality, which is a synchronized direct or indirect view that has been enhanced or expanded by the sequential addition of virtual, computer-generated items (e.g., AR) [32].

Augmented reality (AR), one of the most rapidly developing technologies, generates virtual objects and graphics in a live environment. Due to its capacity to manipulate 3D objects without worrying about negative consequences for making mistakes, AR is frequently seen as a crucial tool for visualizing abstract concepts. As a result, it is often engaged in education; it is one sector that technology and digitization actively disrupt. Studies have shown that computer simulations work better for learning than conventional classroom settings. It enables underachievers to quickly learn and comprehend difficult ideas, which lead to the improvement of their skills.

Because AR has spatial capabilities, researchers can potentially use technology to teach students in higher education. The classroom might be enhanced by utilizing AR. Students that concentrate in the fields of architecture, civil engineering, and mechanical engineering benefit greatly from AR because it allows for visualization outside of the classroom. The most contemporary AR technology (such as computer vision, program that may deliver AR experiences via smart phone cameras) allows for the interactive and digital manipulation of the user's environment. Because of the increasing demand for tools and techniques for special needs education, educators, engineers, researchers, and practitioners have been developing solutions that combine AR and that improve teaching and learning experiences in this context [17].

It is widely known that the field of education has benefited from technology like AR and VR. It has also assisted children with disabilities. Students with cognitive and down disorders also benefit from it.

The two main risks linked with AR are security and privacy.

Privacy is a concern since AR systems can detect user activity.

Through social media networks or other technologies, AR gathers a lot of data on the user's activities.

Unreliable material, social engineering, malware, network credential theft, denial of service, man-in-the-middle attacks, and other security risks are all connected to AR technology.

Since VR is restricted to enclosed spaces and does not include interaction with the outside world, it differs somewhat from AR in terms of security issues. Virtual reality headsets completely block the user's vision, which makes them risky if hackers get control of the system. For instance, a hacker could alter the information so that the consumer experiences nausea and dizziness. The capture of data like voiceprints, iris or retina scans, and biometric scans are among the privacy concerns with VR. Examples include deep fakes, fake identities, eye tracking, and finger tracking. Apart from cybercrimes, one of the greatest limitations of VR is that it entirely isolates a user's auditory and visual link to the outside world.

## 10.2 Augmented Reality/Virtual Reality

Augmented reality makes it possible for virtual data to be positioned in the user's immediate environment to improve interaction and perception of the real world.

Like how VR is applied, AR can engage all the senses. By adding helpful information to the real world and replacing those senses that are impaired, AR provides additional benefits. Augmented reality merges the real world with the virtual world to deliver additional information about anything in the real world that includes data in the virtual world [15].

Furthermore, AR may be used both indoors and outdoors because its fundamental benefit is interaction with the real environment [21].

The complete cut-off of a user's visual and auditory link to the outside world is one of the primary threats of VR, aside from cybercrimes.

Educational institutions can integrate interactive classrooms into their courses by employing these fundamental AR components. Why should AR be used in education? Augmented reality in the classroom can improve learning by helping teachers design interactive spaces that increase student engagement. Thanks to developments in software and hardware, several industries, including advertising, entertainment (games), marketing, health, engineering, and many others are proactively utilizing AR technology [19].

### 10.2.1 Benefits of AR

Learning environments may be significantly impacted by AR:

#### *10.2.1.1 Higher Attention*

Augmented reality is useful since the user gives more attention to technology rather than course material [31].

#### *10.2.1.2 Student Engagement and Interest*

Students' interest increases when they can contribute to the creation of educational content. Thanks to AR technologies, they can add to the curriculum, create virtual worlds, and find new hobbies.

#### *10.2.1.3 Learning Environment*

Students' participation can be promoted in classes that use AR. The possibility to apply efficient teaching methods that can enhance the educational process and motivate learners to perform and master new skills is provided by an interactive learning environment.

### *10.2.1.4 Indulging the Content*

There is a dearth of excellent information that is oriented on instruction rather than enjoyment, which teachers who are hesitant to use AR in the now autonomously create immersive educational experiences to make sure that their students understand the topics provided in the syllabus.

### *10.2.1.5 Collaboration*

Information exchange is extremely easy because AR content is digital. For instance, a group of teachers and students might work together frequently to enhance the curriculum. Students are more inclined to learn in a collaborative learning atmosphere because they are involved in the process of developing educational content.

### *10.2.1.6 Memory*

Augmented reality is a powerful tool for making lessons more interesting and for helping students retain important information. A teacher might use AR technology to construct an immersive story about life in Colonial America rather than just presenting pictures.

### *10.2.1.7 Sensory Development*

Augmented reality technology can help teachers create lesson plans that use a variety of senses. Students benefit from immersive virtual content that employs an experiential learning approach, where students engage in physical actions rather than only watching a demonstration. With this strategy, sensory development may be aided.

### *10.2.1.8 Cost-Effectiveness*

Adoption of AR is frequently cited as being hampered by the cost of the hardware. However, employing AR in education is becoming more accessible because young Americans are using smartphones more frequently and because smartphones already have the hardware required to run AR apps. Additionally, by substituting pricey textbooks, AR can reduce educational costs.

### 10.2.2 Classroom Examples of AR

The following use cases of AR in education and teacher aids:

#### *10.2.2.1 Math*

AR technologies can assist teachers in developing interesting and instructive math materials that pique students' interests and aid in their academic performance. With the help of AR software Photomath, students can detect a math problem from a physical worksheet and be led digitally through the calculations. Augmented reality apps can also help students learn the concepts and theorems of mathematics through visualization and interactive 3D models. For instance, Merge Cube provides students with an interactive way to study geometry by allowing them to hold, examine, and rotate a virtual cube.

#### *10.2.2.2 Chemistry and Biology*

Teachers can use AR apps to create interactive lessons that will make learning science more interesting. By combining all the components of AR with movies and animation, teachers may support students with their scientific doubts. For instance, Chem101 AR helps students understand complex compounds like oxides and acids. Students can virtually amend molecular structures and yield new materials using dedicated cards.

#### *10.2.2.3 History*

Educators can use AR systems to offer students an interactive records lesson. Virtual journeys to places global are made viable via gears like Timelooper and 360Cities, which assist college students study diverse cultural and historic viewpoints. Students and teachers can use their own smartphones to use AR apps at museums and historical sites that give more details and context about the historical artefacts on show.

#### *10.2.2.4 Coding*

The ability for teachers and students to work together on lesson ideas is one of the key advantages of AR technology. Educators can use platforms to develop coding classes that make advantage of AR technology. For instance, Tynker provides materials for teachers to teach coding for video games. Students can also produce AR projects for the classroom.

#### *10.2.2.5 Educational AR Apps*

Augmented reality is used in on-campus and online schools and colleges to enhance existing curricula and increase interactivity. The following are AR educational apps:

#### *10.2.2.6 Human Anatomy Atlas*

Students and medical professionals can better grasp how the human body systems work by using 3D simulations and models of the male and female anatomies from the Human Anatomy Atlas 2021. Users can look at animations, analyze muscle movement, conduct virtual dissections, and more.

#### *10.2.2.7 Holo-Human*

Users of the AR app Holo-Human can study human anatomy models in a group setting with access to internal and 360-degree views. Lesson plans can also be written by teachers.

#### *10.2.2.8 VR Frog Dissection*

Ribbit-ing new findings in biology schools throughout the world, students dissect frogs to learn about bodies. By using this system in place of that technique, instructors and students can do virtual dissection studies to learn about frog anatomy.

#### *10.2.2.9 GeoGebra AR*

With the aid of AR elements, this interactive application enriches STEM teaching by enabling students to explore shapes and 3D operations, exercise analytical reasoning, and more. All subjects are covered, including math, geometry, and statistics.

#### *10.2.2.10 Expeditions*

This flexible program allows teachers and students to create and experience dynamic, virtual worlds. It has hundreds of AR tours.

#### *10.2.2.11 Exoplanet*

Exoplanet is an app that offers an interactive list of planets that are known to be orbiting stars in the Milky Way. It was created by a professional astronomer.

#### *10.2.2.12 Star Walk*

Through the VR app Star Walk, users can view and identify constellation and stars in real time while discovering interesting facts and amusing astronomy trivia.

#### *10.2.2.13 Touch Surgery*

Using this software, surgeons and medical professionals can learn about different surgical procedures and prepare for surgical cases.

#### *10.2.2.14 4-D Interactive Anatomy*

With the aid of the 4D interactive anatomy app, both teachers and students can assess their understanding of the human body.

#### *10.2.2.15 Visible Body*

With the help of the AR dissection features in the app Visible Body, students without easy access to a lab can view 3D representations of the human anatomy within the actual world.

#### *10.2.2.16 Plantale*

This interactive AR software lets you observe about the anatomy and life cycle of plants.

#### *10.2.2.17 Boulevard AR*

The National Portrait Gallery's artwork comes to life with the use of AR technology, as long as viewers with access to a museum-like experience regardless of their location.

*10.2.2.18 3DBear*

This approach integrates AR, VR, 360-degree photography, scanning, and 3D printing to enhance learning both online and in person.

## 10.3 Virtual Reality

A virtual experience that resembles or is completely unconnected to reality is called VR. Around the world, VR was first used as a tool for psychological therapy [32]. Many industries, including business, education (including medical and military training), and entertainment (including video games), use VR (e.g. virtual meetings). Augmented reality and XR are additional variants of VR-style technology.

To deliver realistic visuals, sounds, and other sensations that mimic a user's physical presence in a virtual world, current mainstream VR systems either use VR headsets or multi-projected environments. A user can gaze around the virtual environment, move around in it, and interact with virtual features or objects when using VR technology. However, VR headsets—which have a head-mounted display with a small screen in front of the eyes—typically produce the impression. Additionally, specifically designed rooms with numerous gigantic screens might give the appearance. Virtual reality normally includes auditory and visual input, but this type of technology may also enable extra sensory and force feedback.

### 10.3.1 Virtual Reality in Real World

A simulation that might closely match the real world or be very different from it is called VR. Business, amusement (like video games), and education (like medical or military training) all have uses for VR (e.g. virtual meetings). Additional iterations of VR-style technologies include AR and XR.

Currently available commercially VR systems either use VR headsets or multi-projected environments to provide realistic sights, sounds, and other sensations that duplicate a user's physical presence in a virtual world. Using VR technology, a person can roam around in the virtual environment and interact with fictional things or creatures. Virtual reality headsets, which have a helmet display with a small screen in front of the eyes, often give the impression. Additionally, the look could be created by specially created spaces that feature multiple enormous screens. While haptic technology may potentially offer additional sensory and force response in VR, it typically only comprises aural and visual input.

Virtual reality is not a brand-new idea; it has been around since the late 1960s in a variety of formats. Before it was extensively used, VR was referred to by terms like artificial reality, cyberspace, simulator technology, and more. Desktop VR is also known as non-immersive VR (Onyesolu, 2006) and Window on World (WoW). Due to the widespread use of desktop VR, less immersive applications have continued to be created using the technology. These non-immersive VR applications have made progress in industry training and development despite being much less expensive and technically challenging. By creating a virtual world, VR has the probability to alter the way that instructional content is presented. The creation of a real and imagined world aids in a student's comprehension of the material being taught [16].

Finally, VR has the potential to be developed and used extensively, particularly in education sector where computer-based interactive learning environments (VLE) are being pushed as desktop VR. Thus, educational programs ought to make use of it (Ausburn & Ausburn, 2004). Physics, engineering, and other disciplines now have a wider range of things that may be studied, taught, and done, thanks to these computer-based virtual learning environments (VLEs). Virtual learning environments give students the chance to meet their educational goals. As a result, VLE-based applications have become widely used in colleges and schools as effective tools to supplement conventional teaching techniques. It has been found that these learning settings are more pedagogically beneficial for learners.

In virtual learning environments, it is possible to get insights into the components and operations of any system in three dimensions. Students can quickly, effectively, and enjoyably learn the foundations of such a system by engaging with and navigating around the environment created for such a system. The ability of VR to create artificial objects that are as realistic as or perhaps more so than the genuine ones is widely acknowledged.

### 10.3.2 Advantages

For manipulating virtual objects in VR, the student simply requires head mounted display (HMD), haptics, and sensors [33].

Additionally, PTSD and phobias have been successfully treated with VR (including a phobia of flying, spiders, and heights). Since it has been demonstrated to be successful in an academic setting, many commercial organizations are now able to provide patients with this form of therapy. The computer-based simulations nevertheless had a number of advantages over live training, even if it had been demonstrated that employing standardized patients for such training was more realistic. Their objective was to reduce psychological stress while increasing performance and decision-making by exposing more people to actual emergency scenarios.

### 10.3.3 Disadvantages

Some psychologists worry that complete immersion in virtual environment can have a negative psychological impact on a user. They contend that virtual environment (VE) systems that expose a user to violent scenarios, particularly when acting as the perpetrator of violence, may lead to desensitization in the user. In essence, there is concern that the VE entertainment industry may produce a generation of sociopaths. Virtual environments that are interesting could be more addictive. Criminal activity is another growing issue. It has been difficult to define crimes like sex crimes or murder in the virtual world. Since studies have shown that people can have genuine physical and emotional reactions to stimuli in a virtual world, a victim of a virtual attack might suffer from emotional disturbance.

## 10.4 Algorithms of AR Used in Education

### 10.4.1 Variance Inflation Factor (VIF)

As part of the pre-test for candidate teachers, intestines were asked to be represented in a human model and implanted in the gaunt structure. The teaching materials created using the AR application were then made available for teacher candidates to use [22].

### 10.4.2 The Hum-AR Library

Programmers can easily construct AR apps, thanks to the Hum-AR (HuAR) software library, which is available for the C and C++ programming languages. There are several potential uses for AR, which is the overlay of virtual computer graphic images on the physical world that defines the technique for calculating posture. A numerical solution to the problem of minimizing a function—typically a nonlinear function—over the space of its parameters is provided by the Levenberg–Marquardt algorithm, also referred to as LMA. Nonlinear programming and least squares curve fitting are two areas where these minimization problems are very common [23].

### 10.4.3 SketchAR

One of the programs that artists have recently liked regularly is SketchAR, which mixes drawing with AR. Since SketchAR is a drawing software that is made available to artists, attests to the originality and uniqueness of digital works produced by artists, non-fungible token (NFT) is accepted for them (data unit). By fusing drawing with AR technology and AI assistance, Aleksandr Danilin, Alexander Danilin, and Andrey Drobitko's initiative SketchAR—founded in 2017 in Lithuania—offers its users a unique drawing experience.

### 10.4.4 Virtual Reality-Collaborating Classroom Grounded on Deep Learning Algorithm

The invention of interactive teaching activities based on the deep learning algorithm can help teachers carry out teaching activities productively in addition to addressing the outlook of individualized learning. Based on the features of the environment, VR-interactive classroom teaching activities are divided into in-class learning activities and after-class learning activities [26]. The VR-interactive classroom's curriculum is broken up into four parts. The interactive test, learning objective, video content, and learning summary are some examples. A VR classroom can be created using the associated model [24].

### 10.4.5 Security Risks for AR

The serious security, privacy, and safety risks that developing AR technology bring are now being recognized and addressed by the computer security and privacy sector. Many of these actions are based on the dangers that specific AR users can encounter from harmful or shady apps on their devices. Some people deal with input privacy by, for instance, limiting the passage of private sensitive information (such as pictures of people's faces or confidential papers) to unapproved programs. Others take into consideration output security, which stops apps from showing offensive or hazardous content. Additionally, research into security and privacy safeguards for multi-user interactions has just recently started [20]. Figure 10.1 provides the framework for security techniques of AR/VR. It mainly describes the flow of information that is adopted while carrying out the research.

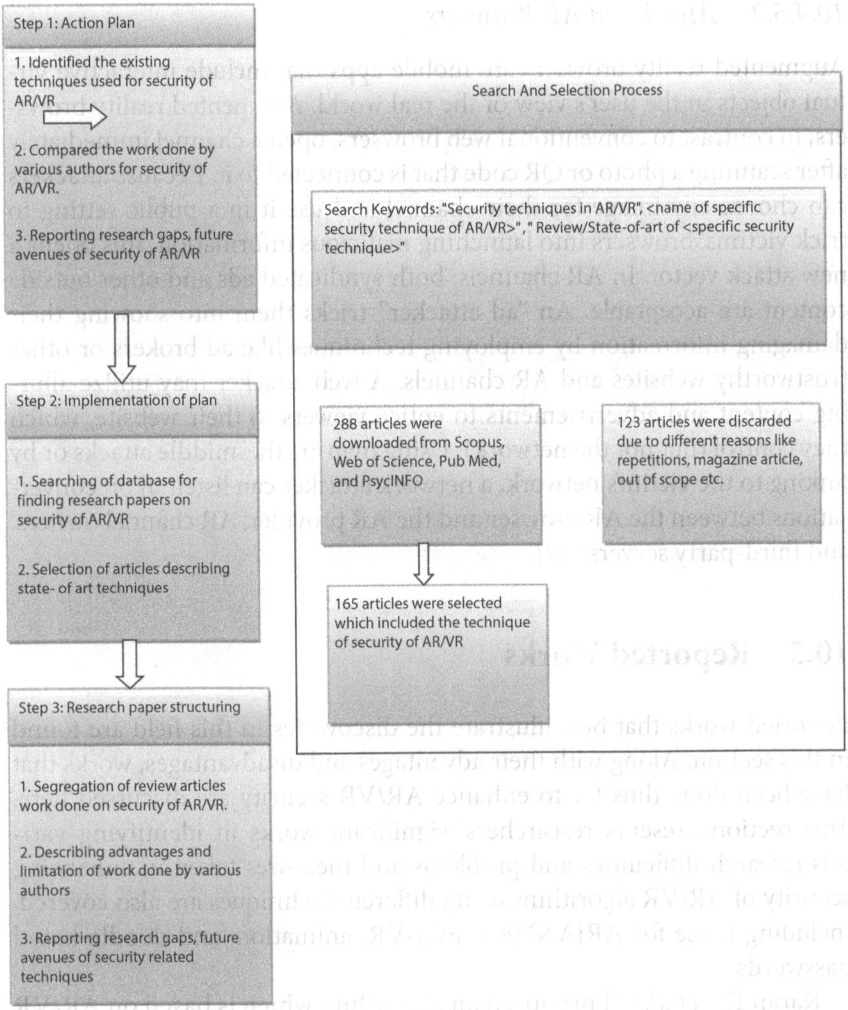


**Figure 10.1** Framework for security techniques of AR/VR.

### *10.4.5.1 Cybersecurity Risks in AR*

Since all Internet of Things (IOT) devices communicate with the Internet, AR gadgets are just like any other IOT device subject to dangers (i.e., The Internet is seen as an unsafe network). Risks are defined as potential exploitable vulnerabilities. The major issues of data security and privacy are maintaining the confidentiality, integrity, and availability of the data [25].

#### *10.4.5.2 Attacks on AR Browsers*

Augmented reality browsers are mobile apps that include interactive virtual objects in the user's view of the real world. Augmented reality browsers, in contrast to conventional web browsers, open a channel immediately after scanning a photo or QR code that is connected to it. Because attackers can choose any image for their channel and use it in a public setting to trick victims' browsers into launching malicious information, this opens a new attack vector. In AR channels, both syndicated ads and other outside content are acceptable. An "ad attacker" tricks them into showing their damaging information by employing techniques like ad brokers or other trustworthy websites and AR channels. A web attacker may utilize alluring content and advertisements to entice viewers to their website, which they control (but not the network). Using man-in-the-middle attacks or by linking to the victim's network, a network attacker can listen in on conversations between the AR browser and the AR provider, AR channel owners, and third-party servers [27].

## 10.5 Reported Works

Reported works that best illustrate the discoveries in this field are found in this section. Along with their advantages and disadvantages, works that have been done thus far to enhance AR/VR security are discussed here. This section presents researchers' significant works in identifying various research difficulties and problems and measures taken in enhancing security of AR/VR algorithms using different techniques are also covered, including those for ARIANNA+, Edu-VR, animation, and doodle-based passwords.

Karan KV *et al.* [1] proposed an algorithm, which is based on AR/VR virtual environment, which used a technique "EDU-VR". In this study, the researcher developed a method that enables instructors to create or download their own AR model for instruction. This algorithm revealed some flaws that were not overlooked, resulting in poorer accessibility for students when they begin accessing their lessons. Students, as well, cannot take notes during lectures. Song Chen *et al.* [2] proposed an algorithm based on the ZED stereo camera and the Samsung Gear AR/VR device. Researchers have successfully attacked 4-digit numerical passwords using this algorithm at 1.5 meters with a success rate of 90%. Some drawbacks of this algorithm is security, which showed an issue for other AR devices like HoloLens. Alice Lo Valvo *et al.* [3]

created the ARIANNA+ tool, which is very useful for people with physical disabilities because it enables them to design pre-defined pathways without any physical assistance. The disadvantage of this strategy is that wearable technology, such as camera (vision) sensors and smart watch (vibration) gadgets, are not integrated to give blind people a more comfortable experience. A web-based animation was suggested by Husnu S. *et al.* [4] to engage students and improve knowledge, however, it only works with a small quantity of data. Waqas Wazir and others [5] developed a hybrid of graphical and doodle-based methods, which are challenging to decipher due to the wide range of doodle shapes, but it has scant evidence to back it up. Barbara Leporini *et al.* [6] proposed an E-learning system. Virata, R.O *et al.* [7] developed a Plan-Do-Study-Act (PDSA), which helped in improving and having more satisfactory learning outcomes. One limitation is that teachers find it difficult to use. Kesim and Ozarslan [8] conducted an exploratory study that allows a smooth transition between virtuality and reality on a group learning, which improves learning outcomes. It promotes critical thinking skills in learners. Angel Lu *et al.* [10] developed an AR software, which describes relations between AR software and environment. However the knowledge it provides is less technical as compared to other technologies. Wu *et al.* [11] developed an application that helped in improving learning achievements. However, it increases the cognitive load among students. Alkhattabi *et al.* [12] conducted an exploratory study, which shows there is a high acceptance rate among users of AR, but there is a lack of proper training among teachers. Elmqaddem *et al.* [13] carried out an exploratory study that found AR applications are highly interactive, but has limitations on technical details being high. Ozkan Yilmaz [14] conducted a theme analysis with which students feel comfortable. It was concluded that AR software requires a lot of improvement. Martin *et al.* [25] developed educational games that enhance the experience of visitors. It focused on theoretical data. More experimental data need to be considered. Kimberly Ruth *et al.* [26] proposed Microsoft HoloLens that meets design goals and experience. However, interaction between multiple users using the same AR device is an issue in HoloLens. Mark Roman Miller *et al.* [28] conducted a psychological analysis, which shows social presence of users. However, realism was not systematically controlled. Nitika *et al.* [29] created a WebAR with 3D modeling to reduce the barrier of downloading. Bhupinder Singh *et al.* [30] proposed the use of electromagnetic devices using AR, which provides virtual information to its nearest neighbor. However, it has limitations for physically disabled people.

### 10.5.1 Comparative Analysis

| Author | Year | Approach used | Advantage of work | Drawback |
|---|---|---|---|---|
| Karan KV *et al.* [1] | 2021 | VR/AR based virtual environment "Edu-VR" | It enables educators to create or download their own AR model for instruction. | Classes are less accessible to students. Students cannot take notes during lectures. |
| Song Chen *et al.* [2] | 2019 | Augmented reality system constructed on the ZED stereo camera and the Samsung Gear VR | The attack is successful at 1.5 meters, with a decent success rate of 90% for 4-digit numerical passwords. | Security is an issue for other AR devices like HoloLens. |
| Alice Lo Valvo *et al.* [3] | 2021 | ARIANNA+ | Assists those who are blind in navigating along established routes; removes the need for any physical assistance. | Integration of wearable technology to improve the perception of one's surroundings for those who are blind or visually challenged, such as integrating camera (vision) sensors and smart-watch (vibration) gadgets. |
| Husnu S *et al.* [4] | 2020 | Standard and web-based animation | These programs would help kids become more interested in studying and more engaged with challenging subjects. | Worked on small data sets |
| Waqas Wazir *et al.* [5] | 2018 | Combination of AR environments and the graphical doodle password technique. | Modern authentication methods that are easier to use and are more effective. Due to the vast array of doodle shapes that can be used, doodle passwords are challenging to hack. | The doodle password approach is the initial step. More research needs to be done. |

*(Continued)*

(*Continued*)

| Author | Year | Approach used | Advantage of work | Drawback |
|---|---|---|---|---|
| Barbara Leporini *et al.* [6] | 2022 | E-learning systems (LMSs and LOs) | Virtual learning is facilitated. | More challenging for a user who is blind than for a user who is not blind. When creating the UI code, the requirements of blind users should also be taken into consideration. |
| Virata, R.O *et al.* [7] | 2019 | PDSA | Increased understanding of subjects like chemistry; better learning outcomes; ease of use; increased motivation and learning satisfaction. | Teachers may struggle with technology use; they may not be able to discover apps that are appropriate with their pedagogical demands, and technology may oversimplify visualization. |
| Kesim and Ozarslan [8] | 2012 | Exploratory, qualitative study | Allow for connections between the physical and virtual worlds, a smooth transition between the two, and the use of a physical interface as an analogy for manipulating objects. | The main issue is the need for instructional designers to provide AR learning experiences. |
| Chu *et al.* [9] | 2019 | Randomized skillful study; experimental peer learning | AR-based education enhances learning outcomes and fosters student motivation and engagement. | There are still some issues with the research design's validity for AR-based learning environments, which encourages students to develop their critical thinking abilities. |

(*Continued*)

(*Continued*)

| Author | Year | Approach used | Advantage of work | Drawback |
|---|---|---|---|---|
| Angel Lu *et al.* [10] | 2021 | AR software | A good relationship between learner attitude and how the AR program was perceived. | Less content, fewer gaming components and interactions, fewer scenes in AR software, and fewer instructions and training materials |
| Wu *et al.* [11] | 2013 | Experimental, app development | One of the main advantages was that using AR can help students attain better learning results. | One of the main obstacles to adoption and implementation was a potential, unmanageable rise in the cognitive load of the students. |
| Alkhattabi *et al.* [12] | 2017 | Exploratory research Study | According to the report, there is an increasing overall adoption rate of AR use and a willingness to adopt it when it becomes available. | The key issues, according to the survey, are a lack of proper teacher preparation, a resistance to change, and a reluctance to adopt new technologies. |
| Elmqaddem *et al.* [13] | 2019 | Exploratory study | Augmented reality improves entertainment, object manipulation, student participation, and interactivity to a high extent. | The study identified significant technical and social obstacles, such as uncomfortable gadgets and health problems, that prevented the use of AR in academic contexts. |
| Ozkan Yilmaz [14] | 2021 | Theme analysis | Augmented reality is the best method for learning about abstract concepts. Students feel comfortable with the software. | It comprises only subjective data that can vary. There is no integration of pedagogy with AR. The AR software of AR requires a lot of improvement. |

(*Continued*)

(*Continued*)

| Author | Year | Approach used | Advantage of work | Drawback |
|---|---|---|---|---|
| Martin *et al.* [25] | 2011 | Mobile AR educational games | To collect data and improve the experience of guests at cultural institutions (such as museums and archaeological sites). | Only theoretical data are considered. More research needs to be carried out to focus on experimental data. |
| Kimberly Ruth *et al.* [26] | 2019 | Microsoft HoloLens | It meets the design goals and imposes minimal performance overhead. | Interaction between multi-users using the same AR device is an issue. |
| Mark Roman Miller *et al.* [28] | 2021 | Psychological analysis | The findings demonstrated that even when both individuals were physically present in the same space, those who were wearing headsets felt noticeably less related to them. | Realistic depictions, whether behavioral or visual, were not routinely controlled. Previous studies have demonstrated that agents influence society, and that agency and reality help mitigate that influence. |
| Nitika *et al.* [29] | 2021 | WebAR | To eliminate the need to download any application-based AR software, 3D data modeling was used to create an experience that can also be used in a web browser. | For the computing needs of browsers, more efficient object optimization approaches can be used. |
| Bhupinder Singh *et al.* [30] | 2021 | Electromechanical devices using AR | People's lives are made easier with virtual information provided to their nearby regions, as well as any indirect view of the real-world environment, such a live video stream. | With limitations for people with physical disabilities |
| Danial Weber *et al.* [18] | 2022 | Combination of AR and eye-tracking to make robots flexible | High speed and user-friendly, achieving reasonable accuracy as compared to traditional approaches. | Training data are not available |

## 10.6 Conclusion

Augmented reality and virtual reality have numerous benefits for instruction. Most VR instructional contents developed take the form of concept-focused guided experiences. Because it enables educators to create or download custom AR models for teaching various concepts, Edu VR is distinctive. Instead of focusing on the creation of models, teachers can focus on the subject. The purpose of this study is to evaluate how well a VR education functions as a teaching tool. Various technologies are used, and advantages and disadvantages of each technique are studied. A virtual reality classroom is created where users may roam around and engage in peer-to-peer learning, as well as student–teacher communication. However, there is still work to be done on the representation of the AR objects for instruction, the systems for AI-proctored exams, and the concept of text pattern recognition for judging descriptive replies.

Emerging technologies in the quickly growing area of VR may be able to assist VR classrooms in overcoming some of its initial problems. The issue of enabling pupils to take notes during lectures may be solved by future developments in AR.

## Acknowledgement

The authors thank the Chandigarh Group of Colleges Landran, for providing the opportunity to complete this book chapter. Suggestions and encouragement from colleagues helped the authors develop and finish this chapter. Without their contributions, this work would not have been possible.

## Conflict of Interest Statement

The authors have no conflicts of interest to declare and they have agreed to and have seen the contents of the manuscript. Furthermore, there is no financial interest to report. The authors certify that the submission is an original work and is not under review at any other publication.

## References

1. Karan KV, Yashwanth Krishnan B, R. Ranjana and T. Subha. "Edu VR: Design and Implementation of Virtual Classroom Environment in VR for Remote Learning."DOI: 10.20944/preprints202106.0447.v1 (2021).

2. Song Chen, ZupeiLi, Fabrizio DAngelo, Chao Gao, Xinwen Fu. "A Case Study of Security and Privacy Threats from Augmented Reality (AR)".
3. Alice Lo Valvo 1, Daniele Croce 1, Domenico Garlisi 1,2, Fabrizio Giuliano 1 and Laura Giarré 3,* and Ilenia Tinnirello 1,2. "A Navigation and Augmented Reality System for Visually Impaired People" *Sensors*, 2021, 21(9), 3061.
4. Husnu S. Narman, Cameron Berry, Alex Canfield, Logan Carpenter, Jeremy Giese, Neil Loftus, and Isabella Schrader." Augmented Reality for Teaching Data Structures in Computer Science". marshall.edu Department of Computer Sciences and Electrical Engineering, Marshall University, Huntington, WV 25755.
5. Waqas Wazir1, Hasan Ali Khattak2, (Senior Member, IEEE), Ahmad Almogren2, (Senior Member, IEEE), Mudassar Ali Khan3, Ikram Ud Din. "Doodle-based Authentication Technique Using Augmented Reality" Vol 4, 2018.
6. Barbara Leporini1, Marina Buzzi. "Learning by e-Learning: Breaking Down Barriers and Creating Opportunities for the Visually-Impaired", 2022. DOI: 10.1007/978-3-540-73283-9_75 · Source: DBLP.
7. Virata, R.O.; Castro, J.D.L. "Augmented reality in science classroom: Perceived effects in education, visualization and information processing". In *Proceedings of the 10th International Conference on E-Education, E-Business, E-Management and E-Learning*, Tokyo, Japan, 10–13 January 2019; pp. 85–92.
8. Kesim, M.; Ozarslan, Y. Augmented reality in education: Current technologies and the potential for education. *Procedia-Soc. Behav. Sci.*, 2012, 47, 297–302.
9. Chu, H.C.; Chen, J.M.; Hwang, G.J.; Chen, T.W. E_ects of formative assessment in an augmented realityapproach to conducting ubiquitous learning activities for architecture courses. *Univers. Access Inform. Soc.*, 2019, 18, 221–230.
10. Angel Lu, Crusher S. K. Wong, Richard Y. H. Cheung and Tarloff S. W. Im "Supporting Flipped and Gamified Learning With Augmented Reality in Higher Education" *Digital Learning Innovations, a Section of the Journal Frontiers in Education*, April 2021.
11. Wu, H.K.; Lee, S.W.Y.; Chang, H.Y.; Liang, J.C. Current status, opportunities and challenges of augmented reality in education. *Comput. Educ.*, 2013, 62, 41–49.
12. Alkhattabi, M. Augmented reality as E-learning tool in primary schools' education: Barriers to teachers', 2017.
13. Elmqaddem, N. Augmented Reality and Virtual Reality in Education. Myth or Reality? *Int. J. Emerg. Technol. Learn. (IJET)*, 2019, 14, 234–242.
14. Ozkan Yilmaz "Augmented Reality in Science Education: An Application in Higher Education". *Shanlax shanlax Int. J. Educ.*, [2021].

15. Anand Nayyar, Bandana Mahapatra, Dac NhuongLe, G. Suseendran "Virtual Reality (VR) and Augmented Reality (AR) technology for tourism and hospitality Industry" *Int. J. Res. Technol.*, 2018.
16. Yosr Chamekha* , Mohamed Amin Hammami "Impact of Virtual Reality on Modern Education" *Int. J. Sci.: Basic Appl. Res. (IJSBAR)*, (2020) Volume 50, No 2, pp 1-8.
17. Malek Turki Jdaitawi, Ashraf F Kan'an "A Decade of Research on the Effectiveness of Augmented Reality on Students with Special Disability in Higher Education", 2022.
18. Daniel Weber, Enkelejda Kasneci, Andreas Zell "Exploiting Augmented Reality for Extrinsic Robot Calibration and Eye-based Human-Robot Collaboration", 2022.
19. Olena Ie. Piatykop, Olha I. Pronina, Iryna B. Tymofieieva and Ihor D. Palii "Using augmented reality for early literacy" CoSinE 2021: 9th Illia O. Teplytskyi Workshop on Computer Simulation in Education, co-located with the 17th International Conference on ICT in Education, Research, and Industrial Applications:Integration, Harmonization, and Knowledge Transfer (ICTERI 2021), October 1, 2021, Kherson, Ukraine.
20. Kiron Lebeck, Kimberly Ruth, Tadayoshi Kohno, Franziska Roesner Paul G. "Towards Security and Privacy for Multi-User Augmented Reality: Foundations with End Users" Allen School of Computer Science & Engineering, University of Washington 2018 IEEE Symposium on Security and Privacy.
21. Joel Weijia Lai and Kang Hao Cheong "Adoption of Virtual and Augmented Reality for Mathematics Education: A Scoping Review" Digital Object Identifier 10.1109/ACCESS.2022.3145991.
22. Ebru Turan Güntepe, Necla Dönmez Usta." Augmented Reality Applicationbased Teaching Material's Effect on Viscera Learning Through Algorithmic Thinking". *J. Sci. Learn.*, 2021. 4(4). 365-374.
23. Mariano Alcañiz, Manuel Contero, David C. Pérez-López and Mario Ortega "Augmented Reality Technology for Education".
24. Weijie Chen, Xiaoxi Liu, Lei Qiao, Jian Wang, and Yanheng Zhao." Construction of Virtual Reality-Interactive Classroom Based on Deep Learning Algorithm" *Hindawi Wireless Commun. Mobile Comput.*, Volume 2020, Article ID 8870536, 9 pages https://doi.org/10.1155/2020/8870536.
25. Martin, S., Diaz, G., Sancristobal, E., Gil, R., Castro, M., & Peire, J. (2011). New technology trends in education: Seven years of forecasts and convergence. *Comput. Educ.*, 57, 1893-1906. http://dx.doi.org/10.1016/j.compedu.2011.04.003.
26. Kimberly Ruth, Tadayoshi Kohno, and Franziska Roesner" Secure Multi-User Content Sharing for Augmented Reality Applications:" Paul G. Allen School of Computer Science & Engineering, University of Washington https://ar-sec.cs.washington.edu/.

27. Richard McPherson, Suman Jana, Vitaly Shmatikov." No Escape From Reality: Security and Privacy of Augmented Reality Browsers".
28. Mark Roman MillerI, Hanseul JunI, Fernanda Herrera, Jacob Yu Villa, Greg WelchI, Jeremy N. Bailenson," Social interaction in augmented reality" Department of Computer Science, Stanford University, Stanford, CA, United States of America.
29. Nitika, Tanuja Kumari Sharma, Saumya Rajvanshi, Keshav Kishore. "A Study of Augmented Reality Performance in Web Browsers (WebAR)" *2021 2nd International Conference on Computational Methods in Science & Technology (ICCMST).*
30. Bhupinder Singh, Dr. Rajneesh Talwar, "Learning of Standard Electromechanical Devices Using Augmented Reality: A Reality", *International Journal of Informative & Futuristic Research (IJIFR).*
31. Phil Diegmann, Manuel Schmidt-Kraepelin, Sven Eynden, Dirk Basten "Benefits of Augmented Reality in Educational Environments - A Systematic Literature Review".
32. Martijn J. Schuemie, Peter van der Straaten, Merel Krijn, and Charles A.P.G. van der Mast "Research on Presence in Virtual Reality: A Survey". 5th july 2004.
33. Magar, Sunny Thapa, Suk, Hae Jung "The Advantages of Virtual Reality in Skill Development Training Based on Project Comparison". 28.6.2020.

# Index

3D imagery, 33

Adaptability, 168
AR-based learning, 1, 192, 225
Artificial intelligence, 3, 33, 50, 54-56, 121, 123-124, 133-134, 190, 205, 210
Assessment, 14-15, 19, 23, 37-38, 40, 67, 154, 161, 183-184
Attention deficit hyperactivity disorder (ADHD), 177, 209
Audio-visual effects, 33
Augmented reality (AR), 1-2, 51, 54-55, 65-66, 91-92, 103-104
Autism spectrum disorder (ASD), 65, 80, 94, 105

Behavioral traits, 103
Business logistics, 33

Challenging, 66, 93, 161, 182, 218, 224
Cognitive level, 161
Collaborative VR settings, 65, 75-76
Communication challenges, 65, 80
Communication issues, 66, 83
Communication training, 73-74
Comparative analysis, 210, 224
Concentration, 13, 161
Controlled environments, 105, 191, 199
Controlled virtual environments, 103
Customized experience, 189, 195

Dan Brown, 91
Data retention, 161
Developmental disabilities, 141, 158
Digital campus management, 103
Digital learning environments, 1, 21
Digital media, 1, 3, 147, 193
Digital transformation, 189
Disabilities, 39, 72, 91, 105-107, 109, 192, 201, 204, 211
Disadvantages, 23, 57, 77, 219, 222, 228
Down syndrome, 209
Dyslexia, 161, 162, 164, 170, 183

Early training scenarios, 103
Education, 136, 145, 189
Education pattern shifts, 1
Education sector, 26, 36, 91, 218
Educational applications, 1, 204
Educational content, 141, 163, 213
Educational facilities, 141
Educational technology, 33, 91-92, 95, 171, 210
Emotional disturbance, 161, 219
Empathy, 65, 67-70, 72-75
Engagement, 12-13, 76, 80, 107, 171, 179, 225
Ethical issues, 65, 83, 134, 137, 179
Evolution, 55
Experiential learning, 26, 55, 92
Extended reality (XR), 124, 128, 209

Flight simulation, 35

Groundbreaking technology, 121
Group problem-solving, 121

Hardware and software requirements, 122
Higher education, 1-2, 47, 54-55, 93-94, 96-97
Human society, 91

Immersion experiences, 33
Immersion, 10, 54, 72, 83, 150, 181
Immersive environments, 109, 126
Immersive experience, 10, 95, 169, 189, 200, 203
Immersive technologies, 9, 33, 92, 94-95
Implementation challenges, 168
Inclusive educational ecosystem, 122
Inclusive learning environments, 137
Individualized instruction, 125, 161
Individualized learning pathways, 122
Instructional design, 184
Integrated learning tool, 1
International Data Corporation (IDC), 91

Knowledge exchange, 141

Learner engagement, 157
Learners with disabilities, 91, 197, 205
Learning content, 8, 33
Learning difficulties, 96, 161
Learning environment, 21-22, 41, 123, 170, 210
Learning needs and disabilities, 122, 132
Learning outcomes, 33, 57, 98
Learning process, 4, 12. 133, 182
Learning theories, 27
Linguistic impairments, 209

Machine learning, 28, 157, 190, 205
Mars landing
Medical field, 33
Metaverse platform, 189, 193, 197, 200-202, 204-205
Metaverse, 189, 193, 197, 200-202, 204-205
Mixed reality (MR), 1-2, 93, 189, 193

Navigation, 11, 78, 175,
New technologies, 12, 141, 179

Pedagogical concerns, 122
Personalized therapies, 103
Perspective-taking skills, 65

Real-life scenarios, 1, 79, 107
Real-world examples, 65, 80, 83
Remote learning, 1-2, 94, 130, 202, 206

Science and mathematics education, 86
Security risks, 210, 220-221
Self-confidence, 65, 80, 110-112, 115-116, 164, 171
Simulation, 9, 13, 15, 33-35, 39, 51, 54, 66, 69, 70, 72-73, 83, 93, 104, 121, 126, 137, 146-147, 154, 164, 166, 219
Skill improvement, 34
Smart campuses in India, 103
Smart educational campuses, 103
Social anxiety, 84, 156, 209
Social communication, 106, 129
Social engagement, 27, 65, 76-77, 79, 123
Social skills development, 65-67, 69-71, 75-76, 78, 80-83
Social skills, 65, 67, 69-70, 75-76, 78, 80-81
Socially aware virtual agents, 65
Socioeconomic effects, 122
Special education, 65, 96, 103, 105, 106, 121, 125, 127, 129, 132, 144-145, 150, 190, 194, 197, 199-204
Special needs, 65-67, 71, 141,145, 199
Specialized instructional tools, 161

Spread of knowledge, 122
Student assessment, 161
Student participation, 121-122, 226

Teaching reforms, 34
Technical difficulties, 122, 134
Technological advancements, 91, 100, 200
Telecommunications, 33
Theoretical foundations, 1, 66
Theoretical frameworks, 65-67, 83
Three dimensions, 1, 93, 153, 218
Training resources, 161
Transformative technology, 122

User experiences, 122, 134, 190

Virtual characters, 69, 70, 103, 175
Virtual classrooms, 35, 123, 133
Virtual reality (VR), 1-2, 55, 65-66, 91-92, 103-104, 123, 141, 161-163, 189, 191, 209
Virtual social interactions, 65, 73-74, 83, 126

# Also of Interest

## Check out these other related titles from Scrivener Publishing

*TRANSFORMING EDUCATION WITH VIRTUAL REALITY,* Edited by Reena Malik, Ambuj Sharma and Prashant Chaudhary, ISBN: 9781394199990. The book provides an in-depth and comprehensive knowledge review of the use of virtual reality in the education industry and businesses.

*HUMAN MACHINE INTERFACE: Making Healthcare Digital,* Edited Rishabha Malviya, Sonali Sundram, Bhupendra Prajapati and Sudarshan Kumar Singh, ISBN: 9781394199914. The book contains the latest advances in healthcare and presents them in the frame of the Human-Machine Interface (HMI).

*ARTIFICIAL INTELLIGENCE FOR BONE DISORDER: Diagnosis and Treatment,* By Rishabha Malviya, Shivam Rajput and Markarand Vaidya, ISBN: 9781394230884. The authors have produced an invaluable resource that connects the fields of AI and bone treatment by providing essential insights into the current state and future of AI in bone condition diagnosis and therapy, as well as a methodical examination of machine learning algorithms, deep learning approaches, and their real-world uses.

*ENABLING HEALTHCARE 4.0 FOR PANDEMICS: A Roadmap Using AI, Machine Learning, IoT and Cognitive Technologies,* Edited by Abhinav Juneja, Vikram Bali, Sapna Juneja, Vishal Jain and Prashant Tyagi, ISBN: 9781119768791. The book explores the role and scope of AI, machine learning and other current technologies to handle pandemics.

*SOULWARE: THE AMERICAN WAY IN CHINA'S HIGHER EDUCATION,* By Way Kuo, ISBN: 9781119509899. The book adopts a critical perspective and draws on abundant empirical evidences and valuable data to substantiate its analyses of the major higher education systems under scrutiny.

Printed in the USA/Agawam, MA
September 16, 2026

910661.059